WISDOM HAS TWO SIDES

Calvinism - is it Biblical?

By
James F. Billton

Published by
Grace Mount Publishers
P.O. Box 27048 Edinburgh EH10 6YP

COPYRIGHT ACKNOWLEDGEMENT

All Scripture texts in this book are quoted from the King James Version unless otherwise stated.

INADVERTENT INFRINGMENT OF COPYRIGHT

Should we have in any way inadvertently infringed anyone's copyright, in referring to or quoting from their writings, which are mentioned in this book, we do apologize for this oversight.

Paperback **ISBN 0-9540427-1-9**
Hardback **ISBN 0-9540427-0-0**

First printed in May 2001

A WORD OF THANKS TO THOSE WHO HAVE HELPED ME WITH THIS BOOK

My very grateful thanks to my dear friend John McLeod for all his hard work in checking and rechecking the manuscript for this book and for his wise advice and encouragement to continue until the task was finished.

To my young friend Ewan Aitken for his help in sorting out the manuscript to the correct format and helping me with the computer. For the help of the late Albert Long who gave me all his unpublished writing against the doctrine of Calvin and in so doing encouraged me to continue with my writing.
To those who read the work and made comments on it, I am grateful.

THIS BOOK IS DEDICATED TO THE LATE BRIAN R. JONES AND MY DEAR WIFE MARJORIE.

Brian and his wife Isabel came for a holiday to our home in July 2000 and at the time we never dreamt that within a few months both Brian and Marjorie would be with the Lord. Marjorie died on the 27th and Brian on the 30th of November 2000. Brian read the book while he was visiting us and his brief comment is on the back cover of the book. He told me that the passion of his life was evangelism.

This book is written against the doctrine of Calvinism, which by its very nature is against the need for evangelism.

If you find difficulty in obtaining additional copies of this book they can be had directly from the publishers.

FOREWARD

James Billton follows a correct and essential hermeneutic of literal interpretation allowing for the context. He gives words their normal, their usual, their customary meaning contextually. Following the inductive method he allows the Bible to speak for itself rather than forcing a system into the Bible. In doing this he presents a clear harmony between theology and soteriology – the essence of God and salvation of mankind.

Billton's simple, clear style is devoid of academic stuffiness but alive with Biblical truth and relevance. He continually challenges the "Calvinist system" with the clarity of Scripture while at the same time he does not fall into an Arminian straitjacket. The development of his theme, the Gospel, not only brings a theological harmony but also a psychological harmony. God does love everyone, and has made provision for everyone at the cross and is not willing that any should perish but all should come to the knowledge of the truth.

Billton points out clearly the problem of sin, which separates humankind from God and the Good News that "God was reconciling the world to himself in Christ, not counting men's sins against them." (2 Corinthians 5:-19). "You see that at just the right time, when we were still powerless, Christ died for the ungodly." (Romans 5:-6) N.I.V.

He points out that the incarnation was essential for the atonement to take place. "For since death came through a man, the resurrection of the dead also comes through a man." (1 Corinthians 15:-21) N.I.V. "We see Jesus, who was made a little lower than the angels, crowned with glory and honour because he suffered death, so by the grace of God he might taste death for everyone." (Hebrews 2:-9) N.I.V. The atonement, he points out, is first God-ward and second man-ward. "He did it to demonstrate at the present time, so as to be just and the one who justifies those who have faith in Jesus." (Romans 3:-26) N.I.V. The cross was essential for God's justice to be satisfied. Jesus' death was acceptable to God not because of who he was but because of what he was, "The lamb without blemish or defect." (1 Peter 1:-19) N.I.V. Christ became the ground on which God can "Be just and the one who justifies those who have faith in Jesus."

Billton states the teaching of the New Testament that Jesus died for the world. "Look, the Lamb of God, who takes away the sin of the world!" (John 1:-29) N.I.V. "For God so loved the world that he gave his one and only Son, that whoever believes in him shall not perish but have eternal life." (John 3:-16) N.I.V. "This bread is my flesh, which I will give for the life of the world." (John 12:-51); N.I.V. "That God was reconciling the world to himself in Christ, not counting men's sins against them." (2 Corinthians 5:- 19); N.I.V. "And we have seen and testify that the Father sent his Son to be the Saviour of the world." (1 John 4:-14); N.I.V. "He is the atoning sacrifice for our sins, and not only for ours but for the sins of the whole world." (John 2:-2) N.I.V. Billton shows and asserts the normal meaning demands that "world" means world!

Billton continues the New Testament declaration that Jesus died for all men and women, "I, when I am lifted up from the earth, will draw all men to myself." (John 12:-32); N.I.V. "Consequently, just as the result of one trespass was condemnation for all men, so also the result of one act of righteousness was justification that brings life for all men." (Romans 5:-18); N.I.V. "God our Saviour, who wants all men to be saved and come to a knowledge of the truth. For there is one God and one mediator between God and men, the man Christ Jesus, who gave himself as a ransom for all men." (1 Timothy 2:-4-6); N.I.V. "For the grace of God has appeared for the salvation of all men." (Titus 2:-11 RSV); Billton demonstrates that the context demands that "all men" means all men as Paul also said to Timothy; "God...is the Saviour of all men, and especially of those who believe." (1 Timothy 4:-10) N.I.V.

Billton builds a strong apologetic for Jesus not only being the Saviour of all men and women objectively but subjectively only those who believe are saved! Potentially Jesus is the Saviour of all men and women but effectually only those who believe experience salvation.

I believe that most Christians will benefit from this book, but there will be those who will not endorse it for the fear of men.

I endorse it wholeheartedly and ask the "Calvinists camp" to respond using the same contextual hermeneutic.

Evangelist.
Ian Leitch

CONTENTS

"TRUE WISDOM HAS TWO SIDES" Job 11:-6 N.I.V.

INTRODUCTION

"FOR HE WHO STANDS IN AWE OF GOD SHALL
AVOID BOTH EXTREMES."
Ecclesiastes 7:-18. J.M.V.

Calvin in particular among the Reformers went from the carnal doctrine of individuals working their way to heaven, by good works, with the help of rituals and church indulgences, and the assumed God given dictatorial authority which led to the tyrannical extremes of the Roman religion, to the opposite end of the spectrum of doctrine. This is as unscriptural as the dogma of Rome. Calvin resurrected Augustine's teaching, which was rejected by the early church as unacceptable and heretical.

Of the multitudes of books written on theology, perhaps the largest number of contributors are those of the Calvinistic school. Some of the books and booklets have been specially produced to win Christians over to adopting the sterile Calvinistic Thesis and have been in print for very many years. A few of them which tried to explain from Scripture the Five Points of Calvinism came into my hands some time ago.
These books and booklets made some astounding statements which, as far as I am aware, no one has refuted, at least not in the form of a book dealing solely with the outrageous declarations made and the controversy raised.
The basic issues raised attack the very heart of the gospel message, of John 3:-14 to 17 and the teaching of our Lord Jesus Christ.
The first temptation in the Garden of Eden by Satan, **was to sow doubt as to the good intentions and kindness of God towards man.**
The reactionary theology of Calvinism does exactly the same.
What issues from, particularly the first four of the Five Points, which are dealt with in this book, are the following:
God does not love the world (everyone)!
In fact God hates most people and has appointed them to damnation!

Christ did not die for the whole world but only for a few, the elect!

God is partial in His dealings with men; He loves one and hates another!

Those who are saved are saved unconditionally and it has nothing whatsoever to do with the one who is saved!

The sinner is completely passive in the matter of salvation, God's grace is irresistible and God does everything from start to finish!

It is impossible for a sinner to repent of his sins, for man lost his free will after the fall in the Garden of Eden!

It is not possible for a sinner to believe in Christ because he has no faith by which he can do this!

Because all unregenerate sinners are dead to God in the same way and sense that a corpse is to its habitat!

Regeneration is given by God to the elect sinners first, without them believing in Christ, in order to allow God to gift faith and repentance so that the sinner can believe in Christ and be saved.

These are some of the major issues that are put forward by a number of Calvinist writers, Biblical commentators and Professors of Systematic theology, as supposedly Scriptural teaching, which all Christians should believe and follow.

It is true to say that this Calvinistic teaching, because it is held by some of the main stream Protestant Denominations and is held to be Biblical by its leaders, brings confusion to the mind of the man in the pew because he sees the discrepancy between Calvinism and Scripture and the many disagreements between the two.

I am aware that there are many very able theologians who are admirably more able than I am to refute these erroneous teachings, but none as far as I am aware has done so.

To my knowledge there is not one book written (there is a booklet) and published in the United Kingdom which puts forward the Scriptural argument against the five points of Calvinism and all the issues that flow from it.

This is the reason for publishing this book.

The method used in refuting the Calvinistic doctrine has been to take what has been written, examine it, and argue the issues purely from a Scriptural point of view, and not necessarily to promote or, propagate James Arminius's teaching or any other individual's doctrine.

If we are, as we should be **"Ambassadors for Christ"**, we put forward His teaching and message, His interests, His Kingdom, plan and agenda for lost mankind, which is given plainly in the New Testament and which means that the main aim of those of us who are part of the body of Christ is to be engaged in the work of Evangelism, to reach the lost with the message of Christ.

Those who are **"Ambassadors for Calvinism"** defend and put forward Calvin's ideas and doctrine and some have the arrogance to claim this as the gospel message, which in fact contradicts and dishonours Christ and His Gospel. They are far more zealous to win Christians over to Calvinism than they are to win the lost for Christ and His kingdom! They show this in the vast amount of man hours and finance used in promoting and defending Calvinism.

The Lord Jesus said, "No servant can serve two masters, he is bound to hate one and love the other, or give his loyalty to one and despise the other." Luke 16:-13. J.B.Phillips translation.

WHOM DO WE FOLLOW; IS IT THE LORD JESUS CHRIST OR CALVIN?

CHAPTER 1
HOW IT ALL BEGAN

THE DOCTRINE AND CONDITIONS WHICH PRECIPITATED THE REFORMATION
ONE BIG UNITED CHURCH AND THE MEANS USED TO KEEP IT THAT WAY

At the time when we had one united Church, which went under the name Christian and which covered most of the western world, we also had what was termed by historians "the dark ages." The corruption of the Church started when the state and Church became united. At the beginning of the fourth century, after Constantine became the ruler of the Roman Empire, he made Christianity the official religion. This resulted in the Empire-Church and a vast influx of pagan people joining, who, having been used to elaborate pagan rituals, were dissatisfied with the very plain spiritual Christian worship. From then on, bit by bit, heathen beliefs and practices were introduced and the Bible neglected. But there were groups throughout the Empire-Church who would not accept the new pagan introductions into worship and tenaciously kept to the New Testament teaching. By the sixteenth century the mainstream Church had evolved into a grossly corrupt, tyrannical religion, to those who did not accept their rule and beliefs. For a period of about four hundred years prior to the Reformation the instrument of this religion was the *Inquisition, under which horrific atrocities were committed. Many who would not conform to this paganish form of worship were sought out, tortured and killed.

Not a few of them were Jews.

*The Inquisition was brought into being by the Council of Verona in 1184.

The only reason the mainstream Reformation took so long in coming and being established, was the suppression of *Bible truth and the ruthless extermination of all who did not accept the Roman religion. Whole cities in both Italy and France were exterminated whenever larger groups of people started to follow the teaching of the Bible and failed to conform to the rule of Rome. *The Bible was forbidden to the man in the pew by the council of Velencia in 1229, and with the Bible out of the way, there was no challenge to Rome's power and authority, (from within the ranks of the Empire-Church). But in spite of all the suppression, the gospel light was not extinguished.

THE GOSPEL KEPT ALIVE BY THE RIVAL CHURCH

Perhaps the oldest organized Protestant Church in the world is in Northern Italy, The Waldensian Church, where, because of the mountainous terrain, it has managed to survive in spite of thousands of its members being martyred or severely persecuted by the Church of Rome for nearly a thousand years. Prior to the Reformation, in the year 1500, one person, in order to get an understanding of the size of this rival Church, asked a Waldensian, how many Waldensian pastors were there in his area, and he was told, "some four hundred."

There has always been opposition to the Roman Church and its introduction of pagan beliefs and worship and this was widespread throughout Europe, where these groups of Bible believers were referred to as heretics (or the Rival Church).

Note. The word "heretic" has its roots in the Greek word *heirein*, which is a verb and has the meaning "To stand before alternatives and make a choice between them."

THE CELTIC CHURCH PREACHED THE GOSPEL IN SCOTLAND AND ENGLAND

The Celtic Church was another such authentic Christian Church, which thrived in Ireland and throughout Scotland and northern England.

St. Patrick was the one used by God to bring the Gospel to the Irish and who established Celtic Churches Nationally. He was not of or from the Roman Church! From Ireland came Columba with his evangelical zeal who used the island of Iona as his base from which to evangelize Scotland and Northern England. The Celtic Church was suppressed by the Roman Hierarchy at the Synod of Whitby in the year 664 AD.

WYCLIFFE, THE REFORMER AND BIBLE TRANSLATOR

Also in England John Wycliffe (1329-1384), translated the Bible into English and had it widely circulated. He led a formidable group of itinerant preachers who became known as Lollards. They taught Scripture and preached the gospel from Oxford and up through England and into the western parts of Scotland. His influence and teaching were widespread throughout the country and in Europe and continued up until the Reformation. There were Wycliffites or Lollards in Ayrshire at the time of the Reformation.

ANABAPTISTS ACTIVE FROM THE BEGINNING OF THE EMPIRE-CHURCH

Another group of authentic Christians, Anabaptists, (which means re-baptisers), were at the time of Augustine in the fourth century referred to as Donatists. Martin Luther, without any reluctance, when referring to Anabaptist called them "Donatists", so persuaded was he that this Church of his day was the perpetuation of the Rival Church, which existed in Augustine's day.

All the early leaders agreed unanimously that the Church should be made up of those who were true believers and that they should follow strictly the New Testament teaching in Life style and worship. They opposed the sprinkling of infants as unbiblical and a pillar of the Roman Religion.

They also believed they should be separate from the world, and therefore were opposed to being linked to local or national government, as was the case at the forming of the Empire-Church when the Church of Rome was born.

Many thousands were martyred by the Roman Church and they suffered a great deal of persecution at the hands of the Reformers, because they did not accept the doctrine of either Luther, Calvin or Zwingli and opposed the link of Church and government. Luther, Calvin and Zwingli were all for having the power of government behind their Reformation Church and by so doing continued in one of the main errors of Rome.

John Knox, I believe, was far more in tune with Scripture and with spiritual values than the other Reformers.

He was the only one to insist on the separation of State and Church, and it is noteworthy that Scotland was the only country where there was not one Roman Catholic put to death because of being Catholic after the establishment of the Reformation in Scotland.

The Roman Catholic Bishop of Ross, (a contemporary of Knox) John Lesley, a keen supporter of Queen Mary, wrote: 'Yet the clemency of the heretic nobles must not be left unmentioned, since at that time they exiled few Catholics on the score of religion, and imprisoned fewer, AND PUT NONE TO DEATH.' (1)

THE SCOTTISH REFORMATION FOUNDED BY PARLIAMENT BEFORE THE CHURCH WAS FORMED

Note. The Scottish parliament in order to establish the New Protestant

Faith, on the 17th August 1560, acknowledged John Knox's Confession of Faith as being the accepted Creed of the Scottish people and passed an Act banning the Roman Religion from the country. Also an Act for the abolishing of the pope and his usurped authority in Scotland, was passed. So there was a civil establishment of the Protestant Faith before there was an Established Church. The first General Assembly of the New Protestant Church in Scotland was held in Edinburgh on the 20th of December 1560. (2).

Dr. McCrie when writing of the great event of the 17th August 1560 said: 'In Scotland, the people were converted to the Protestant faith, before the civil power had moved a step in the cause: and when Legislature became friendly to the Reformation, nothing remained for it to do, but to ratify the profession which the nation had adopted.' (2).

ANABAPTIST MORE BIBLICAL AND ORTHODOX THAN THEIR PERSECUTORS

The Anabaptists were active throughout Europe from before the birth of the Empire-Church and up to and after the Reformation.

Although the Anabaptists were referred to as heretics they were more orthodox than their persecutors. As Henry C. Lea, in his book on the inquisition, "The Inquisition of the Middle Ages", has said about these "heretics", they are "sectaries holding fast to the essentials of Christianity." Testimony to this is voluminous and virtually unanimous in the writings of the inquisitors.

Unlike the Reformers the Anabaptists, and Waldensians were particularly fond of the book of James. This is clearly evident if you compare the doctrine of James with the life style they adopted.

They believed that faith and works went together as James taught. James 2:-17. "Even so faith, if it hath not works, is dead, being alone." K.J.V.

In an old Waldensian catechism the question is asked: "How many kinds of faith are there?" The answer was: "Two, dead and alive!"

(1)Quoted by D. Hay Fleming, Reformation, p 437.
(2)McCrie, Sketches of Scottish Church History (1841) pp 65,66.

WHAT THE INQUISITORS SAID ABOUT ANABAPTISTS

One inquisitor believed that there were three things that made these "heretics" dangerous. These were that they lived godly lives and were just before all men and believed the Apostles' Creed.

A summary of some of the things said by the inquisitors are as follows: These people excel in outward holiness whereas the priests of the Church follow after vices mainly of the flesh.

These "heretics" are known for their manners and their words. They are composed and moderate in manner and their dress is not costly or splendid, but simple and functional.

They would not follow a merchant's trade for fear of dishonesty or having to swear an oath, which they refused to do.

"But above all, my brethren, do not swear, either by heaven or by earth or with any other oath. But let your "Yes" be "Yes", and your "No" "No", lest you should fall into judgment." James 5:-12. N.K.J.V.

They believed that they should not multiply riches, but were content with the necessities of life. James 5:-1-2-3.

They would not frequent taverns or participate in dances and other such vanities. James 4:-4.

Moreover they were chaste and showed moderation in eating and drinking. They were always working, teaching or learning.

They were known for their scrupulously accurate and moderate speech. James 1:-19-26, "let every man be swift to hear, slow to speak, slow to wrath." K.J.V.

"If any man offend not in word, the same is a perfect man, and able also to bridle the whole body." James 3:-2, K.J.V. They would avoid bickering, back-biting, idle words, lies or swearing. Their sole evil was to be scornful of the Roman Church.

Many of them had learned in the vernacular entire books of the New Testament as well as the Apostles' Creed by heart and they would often repeat these to each other.

JESUS TELLS US HOW TO RECOGNISE FALSE CHRISTIANS

The Lord Jesus said that the way you can tell if a person or a group of people are of God is by their deeds. "By their fruit ye shall know them." He told the Pharisees: "Ye are of your father the devil, and the lusts of your father ye will do. He was a murderer from the beginning, and abode not in the truth, because there is no truth in him." John 8:-44, K.J.V.

ROME TELLS US "WE CHANGE NOT"

The motto of Rome is *Semper idem*, "We change not", or "Always the same", and they tell us they never change or bring into being new doctrine. This is pure fiction. The changes that have taken place in recent years through the second Vatican council are conceived to project to the world an image of tolerance and reasonableness and are an exercise in cosmetic window dressing. They have not rescinded the basic heretical dogmas of Rome. In fact additional idolatrous Dogmas have been brought in since the Reformation, so they do change, but for the worse.

THE REFORMATION HAS CHANGED THE WORLD AND ROME

The mainstream Reformation has changed The Roman Church because she cannot rule as she did with absolute power and terror over all her domain, nor can her iniquitous Inquisition be used in the way it was before the Reformation. With the Reformation came the opening of the Scriptures and, with the truth of God's word, the challenging of the error of Rome.

THERE HAS BEEN A FALLING AWAY OF MEMBERS SINCE VATICAN TWO

To the practicing Roman Catholic the decrees of Vatican Two were devastating, mainly because of the abolition of the Latin mass and eating fish on Fridays. A Roman Catholic author and journalist, Piers Compton, has estimated that in the first seven years since Vatican Two and because of the changes brought into being by the Vatican, the Church has lost 2,500,000 adherents in England alone.

In Scotland the decline is also enormous. The effects are seen in the closing of many private and council schools, convents, monasteries and even Church buildings and I would be surprised if they have even half of the number of adherents they claim they have. The Roman church will never admit to losing any members.

Rome has lost enormous numbers in Canada and America, not just because of Vatican Two, but because of the large numbers of priests who have been charged with sexual abuse of children, some cases going back twenty years. One journalist estimated that in America there were four hundred such cases throughout the country. The cost in damages to Rome is something like one billion dollars.

CHAPTER 2

THE RULE OF THE PAPACY IN SCOTLAND JUST BEFORE THE REFORMATION

The following are just a few examples of the tyrannies practiced by the Roman Church in Scotland prior to the Reformation, when Cardinal Beaton was the head of the Roman religion in Scotland.

In the village of Tullibody the local priest Thomas Cocklaw, fell in love with a wealthy widow named Margaret Jamieson.
At that time, as well as copies of Martin Luther's doctrine, the New Testament was being translated into English and printed in Germany by William Tyndale and they were being smuggled, very often in fishing boats, into both Scotland and England. The priest got his hands on one of these Testaments and thought he would read it to find out if the Bible forbade the marrying of priests. He found that it did not, so he arranged with a priest, Duncan Simpson, in Stirling to marry him and asked two friars to be witnesses. After the marriage he and his wife went down to England for their honeymoon.

THE CARDINAL'S REACTION TO THE MARRIAGE

On hearing about the marriage Cardinal Beaton tried to arrest Thomas Cocklaw, but he was gone, so he arrested the priest who had married the couple and also the two friars. They were charged with heresy and went through an ecclesiastical trial, condemned to death and burned alive at the stake in Edinburgh in 1540.

Margaret Jamieson's house, lands and properties were confiscated. Cardinal Beaton had his own private army.
It is not to be wondered at that, at that time, the Church of Rome owned half of all the land in Scotland.

MURDERED FOR MAKING HIS RELATIONSHIP LEGITIMATE

In 1534, a priest by the name of Norman Gourlay was put to death in Edinburgh for what in the Roman Church is a crime, a priest marrying.

THE VOW OF CELIBACY NEVER KEPT

The cardinal himself was not celibate, he was father (in the true sense) to seven boys and three girls although he was not officially married.
Proof of this can be obtained by anyone who takes the trouble to look up the entries in the Register of the Great Seal of Scotland between 1513 and 1546. They will find the records of the registration of Cardinal Beaton's illegitimate children. The father is designated as 'David, Cardinal priest of the Roman Church, Archbishop of St Andrews, Primate of Scotland.' (1)
(1) "The Story of the Scottish Reformation", By A.M. Renwick.

THE HYPOCRISY OF THE HIERARCHY OF THE ROMAN CHURCH

The blatant hypocrisy of the Cardinal and the hierarchy of the Roman Church is still continuing and prevails to this day.
Priests could have children and very many of them did, as they still do, and still remain in the priesthood; but if they get married officially, they are excommunicated or, if this happened prior to the Reformation, they could have been put to death.

FURTHER INFORMATION FROM A FORMER PRIEST

According to David Rice, a former priest, in his book "Shattered Vows" subtitled "Exodus from the priesthood," apart from those who have just left without giving notice, at the very least 100,000 priests have been excommunicated in recent years because they have done what is right and made legitimate their relationship with a woman. Priests can have children and the Church will support them financially, but whenever they officially marry all financial help stops and the priest is excommunicated, although, if a priest in the Church of England converts to Rome, he is accepted as a priest, wife and all.

THE CRIME OF READING GOD'S WORD IN ENGLISH

Just prior to the Tullibody affair, Thomas Cocklaw's friend the vicar of the town of Dollar, a godly man by the name of Thomas Forret was arrested and brought to trial for what was considered by the Roman church as heresy. Cardinal Beaton had him burned alive at the stake for the so-called crime of reading the Bible to his people in Church, in English.

THE SCOTTISH PARLIAMENT MAKE LEGAL THE READING OF THE BIBLE

I have no doubt that what precipitated the passing of a law by the Scottish Parliament in 1543, making legal the reading of the Bible in the vernacular, was the murder of Thomas Forret and similar instances.

THE CARDINAL REAPS WHAT HE HAD SOWN

Cardinal Beaton was murdered by a group of Scottish nobles fourteen years prior to the Reformation being established in Scotland, and died in 1546. This was done in revenge for the martyrdom of George Wishart in the same year.

1538 is generally taken as the start of the Reformation in Scotland but it was not established until 1560, when Roman rule was banished from Scotland.

THE DEATH KNELL TO THE RULE OF ROME IN SCOTLAND

In March 1558, a deed was done during the time of the successor to Cardinal Beaton, Archbishop John Hamilton, which is looked upon by some as the greatest mistake the Roman Catholic Church in Scotland ever made. Walter Myln a former Priest of Lunan near Forfar, was publicly burned at the stake for believing and preaching the gospel.

He was eighty-two years of age and, when brought before the ecclesiastical court, was scarcely able to stand or walk.

This barbarous execution roused the anger, horror and hostility of the Scottish nation against the Roman Catholic Church and clergy to an incredible pitch. It has been, I believe, correctly assessed that his martyrdom rang the death knell of the rule of the Papacy in Scotland.

SCOTLAND WAS NOT THE ONLY PLACE OF ROMAN TERRORISM

It was not only in Scotland that the Roman terrorists had their way, but in many other countries including England. After the untimely death of Edward VI in 1553, Mary Tudor, daughter of Henry VIII, a fanatical

Roman Catholic ascended the throne, and during her short reign of five years, she earned the infamous nickname, "**Bloody Mary**." During her reign no fewer than 286 Protestants were burned at the stake or died in prison, of whom, the godly Archbishop Cranmer was one.
Most of those who were put to death by Mary were ordinary individuals. One was a blind old lady who had managed to purchase one of Tyndale's English New Testaments and paid people to read it to her. She was burned at the stake for what in the eyes of the Roman church was a crime, listening to the Word of God in a language she could understand.

The behaviour of "Bloody Mary" precipitated an act of parliament forbidding a Roman Catholic from ever being on the Throne of England.

THE MASS MURDER OF THOUSANDS OF PROTESTANTS IN FRANCE

The Roman Church, among her many atrocities, perpetrated one of the most horrific and heinous of crimes in France in 1572, by the torturing and massacre of seventy thousand Huguenots in Paris and other major cities in France. This evil crime commenced at 3 o'clock in the morning of Sunday 24th August and continued until the Tuesday morning. This has become known as the Massacre of St. Bartholomew's Day. This was to the detriment and eternal shame of the French Nation. It was cunningly and deceitfully planned and there were many thousands of perpetrators involved in the massacre.

THE MASSACRE OF ST. BARTHOLOMEW'S DAY AND KNOX'S REACTION

When news of this reached Scotland, John Knox, although aged and unwell, preached the following Sunday in St. Giles Cathedral Edinburgh against the wickedness of the French and the mass murder of so many of God's people. The French ambassador was present at that service and during the sermon Knox addressed him. The gist of the message to the king of France given to his ambassador was as follows: "Go back and tell your master and king, that the Lord's vengeance shall not depart from him nor from his house; that his name shall remain an execration to posterity; and that none proceeding from his loins shall enjoy the kingdom in peace unless he repent." (2)

We read in the book of Revelation 17:-6 and 18:-5-7.
"THEN I SAW THAT THE WOMAN WAS DRUNK WITH THE BLOOD OF GOD'S HOLY PEOPLE AND WITH THE BLOOD OF THOSE WHO WERE KILLED BECAUSE OF THEIR FAITH IN JESUS. Her sins have piled up as high as the sky, and God has not forgotten the wrongs she has done. **Give that city** the same as she gave to others. She gave herself much glory and rich living. Give her the same amount of suffering and sadness." N.C.V.

(2) "The Life of John Knox" by Thomas Mc Crie, 1855, P269.

CHAPTER 3

THE SCRIPTURAL ARGUMENT AGAINST THE DOGMAS OF ROME

For the sake of those not so familiar with Church history and the controversy of the dogmas of Rome, and without going into it in too much detail, I will put forward the Scriptural refutation of these dogmas, which were the means and power behind the Reformation. It has been truly said that the mainstream Reformation was bringing the Church "back to the Bible."

JUST A FEW OF THE DOGMAS DECREED SINCE THE REFORMATION

The Dogma of the Immaculate Conception of the Virgin Mary, (Mary being born without sin) was made in 1854. Mary herself speaks in Luke 1:-46-47 **"And Mary said, My soul doth magnify the Lord, And my spirit hath rejoiced in God my Saviour." K.J.V.**

We only need a Saviour if we are sinners.

The dogma of the infallibility of the pope, was promulgated in 1870, and the dogma of the Assumption of the virgin Mary, promulgated in 1950, states that after her death, Mary's body ascended into heaven.

When the present pope visited southern Ireland he stated that the Virgin Mary was the fourth part of the Godhead.

This I have little doubt will be confirmed as a dogma in the future.

THE BLASPHEMOUS WORSHIP OF FALSE GODS: RELICS, SAINTS AND MARY

They worship idols and relics, and pray to a multitude of saints and the Virgin Mary, as the mother of God, when the commandment tells us clearly, **"You must not have any other gods except Me." Exodus 20:-3. N.C.V.** There is no verse anywhere in the New Testament, which asks us to pray either to Mary or the saints.

ERRONEOUS BELIEF LEADS TO ERRONEOUS BEHAVIOUR

Our beliefs determine our behaviour and there is no doubt that this was the reason for such wickedness, because Rome falsely believes that Peter was the rock on which Christ was going to build His Church and he was also given what they term "the power of the keys," the authority to forgive anyone his sins, and this was passed down through so-called apostolic succession, and that the Church of Rome was the one and only true Church.

THE PROSTITUTION OF WHAT GOD HAS GIVEN FREELY THROUGH CHRIST – FORGIVENESS OF OUR SINS.

It was the selling of the forgiveness of sins, which was called "indulgences", which triggered the Reformation in Germany. The indulgence was not just the forgiveness of sins; **it was the right to sin with impunity.**

Because of a need for money in order to build St. Peter's in Rome, pope Leo X used "the power of the keys" by offering for sale *plenary indulgences and sending his agents to every country, promising to those living, pardon for sins yet to be committed as well as those of the past, and instant freedom from the pains of purgatory for the dead.

*The word "Plenary" means complete. In this case unimpaired freedom to sin.

THE POPE'S MOST ZEALOUS SALESMAN

A priest by the name of John Tetzel a Dominican monk went to Germany and was among the most enthusiastic salesmen for these indulgences and at the beating of a drum, his infamous sales slogan was heard throughout Germany, **"A soul is released from *purgatory and carried to heaven as soon as the money tinkles in the box."**

*Purgatory was brought into being as a dogma by the council of Florence in 1439.

MARTIN LUTHER'S REACTION

The result was the "Ninety-five Theses" Nailed to the church door in Wittenberg on October 31st 1517.

At that time Martin Luther did not disagree with indulgences as such, but in the commercialization of them and the excesses to which John Tetzel and others went, in the selling of them. As a result the debate started, based upon what Scripture had to say about these issues, and through this the Mainstream Reformation began.

ROME TELLS US MARY HAD ONLY ONE CHILD CHRIST

They also have the belief of the "Ever Blessed Virgin Mary," meaning that Mary throughout her life was a virgin, which is untrue.
Scripture informs us that:
"Then Joseph being aroused from his sleep, did as the angel of the Lord had commanded him; he took [her to his side as] his wife, But he had no union with her as her husband until she had borne her first-born Son, and he called His name Jesus." Matthew 1:-24-25. The Amplified New Testament.
Later, "Some one said to Him, Listen! Your mother and Your brothers are standing outside, seeking to speak to You." Matthew 12:-47. The Amplified New Testament.
"Where did this Man get this wisdom and these miraculous powers? Is not this the carpenter's Son? Is not His mother called Mary? And are not His brothers James and Joseph and Simon and Judus? And do not all His sisters live here among us? Where then did this Man get all this?" Matthew 13:-54-56. The Amplified New Testament.
According to this verse Jesus had at the very least six brothers and sisters
So Mary was not the "Ever Blessed Virgin Mary."

Note. In order to make their doctrine of the "Ever Blessed Virgin Mary" fit Scripture, Jerome came up with the idea that the brothers and sisters of Christ were cousins.
The Greek for brother is Adelphos and for sister Adelphe and for cousin Sungenes.
The word Adelphos is used in Mat:-1-2, **"Jacob begot Judah and his brothers" (Adelphos) also Mat 1:-11, "Josiah begot Jeconiah and his brothers." (Adelphos).**

In Mat 4:-18 and 21 the same word is used of Peter and Andrew, **"Now Jesus **** saw two brothers," (Adelphos) "Simon called Peter, and Andrew his brother." Jesus "Saw two other brothers," (Adelphos) "James the son of Zebedee, and John his brother" N.K.J.V.**
"While He was still speaking to the multitudes, behold His mother and **brothers**" (Adelphos) "stood outside, seeking to speak with Him." N.K.J.V. Luke uses the word Adelphos of Jesus' **Brethren** in Luke 8:-19, but of Mary's cousin he uses the word Sungenes. Luke 1:-36.
Jerome's doctrine has no basis in Scripture and is another Roman fiction.

PETER, THE LEADER AND FOUNDATION OF THE CHURCH?

Rome believes that Peter was a prince among the Apostles, the first leader of the Church and bishop of Rome; but there is no Scriptural basis for this.
The Christian Church began on the Day of Pentecost in Jerusalem and Rome does not come into the picture until the beginning of the fourth century, when Imperial Rome decided to make Christianity the religion of the Empire.
Peter was never a cleric and I believe would never have seen Rome.

PETER WAS NOT CELIBATE AND NEITHER WERE MOST OF THE APOSTLES

Peter was married as were most of the other apostles and none of the apostles were priests. There were no clerics, nor is the word "layman" ever used at all in the New Testament.
The only priests in the early Church were those converted to Christ from the Jewish faith.
Matthew 8:-14. "And when Jesus was come into Peter's house, he saw his wife's mother laid, and sick of a fever." K.J.V.
1 Cor 9:-5, "Do we not have the right to bring a believing wife with us when we travel **as do the other apostles and the Lord's brothers and Peter?" N.C.V.**

JAMES, LEADER OF THE CHURCH

The first major theological problem which confronted the Church and which brought about the convening of a council of all the Apostles and Elders, took place after the gospel was opened up to the Gentiles when numbers of them turned to Christ. The first being Cornelius and his household mentioned in Acts chapter 10.
The question confronting the assembly was, 'Should the Gentiles be circumcised, as all Jews were, to conform with Jewish Law?'
Scripture indicates that James, the brother of Christ, was the head of the Church in Jerusalem where the Church started.
He is believed to have led the Church for over thirty years, and was the author of the book of James.
(Acts 15:-13 and 19).It is obvious from Acts 15 that James was not only the leader of the Church in Jerusalem, but that he chaired the council of Apostles and Elders.

After the debate on the issues under discussion, in which Paul, Barnabus and Peter took part, James did the summing up and brought it to its conclusion. Verse 13, "When they had finished speaking James summed up:" Verse 19, "My judgment therefore is that we should impose no irksome restrictions on those of the Gentiles who are turning to God." Acts 15. N.E.B.

So Scripture puts James, not Peter, as the leader of the whole Church with James presiding over the assembly. The proceedings were carried out democratically with all the Church leaders having the opportunity to take part in the debate, the outcome of which was reached by a consensus of opinion, with James bringing the debate to its final conclusion.

PAUL THE APOSTLE TO THE GENTILES; PETER APOSTLE TO THE JEWS

Galatians 2:-7-9. "But these leaders saw that I ("Paul") had been given the work of telling the Good News to those who were not Jewish, just as Peter had the work of telling the Jews. God gave Peter the power to work as an apostle for the Jewish people. But He also gave me the power to work as an apostle for those who are not Jews. James, Peter and John...They agreed that they should go to the Jewish people and that we ("Paul and Barnabas") should go to those who are not Jewish." N.C.V.

THE JEWS EXPELLED FROM ROME

In Acts 18:-2 we read that Claudius expelled all Jews from Rome and among them were Aquila and his wife Priscilla, whom Paul met when he was in Corinth. "But Aquila and his wife, Priscilla, had recently moved to Corinth from Italy, because Claudius commanded that all Jews must leave Rome." N.C.V. Aquila, like Paul, was a tent maker. If all Jews were expelled from Rome then Peter would not have been allowed to stay in Rome.

PAUL WAS THE FOUNDER OF THE CHURCH IN ROME NOT PETER

Scripture teaches us that there were Jews in Rome during Nero's rule. But it is also clear from Acts chapter 28 that the Jews had not heard the gospel of Christ until Paul preached to them, and that it was Paul, not Peter, who started the Church in Rome.

In verses 21-22 we read what the Jews said to Paul:
"But we think it fitting and are eager to hear from you what it is that you have in mind, and believe, and what your opinion is, for with regard to this sect it is known to all of us that it is everywhere denounced." Acts 28:-22. Amplified New Testament.

"They said, 'Nobody wrote warning us about you. And no one has shown up saying anything bad about you. But we would like very much to hear more. The only thing we know about this Christian sect is that nobody seems to have anything good to say about it.'" Acts 28:-21-22.
The Message.

THE BIBLE MAKES NO MENTION OF PETER EVER BEING IN ROME

The first group to which Peter would have gone to preach the gospel had he ever been in Rome, would have been the Jews, because he was the Apostle to the Jews. According to the Roman Church Peter started his rule in Rome in AD 43. Rome claims that Peter was allegedly pope for 25 years until 64 AD.
So Paul was in Rome during the period Peter was supposedly pope and yet they never met, nor is it recorded in the Bible!
The fact that the Jews knew nothing about the Gospel until Paul preached to them and that Peter never met Paul during his stay in Rome is evidence that the Roman claim is pure fiction. Paul was martyred by Nero.
Peter was in prison in Jerusalem in 44 AD.

Paul the Apostle stayed with Peter in Jerusalem in the year 58 AD, for we are told: (1) "Then after three years I went up to Jerusalem to see Peter, and abode with him fifteen days. But other of the apostles saw I none, save James the Lord's brother." Gal 1:-18-19. K.J.V.
Claudius ruled in Rome from 41-54 AD, and Nero from 54-68 AD.
(1)
"(Handbook To The Controversy With Rome)" By Karl Von Hase.1909.

ANOTHER ROMAN ASSUMPTION PROVED WRONG

It is generally assumed that Augustine, sent by pope Gregory in the year 597 AD, was the one who brought Christianity to England, albeit the

Roman Catholic version. This was not the bishop of Hippo, but the Augustine who landed in Kent in the year 597 AD.
In a recent TV programme which featured excavations at Hadrians wall they discovered Christian artifacts in a building which they believed had been used for Christian worship.
Claudius was the Emperor who conquered England in 43 AD. although Hadrian's wall would not have been built until between 117-138 AD.
The Emperor Hadrian, either himself or his command was at Hard Knott Fort until the year 129 AD, when he left. A broach in the form of a fish, an early Christian symbol was found there, believed to date from about 125 AD.
David E Gardner in his book "The Trumpet Sounds For Britain" puts forward a convincing argument, that because of the road system built by the Romans, which allowed easier travel, that Authentic Christianity arrived even before the Roman occupation of England and Wales, which was in 43 AD.
There is little doubt that the Gospel would have followed the Romans and that England had the authentic Christian message at the very least by the beginning of the second Century, which means nearly 500 years before Augustine ever set foot on its shores.

What do I mean by authentic Christianity?
It is obedience to the New Testament teaching of Christ in both life style and worship.

CHAPTER 4

THE TRUE CHURCH FOUNDED ON THE ROCK OF CHRIST, THE ROMAN CHURCH ON PETER AS THE FOUNDATION.

The Roman claim is based on Matthew 16:-18-19. "And I say also unto thee, That thou art Peter, and upon this rock I will build my Church; and the gates of hell shall not prevail against it. And I will give unto thee the keys of the kingdom of heaven: and whatsoever thou shalt bind on earth shall be bound in heaven: and whatsoever thou shalt loose on earth shall be loosed in heaven." K.J.V.

The Amplified New Testament makes Matthew 16:-18-19 clear by giving the Greek words Petros and Petra which are used in the text.

"And I tell you, you are Peter [Petros, masculine, a large piece of rock], and on this rock [Petra, feminine, a huge rock like Gibraltar] I will build My church, and the gates of Hades (the power of the infernal region) shall not overpower it – or be strong to its detriment, or hold out against it.

I will give you the keys of the kingdom of heaven, and whatever you bind – that is, declare improper and unlawful – on earth must be already bound in heaven; and whatever you loose on earth – declare lawful – must be what is already loosed in heaven."

The Greek word Petros literally means a stone.

It was on Peter's Proclamation "THOU ART THE CHRIST, THE SON OF THE LIVING GOD" that the Lord was going to build His Church.

"For their rock <u>is not as our Rock</u>." Deuteronomy 32:-31. K.J.V.

CHRIST ALONE IS THE TRUE ROCK ON WHICH OUR SALVATION DEPENDS

Scripture interprets Scripture, and it is emphasized again and again throughout Scripture that **God alone is the foundation for our trust and He is our salvation.**

2 Sam 22:-32. **"Who is a rock save only our God?"** K.J.V.

2 Sam 22:-2. **"The Lord is my Rock, and my fortress."** K.J.V.

1 Sam 2:-2. **"Neither is there any Rock like our God."** K.J.V.

Ps 28:-1 **“Unto thee will I cry. O Lord my Rock.”** K.J.V.

Ps 62:-2. **“He only is my Rock and my salvation.”** K.J.V.

Ps 89:-26. **“God, and the Rock of my salvation.”** K.J.V.

Ps 94:-22. **“And my God is the Rock of my refuge.”** K.J.V.

1 Cor 3:-11. **“For other foundation can no man lay than that is laid, which is Jesus Christ.”** K.J.V.

“The foundation that has been laid is Jesus Christ, and no one can lay down any other foundation.” 1 Cor 3:-11, from the N.C.V

“For they drank from the spiritual Rock that accompanied them, and that Rock was Christ.” 1 Cor 10:-4 N.I.V.

The true spiritual Church which Christ is building is founded on Christ Jesus the Lord.

PETER HAD THE PRIVILEGE OF GIVING THE GOSPEL TO JEWS, THEN TO THE GENTILES

Peter was told by the Lord Jesus “I will give you the keys of the kingdom of heaven.” Matthew 16:-19. The keys the Lord Jesus was speaking about were to be used to unlock the door to the forgiveness of our sins and the Kingdom of Heaven. The Gospel is that key. Acts 2:-38.
Peter was given the privilege of being the first of the apostles to Preach the **“Glad Tidings”** to the Jews on the day of Pentecost and also the first to open up the Kingdom to the Gentiles when he preached Christ to Cornelius and his household the first Gentiles to come into the Kingdom. Acts 10.
In the exercising of the “power of the keys” on the day of Pentecost Peter says: “It shall come to pass, that whosoever shall call on the name of the Lord shall be saved.” Acts 2:-21. K.J.V.

An example of this is found in Acts 16:-30-31: “Sirs, what must I do to be saved? And they said, Believe on the Lord Jesus Christ, and thou shalt be saved, and thy house.” K.J.V.

ALL THE DISCIPLES AND APOSTLES RECEIVE THE KEYS OF THE KINGDOM

The keys of the Kingdom were not given exclusively to Peter, but to all the disciples and apostles and this is made clear in Matthew 18:-1-18. Verse 1, says: "At that time the disciples came up and asked Jesus, Who then is [really] the greatest in the kingdom of heaven?"

And verse 18 says: "Truly, I tell you, whatever you forbid and declare to be improper and unlawful on earth must be what is already forbidden in heaven, and whatever you permit and declare proper and lawful on earth must be already permitted in heaven." The Amplified New Testament.

As believers we have the keys of the Kingdom of Heaven, the gospel message and we can unlock and open up the Kingdom to the lost by explaining to them the "Glad Tidings" of Christ the Saviour, so that they can believe in Christ and enter in.

THE BLASPHEMY OF TRANSUBSTANTIATION

The Roman Church claims that its priests have the power to change the wafer and wine into the literal body, blood and divinity of Christ. This is called Transubstantiation.

THERE WERE NO MINISTERING PRIESTS IN THE NEW TESTAMENT CHURCH

Read it as often as you will but in the New Testament you will not find clerics or practicing priests in the New Testament Church offering up sacrifices and interceding on behalf of the people, as is done in the Roman Church.

Nor was Peter ever a Bishop in the Roman Catholic sense, let alone of Rome.

The whole point of the Gospel is that Christ: "taketh away the first, that He may establish the second." **"Through the offering of the body of Jesus Christ once for all." Hebrews 10:-9-10. K.J.V.**

JOB CREATION IS NOTHING NEW

In justifying the priesthood, Rome has to invent a ministry for its priests. Rome claims that its priests have the power to bring the body of Christ

down from heaven and re-sacrifice Christ every day and turn the basic elements of the bread and wine into the literal body, blood and divinity of Christ, which is complete fantasy and blatant blasphemy.
They take the verses of Matthew 26:-26-28, and interpret them literally: "And as they were eating, Jesus took bread, and blessed it, and brake it, and gave it to the disciples, and said, Take, eat; this is my body. And he took the cup, and gave thanks, and gave it to them saying, Drink ye all of it; For this is my blood of the new testament, which is shed for many for the remission of sins." K.J.V.

CHRIST'S MEANING MADE PLAIN

We know that Christ meant the bread and wine to be taken symbolically and with true spiritual understanding – not literally – because of what He said in the next verse (29).
"But I say unto you, **I will not drink henceforth of this fruit of the vine,** until that day when I drink it new with you in My Father's kingdom." K.J.V.

DRINKING BLOOD WAS FORBIDDEN IN JEWISH LAW AND BY THE APOSTLES

In Acts 15:-28-29, James, when he had finished summing up a debate on whether Gentiles should be circumcised and conform to the Jewish law said:
"For it seemed good to the Holy Ghost, and to us, to lay upon you no greater burden than these necessary things: that ye abstain from meats offered to idols and from blood, and from things strangled, and from fornication." K.J.V.
One of the few things new Gentile converts to the Christian faith had to do, which was part of the Jewish Law, was **to abstain from drinking blood.** It was forbidden in the Jewish law to drink animal or human blood, hence the prohibition to the new Gentile converts, so it would have been sinful to drink the literal blood of Christ. The apostles forbade such a thing!
Jesus said in Matthew 5 :-17: "Do not think that I have come to do away with or undo the Law and the prophets; I have come not to do away with or undo, but to complete and fulfill them." The Amplified New Testament. The Old Testament reference is found in Leviticus 17:-10-11.

THE BODY OF CHRIST IS IN HEAVEN

The physical body of Christ is in Heaven since Christ's ascension and it is contrary to commonsense for the physical body of Christ to be in a multitude of places at the one time! Speaking of Christ's sacrifice, Scripture tells us: "But Christ did not offer Himself many times." Hebrews 9:-25. N.C.V.

CHRIST'S CRUCIFIXION FINISHED ALL SACRIFICES

In chapter 7 of the epistle to the Hebrews we are told, in verse 27, "He is not like other priests who had to offer sacrifices every day, first for their own sins and then for the sins of the people. **Christ offered His sacrifice only once and for all time when He offered Himself."** N.C.V.
In Hebrews 9:-25-26. "Nor yet that He should offer Himself often, as the high priest entereth into the holy place every year with blood of others; For then must He often have suffered since the foundation of the world: **But now once in the end of the world hath He appeared to put away sin by the sacrifice of Himself." K.J.V.**

"He doesn't do this every year as the high priests did under the old plan with blood that was not their own; if that had been the case, He would have to sacrifice Himself repeatedly throughout the course of history. But instead He sacrificed Himself once and for all, summing up all the other sacrifices in this sacrifice of Himself, the final solution of sin. **Everyone has to die once, then face the consequences. Christ's death was also a one-time event, but it was a sacrifice that took care of sins forever." Hebrews 9:-25-26-27.** The Message.

WHAT JOHN KNOX THOUGHT OF THE MASS

John Knox, who had been a Roman Catholic priest, as had been most of the Protestant leaders, believed transubstantiation to be 'Manifest wickedness' and a 'Detestable idolatry.' John Knox thought the mass so blasphemous that he said:
He would rather hear of an invading army landing on the shores of the land, than to hear of one mass said in the kingdom.

THE CLAIM BY ROME OF APOSTOLIC SUCCESSION

Rome says that the power given to Peter was absolute and this power is passed down by so-called apostolic succession, although it has to admit there is not one text in the Bible that can be found to back up this fictional Roman claim.

But their claim I believe can be justified from Scripture and proved by their behaviour, but it is not apostolic power but purely carnal belief (and with Satan's help) which is expressed in their deeds and not from the texts they use, but from the verses following, in Matthew 16:-21-23, verse 21 and 22 which read: "From that time forth began Jesus to shew unto His disciples how He must go unto Jerusalem, and suffer many things of the elders and chief priests and scribes, and be killed, and be raised again the third day. Then Peter took him, and began to rebuke Him, saying, Be it far from thee, Lord: this shall not be unto thee." K.J.V.

A REBUKE AND A PROPHETIC WORD TO PETER

I believe that the reply Jesus gave to Peter was prophetic, and was applicable not only to him but to all who would follow Peter's carnal example:

"But when He had turned around and looked at His disciples, He rebuked Peter, saying, 'Get behind Me, Satan! For you are not mindful of the things of God, but the things of men'" Mark 8:-33. N.K.J.V.

In his arrogance Peter, in rebuking Christ, was telling Jesus to be obedient to him and in so doing was asking Christ to follow him.

Jesus tells him to ***get behind Him*** (Where he ought to have been) in order to follow Him. In calling Peter "Satan" he was telling Peter that he was doing Satan's work in trying to frustrate the plan of God for the Salvation of the world.

THOSE WHO WOULD COME UNDER THIS REBUKE OF CHRIST'S

The modernists in theology as well as Roman Catholics in their intellectual and religious pride would come under Christ's condemnation.

Because like Peter they contradict His Word and try to redirect Christ's work and by so doing hinder people from salvation and following Christ. They are a **"Stumbling-block"** to Christ because they **"Think as men think, not as God thinks."** N.E.B.

THE CROSS OF CHRIST SEEMED FOOLISHNESS TO PETER

Peter was rebuked and called Satan because he was hindering God's plan of salvation for the world and living as a natural man and did not understand the spiritual truth and significance of what the Lord Jesus was conveying to him in verse 21. In fact it seemed foolishness to him. In his carnal thinking he was like the Pharisees who said:
"He saved others; Himself He cannot save." K.J.V.
They, like Peter, did not grasp the spiritual truth, that the supreme principle in redemption is sacrifice.
"The natural man receiveth not the things of the Spirit of God: for they are foolishness unto him: neither can he know them, because they are spiritually discerned." 1 Cor 2:-14. K.J.V.
I have dealt with this text and its reference to Peter more fully in the appendix of this book.
"For the preaching of the cross is to them that perish foolishness; but unto us which are saved it is the power of God." 1 Cor 1:-18. K.J.V.
Jesus preached the cross to Peter and it was foolishness to him.

ROME THE TRUE FOLLOWERS OF PETER, THEIR FOUNDATION

The hierarchy of the Roman religion is truly following Peter, and their church is built upon him, Peter, who, in his unregenerate state had the audacity to contradict and rebuke Christ and then to persuade Him from going to the cross and who later attempted to kill Malchus, the high priest's servant when he cut off his ear at Christ's arrest in the Garden, that Christ "should not be delivered to the Jews:" John 18:-10-36
Rome has the same arrogance and has done its utmost to hinder the Good News of Christ's salvation from being preached, not only by word, but with violence. *In its pride Rome claims to be the only Church and way of salvation, and all outside the Church of Rome are lost.
By their claim, Rome contradicts and rebukes Christ, as Peter did.
The Lord Jesus was emphatic when He said:
"I am the Way, the Truth, and the Life: no man cometh unto the Father, but by Me." John 14:-6. K.J.V.
Christ asserts in His categorical statement of John 14:-6. That He, not Rome is the Way, is the Truth, and the Life. Rome cannot give Eternal Life; Christ Alone Can.

*Pope Boniface VIII (1294 - 1303) demanded that all rulers be subject to him as pope and wrote in his Bull, '*Unam Sanctam*', 'We declare, state, define and pronounce that for every human creature to be subject to the Roman pope is altogether necessary to salvation.'
This is nothing less than the epitome of egotistical arrogance.

WHAT IS CHRIST'S KINGDOM?

What Peter had in mind when he contradicted the Lord and used violence was that Christ was going to set up an earthly visible Kingdom. Jesus said to Pilate,
"My kingdom is not of this world: if my kingdom were of this world, then would my servants fight, that I should not be delivered to the Jews:" John 18:-36. K.J.V.

CHRIST REJECTED PETER'S VIOLENCE

The inference that Christ makes is, that at that time Peter was not a true servant of Christ, and was not serving Christ's purpose because he was acting with violence, in a purely carnal way, that Christ "should not be delivered to the Jews."
The Roman hierarchy have tenaciously clung to Peter as the foundation of their Church and followed his carnal ways of contradicting Christ and His Word and of resorting to violence (which the Lord rejected) in order to establish a visible kingdom, when Christ clearly tells us.' ***"My kingdom does not belong to this world." John 18:-36. "God's kingdom is coming, but not in a way that you will be able to see with your eyes. People will not say, 'Look, here it is!' or, 'There it is!' because God's kingdom is within you."*** Luke 17:-20-21. N.C.V.
To put it another way, the Kingdom of God is invisible and exists in the hearts and lives of all who genuinely repent of their sins and welcome into their lives the living Christ as the only Saviour and Lord.

THE TRUE SPIRITUAL CHURCH WORSHIPS GOD IN SPIRIT AND TRUTH

"But the hour cometh, and now is, when the true worshippers shall worship the Father in spirit and in truth: for the Father seeketh such to worship Him. God is a Spirit: and they that worship Him must worship Him in spirit and in truth." John 4:-23-24. K.J.V.

GOD'S WORD OF TRUTH IS CENTRAL IN TRUE WORSHIP

"Thy Word is true from the beginning." Ps. 119:-160. "Thy law is truth" Ps. 119:-142. "Thy Word is very pure." Ps.119:-140. "Order my steps in Thy Word." Ps. 119:-133. "All thy commandments are truth." Ps.119:-151. K.J.V. The true worshippers of God, do this by obeying His Word and worshipping Him in the Spirit of His Word, not with rituals and religious performances, such as the burning of incense and the ringing of bells and chanting, which are mere substitutes for true spiritual worship.

A CARNAL CHURCH BUILT ON PETER AND ESTABLISHED BY MAN

Rome has established a visible kingdom, the Vatican City, a state within a state, with a king (the pope), and princes, bishops and cardinals. It issues its own passports and has its own political agenda. It has its own bank and displays to the world its great wealth and pomp, and has Ambassadors and Embassies in various countries around the world, but it has little if anything to do with the true spiritual **"Kingdom of God."**

It does not even remotely resemble the New Testament Church set up by Christ!

They have established Peter's unregenerate vision of an earthly kingdom.

Jesus said, "My kingdom does not belong to this world." John 18:36. N.C.V.

Note. You may think that my claim that the Church of Rome was built on the life of the Unregenerate Peter, is incorrect. But this is proved by the purely carnal argument Augustine puts forward justifying the birth of this new Hybrid.

James and John in asking for a position in Christ's Kingdom had, like Peter, the Zealot idea of an earthly kingdom. This is verified by their asking to bring fire down from heaven on people unwilling to co-operate with them. Jesus in answer to the disciples' request in Luke 9:-54 said:

"Ye know not what manner of spirit ye are of. For the Son of man is not come to destroy men's lives, but to save them." Luke 9:-55-56. K.J.V.

Augustine in his enthusiasm for the uniting of the Roman Empire with the Church had at least to try to justify, if possible, from Scripture the rightness in producing such a Hybrid. He did this by creating the doctrine, which Leonard Verduin referred to in his book "The Anatomy of a Hybrid" as the **"Monstrous doctrine of two swords."**

This was worked out so that the power and sword of government would be at the disposal of the Church. The "Two Swords" doctrine was based on Luke 22:-38, "And they said, Lord, behold, here are two swords. And He said unto them, It is enough." K.J.V.

When Peter used one of those swords to try to kill Malchus and instead cut off his ear, Jesus rebuked him and told him he did not need his carnal help. "Thinkest thou that I cannot now pray to My Father, and He shall presently give Me more than twelve legions of angels?" Matthew 26:-53. K.J.V.

By doing this Jesus pointed out to Peter that this battle was spiritual, as was His Kingdom, not an earthly carnal Kingdom.

But Augustine disregards Christ's teaching and puts the carnal help of the sword back into Peter's hand and that of his successors.

Those who conjured up the doctrine began to teach that the sword of government was given to Peter, and it was only by the permissiveness of the pope, who was allegedly Peter's successor, that they had this power to use.

It came to be an unquestioned doctrine of the Roman Church, that both the arm of government and the arm of the Church were part of the body of Christ, and that the pope was the one who was the head of this body.

It was through this doctrine that Augustine justified the persecution and murder of those who would not conform to the Roman doctrine.

Augustine through his doctrine has the blood of millions of devout believers in Christ, as well as Jews and Muslims on his hands!

Jesus tells us in Matthew 7:-15-20-21: "Beware of false teachers who come disguised as harmless sheep, but are wolves and will tear you apart.(16) You can detect them by the way they act, just as you can identify a tree by its fruit.(20) Yes, the way to identify a tree or a person is by the kind of fruit produced.(21) **Not all who sound religious are really godly people. They may refer to me as 'Lord,' but still won't get to heaven. For the decisive question is whether they obey My Father in heaven."** T.L.B.

The words of Christ were, I believe, prophetic when He said: "Get behind Me, Satan! For you are not mindful of the things of God, but the things of men." Mark 8:-33, N.K.J.V.

CHAPTER 5

FROM ONE EXTREME TO ANOTHER

The theology of Calvin was, I believe, reactionary and swung from the Roman religion's carnal way of man-made rules and regulations and salvation being entirely through man's endeavours, with the help of the rituals of Rome, to that of God doing everything and man not being involved in the process at all.

Doctrinally speaking, this is just as erroneous.

Man appears to go from one extreme to the other as a result of his reaction, or should I say over-reaction, and the truth is very rarely, if ever, found in extremes.

Calvinism (All Five Points) originated from the long forgotten teachings of Augustine, bishop of Hippo.

AUGUSTINE'S BACKGROUND AND DOCTRINE

Augustine was born in Tagaste, Numidia, the country we now call Algeria in 354 AD. His father was pagan, but his mother Monica was a devout Christian. He went to Carthage to study and was a keen student of Plato, Cirero and other philosophers, as well as an avid student of the Bible. While there he had a son to his mistress, whom he named Adeonatus. He became a devout Manichaean because it appeared to offer a solution to the problem of evil that was to preoccupy him for the rest of his life. But he later gave up Manichaeanism in disgust. He moved to Rome in 383 to teach and then to Milan and was greatly influenced by Scepticism and later by Neoplatonism. He had a dramatic spiritual crisis and became a convert to Christianity. This is described in his autobiography.

St. Ambrose baptized both Augustine and his son in 387 AD.

Augustine was reputed to have been one of the greatest intellects the world has ever known.

He returned to North Africa and became the bishop of Hippo in 396 AD.

He produced in 413-415 AD. his *DE CIVITATE DEI*, a deep and masterly vindication of the Christian Church, though here, as elsewhere, the mighty intellect is often misled by defective scholarship, for Augustine knew no Hebrew and very little Greek. Augustine published in 428 his Retractions, in which he fully concedes the errors and mistakes in his works. Calvinism is acknowledged as little more than a reassertion of Augustinianism. The Roman Catholic Hierarchy would deny this claim.

S. BARING-GOULD in his book "The Evangelical Revival" states: "With his new dogmas Augustine introduced a whole category of new terms, "Universal human depravity," "Original sin," "Effectual calling," and God's irreversible "Decrees." "Novel altogether Augustine's doctrine was."
"He was the first in Christ's Church to deny that Christ died for all men, to deny to man the exercise of free will, to urge on the persecution of heretics to death, to exalt slavery as a divine institution, to forge a theology so cruel, so shocking, that he himself, as he contemplated his accomplished work, stood aghast at its hideous completeness. He was actually, truly an innovator altering the whole character of Christianity."
S. Baring-Gould continues: "The divine purpose even drives man into horrible and unnatural sins, such as those mentioned by S. Paul (Rom.1.24, 25). On which Augustine comments (De Gratia et Lib.Arbit.xxi), after quoting other passages that he conceives established his point:"
"From these statements of the inspired word, and similar passages it would take too long to quote in full, it is, I think sufficiently clear that God works in the hearts of men, whether to do good deeds, or to evil."
"That the impulse to do evil came from God was what the heathen taught, and the idea was borrowed from them by Augustine."
"Augustine was of the opinion of Naevolus in the ninth of Juvenal's Satires, who said: "Fata regunt homines," to explain and justify his leading a grossly immoral life. But when Naevolus proceeds to draw there from the rigid conclusion that it avails not to pray, as destiny seals up her ears with wax to the voices of petitioners, Augustine would have hesitated to admit a fact that followed inexorably from the premiss.
There is something pitiable in the sight of a man of great intellect and consummate piety, as was Augustine, trying to adjust his system to Scripture, or, to be more exact, torture Scripture to establish his scheme. He was labouring to effect an impossibility. To veil his difficulties he had recourse to quips and evasions, and to envelop his argument in a cloud of words, so as to blind the eyes of his readers to the inconsequences of the writer."

CALVIN'S BIRTH AND BACKGROUND

John Calvin was born on the 10th July 1509, in Noyon, in Picardy. He became a student of Latin in Paris from 1523 and later he studied law in Orleans, then he went to Bourges to study Greek.
It is believed that the "Institutes" were completed by August 1535 when the writer had just reached the age of 26. He married a widow of a converted

Anabaptist in 1539. There are different opinions regarding the time of his conversion. Some suggest early in 1530 and others put it as late as 1533 when it is believed he went through an experience of sudden conversion to Christ. After Calvin and his friend Farel had been expelled from Geneva in 1538 he went to Strasbourg and devoted himself to the study of the New Testament.

The Genevans invited Calvin to return and after a delay, he accepted their invitation. He founded a theocracy, which controlled virtually all the affairs of the city, and after a struggle with the Libertines, which lasted fourteen years, the reformer's authority was confirmed into an absolute supremacy in 1555.

Calvin, like Augustine was familiar with all the Latin and Greek Philosophers and wrote a book, (his first) which was published in 1532, being an exposition on 'Seneca's 'De Clementia', in which he quotes from a large number of Latin and Greek authors, such as Cicero, Horace and Virgil.

CALVIN REVIVES AUGUSTINE'S DORMANT THESIS

There is no doubt that Calvin's teaching was really a rehash of the doctrine, which was created and formed by Augustine and rejected by the early Church as unacceptable.

Calvin had a very similar educational background in pagan philosophy and some of this is imported into his theology and this is possibly why his doctrine, which went to the opposite extreme from Romanism, appealed to him.

CALVINISTS BELIEVE, IF YOU DO NOT HOLD THEIR BELIEF, YOUR FAITH IS INCOMPLETE

After descending from an open-air platform at the Mound in Princes Street Edinburgh, having given my testimony, two young men approached me and engaged me in conversation. They said, that they were interested in what I had said, but that my religion was ***incomplete***, because I had not the revelation of the book of Mormon. **I told them that I had Christ and needed nothing but Him to be complete** and then I quoted two texts from Colossians 2:- 9-10, "**For in Him" (Christ) "dwelleth all the fulness of the Godhead bodily. And ye are COMPLETE IN HIM."** K.J.V.

The two young men said not a word and walked away.

Calvinists believe that if you do not believe what they believe you are in

error and that you are lacking in spiritual insight and understanding, because what they believe, is a revelation of wisdom. They portray the same image of superior knowledge as Job's friends, when Job summed up their attitude with the words:
"No doubt but ye are the people, and wisdom shall die with you." Job 12:-1. K.J.V.

The message of the Reformation was: **"We are saved by Christ alone."** This is correct.
We are not saved by Christ plus Calvinism, or any other ism.
If it was considered by the apostle Paul to be immature and carnal for the Corinthians to follow Peter, Apollos and Paul who were correct and not heretical in their teaching, how much more immature and carnal is it, if we follow Calvin?
It appears to me to be fashionable at the present time to go under the name Calvinists, but it is nevertheless Wrong!

THE OUTCOME OR FRUIT OF CALVINISM

When I was over in Northern Ireland on a preaching and deputation visit a minister told me that a colleague of his was conducting a children's mission in a Baptist Church, and was teaching the children the chorus: **"Jesus loves the little children, all the children of the world, Red and Yellow, Black and White, all are precious in His sight, Jesus loves the children of the world."** When the people in charge heard this, they told him that he would not be allowed to carry on the mission, because he was teaching error, when he taught this chorus, **because Jesus did not love all the children of the world.** So the mission was stopped. Of course this was the outworking of that Church's Calvinistic belief, that God loves some and hates others, even children.
This is not Hyper-Calvinism, but rather the implementation of Calvin's teaching put into effect in Church life, because that is what Calvin taught. What goes under the name of Hyper-Calvinism is really the teaching of Calvin put into practice.
The opposite is that God loves all people and Christ died for them, even the wicked.

THE STRAITJACKET OF CALVINISM ON EVANGELISTIC OUTREACH

An Open Air Mission Evangelist was holding a meeting at some tenement flats in Kilmarnock, Scotland and noticed a woman standing on her doorstep listening eagerly. She was past middle age and her bluish complexion indicated a serious heart condition. He approached her in a kindly way and asked if she were saved.

"Naebody kens that," she replied, and he soon found out that she had been brought up on the "Westminster Confession" and had no way of knowing whether she was "Predestined to everlasting life" or "Fore-ordained to everlasting death". He spent a long time with her, seeking to show her the way of salvation, and that her state of ignorance was a cruel, Satanic perversion of Holy Scripture; that God has taken the initiative in providing salvation for "the whole world", and awaits our response.

He was not sure whether he had succeeded in leading her to lay hold on those **"Exceeding great and precious promises" by which we become "Partakers of the divine nature."** 2 Peter 1:- 4. The Evangelist told me that although he had always disagreed with Calvinism, from that day on he has hated it.

THE DOCTRINE THAT MAKES THE PROMISES OF GOD INVALID

A young man known to me who had become a Christian, was called into full time service and went to a Calvinistic theological college of the denomination in which he was going to become a minister. After studying and finishing his course he had an interview with the committee with a view to becoming an accredited minister of that denomination.

REJECTED BECAUSE HE BELIEVED WHAT THEY TAUGHT

Among the many questions he was asked was one about his assurance of salvation. He had to admit that, although he had assurance when he came into the college, he did not really know now whether he had been Elected to salvation or not. Because of this he was rejected.

Was it not their theology, which he believed that had deprived him of his faith and brought about this doubt and lack of assurance?

CALVIN ADMITS THE PROBLEM OF DOUBT IN HIS DOCTRINE OF ELECTION

When man has no part whatsoever is his own salvation, but has to wait on

God to save him, before he can know if he is of the elect or not, his problems are great indeed.
Calvin admitted: "Among the temptations with which Satan assails believers, none is greater or more perilous than when disquieting them with doubts as to their election.
And this...is the temptation to which...almost all of us are most prone."
"For there is scarcely a mind in which the thought does not sometime arise: But what proof have you of your election? When once this thought has taken possession of any individual, it keeps him perpetually miserable, subjects him to dire torment, or throws him into a state of complete stupor." (Inst.3:-24 - 4)

If you believe in Calvin's thesis it is not only the attacks of Satan you have to contend with, but a false premise and there is no doctrine better designed to bring about perpetual misery, dire torment, or complete stupor, doubt and lack of assurance of salvation than that of Calvinism!
This doctrine has been for many the road to spiritual breakdown and madness.

THE CALVINIST FATALISTIC VIEW

A friend and fellow Evangelist told me he was asked to speak to an Edinburgh Humanist Group. These professed atheists listened to him with rapt attention for nearly an hour, and then they had about an hour's discussion.
After the meeting, one of their number, who came from the Highlands of Scotland, and who had been reared in Calvinism said, it was immaterial what he believed, for if the Bible was true, our eternal destiny had been settled long before we were born, so he might just as well be an atheist as a Church-goer.

Calvin was unable to give an answer to such logical reasoning put forward by people like this Highland gentleman, and so resorted to abuse, which is a poor substitute for reason.

MANY SWINE POLLUTE CALVIN'S DOCTRINE OF PREDESTINATION

In the "Institutes" Calvin informs us: "To overthrow predestination, our opponents also raise the point that, if it stands, all carefulness and zeal for well-doing go to ruin. For who can hear, they say, that either life or death has been appointed for him by **"God's eternal and unchangeable decree"** without thinking immediately that it makes no difference how he conducts himself, since God's predestination can neither be hindered nor advanced by his effort? "

"Thus all men will throw themselves away, and in a desperate manner rush headlong wherever lust carries them. Obviously they are not completely lying (!!), **for there are many swine that pollute the doctrine of predestination with their foul blasphemies,** and by this pretext evade all admonitions and reproofs."

Calvin uses many abusive words in the Institutes against those who disagree with him, such as," Perverse and foreboding prophets," "Insane," "Fanatics," "The foul grunting of these swine," etc.

CALVIN'S FAVOURING OF THE BURNING OF HERETICS

Because of his complete intolerance of any view other than his own, it is not to be wondered at that Calvin endorsed the notion that heretics should be put to death. He wrote: "whosoever shall now contend that it is unjust to put heretics and blasphemers to death will, knowingly or unknowingly, incur their very guilt. This is not laid down on human authority; it is God that speaks and prescribes it as a perpetual rule for the Church." In saying this Calvin was following Augustine instead of Christ. For Augustine expounded this same doctrine. He was confused in his understanding of Old and New Testament theology and obviously ignores all the teaching of Christ who said, "Love your enemies, bless them that curse you, do good to them that hate you, pray for them which despitefully use you, and persecute you."

Heretics included all those who would have a theological opinion differing from his own.

Calvin seems to have forgotten that the Lord Jesus Christ was put to death by religious people who believed Christ to be a blasphemer, because He claimed to be the Son of God!

IRONY OF REFORMERS FOLLOWING THE FOUNDER OF THE ROMAN CHURCH

Although Calvin had a great admiration for the doctrine of Augustine and adopted it in the setting up of his Reformed Church, Augustine's judgment on Calvin and all who follow his path is made clear in a statement he made

against a Protestant of his day.
He said: “Placed outside the Church, severed from the tree of unity, and from the cords of affection, thou shalt be punished with everlasting torments, **even wert thou to give thyself to be burned alive for the name of Christ.”**
It is ironic that the one who was the principal architect of the hybrid Roman Church, and the one who produced much of the erroneous doctrine and practice, which was so despised and hated by the prime movers in the Reformation, was the one chosen by the Reformers as the teacher they should follow.

THE CORRECT PRINCIPLES OF THE REFORMERS

The Reformers correctly believed the Bible to be the inspired Word of God, using it as the only rule of faith and morals.
I believe their deliberate intention was to set aside all appeals to tradition or to the hierarchy. The Word of God was to be the Sword of Protestantism.
What they failed to do was to get rid of all the pillars of the Roman religion, tradition such as the doctrine of Augustine, using the sword of government to persecute those who would not conform to their beliefs.
They failed to rely only on the Word of God.

THE BURNING OF A HERETIC

One such person who was burned at the stake as being a heretic was a man from Spain named Servetus. The burning was a logical outcome of this kind of thinking, and was the continuation of the intolerance by the Roman religion. In a letter Calvin mentioned that if ever Servetus came to the city and under his authority, which he reviles, he would never let him out of the city alive. He kept his word.

When the death sentence was passed, Calvin did try to have Servetus executed by a less painful means, other than by burning, but this was more to ease his conscience than because he realized that the burning of people for heresy was questioned publicly and becoming less acceptable. Perhaps one of the reasons for this was the slow and extremely painful method of death. When a heretic was sentenced to death it was usually stipulated that the execution was to be by “small fire” and it appears in the case of Servetus green wood was used, so that it took three hours before he was pronounced dead.

"Whosoever doeth not righteousness is not of God, neither he that loveth not his brother 1 John 3:-10. Whosoever hateth his brother is a murderer: and ye know that no murderer hath eternal life abiding in him." 1 John 3:-15. K.J.V.

PROTESTS WERE MADE AGAINST THE BURNING OF SERVETUS

There were protests before, during and after the burning of Servetus and this was vexatious to Calvin and caused him much trouble. But he was certain he was right. Not long after the death of Servetus, a book was published anonymously arguing against and strongly condemning the burning of Servetus. Calvin was not persuaded by reason or Biblical argument. He was not in the least dissuaded in his opinion but with the help of Beza wrote in reply a long article arguing and defending the burning of Servetus, specifically, and all heretics generally.

An Anabaptist, during the trial, who was taking refuge from persecution himself and living in Switzerland, wrote to the magisterial reformers who were conducting the trial and argued strongly against the death of Servetus. The gist of his argument was as follows. "Noble, wise, prudent lords, consider what would happen if every liberty were granted to men's opponents to kill heretics. How many men would remain alive on earth if each had the power over the other according to their mutual definition of heresy? Turks and Jews consider Christians to be heretics and Christians treat each other as such. Papists and Lutherans, Zwinglians and Anabaptists, Calvinists and Adiaphorists, all excommunicate each other. Must men hate and kill each other because of differences of belief and opinion? In regard to this Servetus, if he is a heretic in God's eyes, then do not inflict bodily torture upon him. At the worst banish him from your city." This man took considerable risk because Anabaptists were detested and persecuted by those of the Reformed faith. There were many put to death in Switzerland during and after the Reformation.

CONTEMPORARIES HAD DOUBTS THAT CALVIN WAS TRULY REGENERATE

A contemporary of Calvin, Pieter Bloccius, wrote in answer to Calvin's argument: "That heretics are to be killed Christ has nowhere taught....**They who recommend that heretics be put to death show that they are not truly regenerate**, men who would be more blessed if they would seek out a hundred passages from the New Testament dealing with love......**and**

men who belch forth books advocating the killing of heretics want to pass for Christians; this you have not learned from Christ, who rebuked the vengeful disciples."

WE IGNORE CHRIST'S TEACHING AT OUR PERIL

Calvin completely ignored the gospels and, in particular, the teaching of the Lord Jesus Christ, in his understanding and dealings with others, particularly those who disagreed with him. Did Christ not say it is the foolish man who does not do what Christ teaches, and the wise man who does? We know what happens to the foolish man. Matthew 7:-24-27.

IN CALVIN'S PLACE WHAT WOULD CHRIST HAVE DONE?

Certainly not what Calvin did! "If any man have not the Spirit of Christ, he is none of His." Romans 8:-9. K.J.V.
So, it would appear that the man whom many today take as their spiritual guide was regarded, and understandably so, by some of his contemporaries as NOT BEING BORN AGAIN.

THE OUTWORKING OF CALVIN'S APARTHEID THEOLOGY

Because of this Calvinistic apartheid theology, which teaches that God loves one person but hates another, it is not surprising that while John Wesley was campaigning against slavery, the Calvinist preacher George Whitefield was introducing it into Georgia in America.
The founder of the Colony of Georgia was General Oglethorpe, who was a devout Christian man, and compassionate to the needs of others. He made Georgia an asylum for unfortunate debtors from the very harsh penalties inflicted by the cruel penal law of England.

General Oglethorpe also believed that slavery was against the gospel, as well as the basic law of Britain, and looked upon slavery as a dreadful crime and it was completely prohibited by the trustees of the Colony.
Nevertheless Whitefield managed to neutralize the humane intentions of the founder and the trustees and slavery was introduced into the Colony.
When George Whitefield died he left in his will the fifty Negro slaves he owned, to the Countess of Huntingdon.

CHAPTER 6

THE FIVE POINTS OF CALVINISM

The "Five Points" of Calvinism are best known in the "TULIP" form, which are T = Total Depravity, U = Unconditional Election, L = Limited Atonement, I = Irresistible Grace, P = Perseverance of the Saints, and are perhaps less objectionable and repugnant than the generally accepted longer version of the "Five Points" which was produced by the Synod of Dort in 1618-19, in answer to James Arminius's Five Points of doctrine. They are as follows, and are not in the same sequence as the "TULIP" form, and are with headings, which I have added.

UNCONDITIONAL ELECTION

1. God by an absolute decree, has elected to salvation a very small number of men, without any regard to their faith and obedience whatsoever, and has secluded from saving faith all the rest of mankind; and has appointed them, by the same decree, to eternal damnation, without any regard to their infidelity or impenitency.

LIMITED ATONEMENT

2. That Christ Jesus hath not suffered for any other than for the Elect only, having neither had any intent nor commandment of the Father to make any Satisfaction for the sins of the whole World.

THE TOTAL DEPRAVITY OF MAN

3. That, by Adam's fall his posterity lost their free will, being put to an unavoidable necessity to do, or not to do, whatsoever they do, or do not, whether it be good or evil; being thereunto predestinated by the Eternal and Effectual SECRET DECREE OF GOD.

IRRESISTIBLE GRACE

4. That God, to save the Elect from the corrupt mass, doth beget Faith in them by a power equal to that whereby He created the world, and raised up the dead; Insomuch such unto whom He gives grace cannot reject it, and the rest being reprobate cannot accept it.

THE PERSEVERANCE OF THE SAINTS

5. That such as have once received the grace of faith can never fall from it finally. Notwithstanding the most enormous sins they have commited.

WHAT HAVE THE FIVE POINTS OF CALVINISM TO DO WITH THE GOSPEL?

Pastor W. J. Seaton in his booklet, "The Five Points Of Calvinism," which has been in circulation for over twenty five years, and which is produced to promote Calvinism, tries to explain the five points, and on the back cover, and also on page 17 of his article, he makes the following astonishing claim:

"By an accident of history in the 17th century five great Christian truths, formulated by successors of the Reformers at the Synod of Dort to counter a drift from the gospel, became linked with the name of the Genevan Reformer who had died a half a century earlier."

"And again, let us recognize the fact that all that the men at the Synod of Dort [and those who teach likewise] were doing, was putting into small compass in a systematic form, **the teaching of God's Gospel of free and sovereign grace."**

"The "Pastor", on page five of his booklet, also refers to Calvinism as a "System."

Pastor Seaton has the audacity to put forward the man-made Calvinistic points as "God's Gospel."

The Gospel is not based upon a man-made "system," Calvinist or otherwise, but is clearly defined in John 3:-16 which is that God loves all mankind and that Christ died for the whole World, and this is emphasized again by John in his epistle, 1 John 2:-2.

"And He is the propitiation for our sins: and not for ours only, BUT ALSO FOR THE SINS OF THE WHOLE WORLD." K.J.V.

1 Timothy 6:-3, tells us, "If anyone tries to teach some doctrinal novelty which is not compatible with sound teaching (which we base on Christ's own words and which lead to Christ-like living), then he is a conceited idiot!" J. B. Phillips.

"But I certify you, brethren, that the gospel which was preached of me is not after man. For I neither received it of man, neither was I taught it, but by the revelation of Jesus Christ." Galatians 1:-11-12. K.J.V.

"I want you to know that the Good News I preached to you was not made up by human beings. I did not get it from humans, nor did anyone teach it to me, but Jesus Christ showed it to me." Galatians 1:-11-12. N.C.V.

THE CURSE OF GOD WHICH COMES ON THOSE WHO CHANGE THE GOSPEL

There is a curse that comes with changing or perverting the Gospel.
"But even if we, or an angel from heaven, should preach any gospel to you other than what we have preached to you, let him be accursed."
Galatians 1:-8. N.K.J.V.

THE FIVE POINTS ARE NOT REMOTELY CONNECTED WITH THE GOSPEL

What the above Five points have to do with the Gospel message, and rectifying a drift away from it, would baffle all who know and love the Good News, for the five points have nothing whatsoever to do with the "Glad Tidings" which Christ preached in John 3:-14-17, ***which is the true Gospel of Christ, which is free to all who accept and believe.***

"And the Angel said unto them, Fear not: for, behold I bring you good tidings of great joy, which shall be to all people." Luke 2:-10. K.J.V.
*How could the particular points on "Unconditional Election" or "Limited Atonement" even have a remote connection with the Gospel? Let me remind you of what they say.

“UNCONDITIONAL ELECTION”

1. “God by an absolute decree, has Elected to Salvation a very small number of men, without any regard to their faith and obedience whatsoever, and has secluded from saving faith all the rest of mankind; and has appointed them, by the same decree, to eternal damnation, without any regard to their infidelity or impenitency.”

“LIMITED ATONEMENT”

2. “That Christ Jesus hath not suffered for any other than for the elect only, having neither had any intent nor commandment of the Father to make any Satisfaction for the sins of the whole World.”
Calvin also says in his Institutes “(God) has barred the door of Life to those whom He has given over to Damnation.”

GOD’S WILL IS THAT ALL MEN SHOULD BE SAVED

Scripture reminds us in 1 Timothy 2:-3-4 **“For this is good and acceptable in the sight of God our Saviour; who will have all men to be saved, and come unto the knowledge of the truth.” K.J.V.**

“This is right and pleasing in the sight of God our Saviour, who wills all mankind to be saved and to come to the knowledge of the truth.” The same verses from the Weymouth translation.

“Truly God will never do wrong; the Almighty will never twist what is right.” Job 34:-12. N.C.V.
The five Calvinistic points militate against the “Glad Tidings” and are the opposite of good news to all men, and would inhibit anyone who believes in them from preaching the gospel, and to claim that the five points were brought in to “Counter a drift from the Gospel” **is complete nonsense; the very opposite is true.**

CHAPTER 7

TOTAL FALL IN THE GARDEN OF EDEN

Calvinists make hyperbolic statements and expect people to take them seriously when they put up their smoke screen of explanatory words in order to make their statements sound reasonable.

Pastor Seaton on page 4 of the booklet on Calvinism, writes, "Man is totally unable to save himself on account of the Fall in the Garden of Eden being a Total Fall." Then, on page 5, he speaks about those who believe man's fall in the Garden as being Merely Partial, not total.

What is meant by, "Merely Partial?" Partial means not complete.

And "Total Fall" means a complete or entire fall.

If we are to take these words at their universally accepted meaning, we must assume that, from the fundamental moral principle which had to exist in man when he was in full communion with God in the Garden of Eden, which was Goodness and Love, that this was totally reversed to a principle of Evil and Hatred. This is what a Total Fall would mean.

Anything less than this could not be called a complete or total fall, as a total reversal of direction would mean turning and going the opposite way. So a total fall spiritually and morally would mean the exact opposite of the condition and state of man in the Garden of Eden, from Goodness and Love to that of Evil and Hatred, whereas less than this would be, as he put it, "Merely Partial."

THE UNREASONABLENESS OF THE DOCTRINE OF TOTAL DEPRAVITY

It is an uncompromising and exclusive term "The Total Depravity of Man." Without at this moment going into what Calvinist apologists put forward as an explanation of what they mean by "Total Depravity" we will examine the implications of the universally accepted meaning of the two words.

YOU CANNOT HAVE DEGREES OF TOTAL

This would make man Totally Evil and incapable of love, which is, of course, nonsense. It would also mean that there are no degrees of depravity in man, which is also incorrect. The Word of God tells us in 2 Timothy 3:-13 "But evil men and seducers shall wax worse and worse, deceiving, and being deceived." K.J.V.

So the natural state of man is not "Total Depravity". This is an intellectual exercise to establish a point in a theological theory, which has no factual relevance to reality. Doctrine, to be sound, must be true to experience or it is meaningless and serves no real purpose, except perhaps to confuse or mislead.

THE PRINCIPLE WHICH EXISTS IN SOCIETY

Society as we know it could not exist if "Man's Natural State" were, as they insist, that of "Total Fall," i.e. "Total Depravity." The essential unit of the communities we live in, the family, must cherish and care for each other to survive as individuals or as a family.

The fundamental principle in physical life is that which existed in the Garden of Eden with the additional factor of sin, which has brought the separation from God, and not as the Calvinists infer, a total reversal of principle.

MAN IS MADE IN THE IMAGE OF GOD

The acceptance of their conclusion would mean **that man is no longer in the image of God**, because man is totally evil. This could in no way Reflect the Image of God, let alone the Glory of God. 1 Cor 11:-7.

Most theologians believe that the image is not physical because God is Spirit, but is a moral and spiritual likeness and because man, like his creator, is a trinity. Genesis 1:-26, "Let Us make man in our own image, after Our Likeness." K.J.V.

God's own moral character, His Justice and Righteousness are reflected in man and can be said to be part of the Image of God in man.

If man is, as Calvinists say, spiritually dead, because he is "Totally Depraved" how can he be in the Image of God, if he has no spiritual existence and is morally destitute?

In 1 Corinthians 11:-7 we read: "For a man indeed ought not to cover his head, **forasmuch as he is the image and glory of God**." K.J.V.

In the light of this text, **and because you cannot put a hat on moral and spiritual values**, it must be interpreted in a literal sense, to include the physical, as well as the moral and spiritual likeness, also that man is tripartite like God, which includes his physical body.

To say that Calvinists have a problem reconciling their theory with Scripture would be an understatement.

GOD WANTS US TO BE LIKE HIM

It would be true to say that God wants man to be like Him, and Satan wants man to be like Satan. God is completely good, and it is generally believed that Satan is completely evil. But man is neither wholly good nor wholly evil. It would be equally true to say that man could not become, totally good or Godly, without the help of God, nor could he become totally Evil or Satanic without the help of Satan.

There is not only the fact of man's sin, but also the very powerful unseen spiritual forces working upon and in and through individuals for good and evil. And all this hinges on what people believe.

This is why the Lord Jesus put so much emphasis on believing in Him, a very important component in the problem, if we want a proper understanding of what the Bible teaches.

AN EXTREME IDEA TO ESTABLISH THAT IN SPIRIT MAN IS DEAD TO GOD

As I see it, the Calvinist conveys the idea that man is "Totally Depraved" to establish the thought that because he is so, **he is also completely dead to God spiritually**, like a physical corpse is to the world, and therefore concludes the "Total Inability" of man to participate or contribute towards his salvation, not even by believing and repenting.

The link between the moral and spiritual is clear, and is referred to in Scripture in Romans 7:-14, **"For we know that the Law is spiritual:** but I am carnal, sold under sin." K.J.V.

But if man can understand the Law or Commandments of God he must have <u>a spiritual aspect in his life</u> in order to **comprehend these moral laws, which are spiritual. "These commands are like a lamp; this teaching is like a light. And the correction that comes from them will help you have life." Proverbs 6:-23 N.C.V.**

In Romans 2:-14-15,we are told that the Law is written on the very heart of man. "For when the Gentiles, which have not the law, do by nature the things contained in the law, these having not the law, are a law unto themselves. Which shew the work of the law written in their hearts, their conscience also bearing witness, and their thoughts the mean while accusing or else excusing one another." K.J.V.

Those two words, "Total Depravity", are not consistent with actual reality, or Scripture.

HOW CALVINISTS EXPLAIN THIS DOCTRINE AWAY

Calvinists explain it away by saying that what they mean by the words "The Total Depravity of Man" is that every department of man's life has been affected by sin. This no Bible believing person would deny, but this is not total depravity. To the Calvinist total doesn't mean total. All doesn't mean all and world doesn't mean world, but only the elect in the world. Whosoever does not mean whosoever, but only that limited number, they believe, for whom Christ Died.

I quote from the same writer, "When Calvinists speak of total depravity, however, they do not mean that every man is as evil as he could possibly be," ***Why then do they use a phrase that means exactly that?***

"Nor that man is unable to recognize the will of God; nor yet, that he is unable to do any good towards his fellow man, or even give outward allegiance to the worship of God."

"What they do mean is that when man fell in the Garden of Eden he fell in his **"Totality"**. The whole personality of man has been affected by the fall, and sin extends to the whole of the faculties - the will, the understanding, the affections and all else."

This is more or less the same explanation that is given by other Calvinist theologians in their works on systematic theology when trying to explain what "Total Depravity" means.

THE MAIN PRINCIPLE THROUGH WHICH THE FAMILY FUNCTIONS

Because sin has tainted every department of man, he is totally evil.

Let us transfer this logic into another situation in order to get an idea of its sense and rationality.

The basic unit of society is the family. In order for the family, be it Christian or otherwise, to exist, and continue to exist successfully, it must function on the principle of love and care, a great deal of love and care for one another over an extended period of time, even though every member of the family is a sinner.

Would Pastor Seaton describe this group of sinners as being a totally wicked family because every member of the family is a sinner?

The whole family has sinned in its **"Totality"** the father, the mother, and all the individual children. Sin extends to the whole family. Therefore, using this kind of logic, it would be described as a Totally Depraved Family. What utter nonsense!

To say that every department of man has been affected or tainted by sin, may be correct according to Scripture, but when the "Pastor" uses the word **Totality** to describe this, he is wrong.

Totality means the whole sum, or entirety, **and not parts of the parts of the whole.**

There is a vast difference between every department of man being affected by sin, and every department of man being completely sinful, which is what the words "Totally Depraved" mean.

TO ILLUSTRATE THE POINT

If I say that my front door is totally black, and then say, but what I mean by this is that it is totally black, although it has some white panels and white beading, but there is not a part of the door that has not some black on it. Apart from the fact that sane people would look upon me as a lunatic, I could not in honesty say that the door was Totally Black.

In fact I would be telling a deliberate lie if I did.

That is exactly what the Calvinists do. They say that man is "Totally Depraved" and then go on to explain that he is not.

One cannot have it both ways without being dishonest and deceitful.

APPLY THE PRINCIPLE OF LOVE INSTEAD OF SIN

If you apply the same reasoning Calvinists use with sin, and transfer it to one of the other fundamental principles in man, that of love, which is common to all men, using Calvinist logic you could say that, I quote:

"The whole personality has been affected" (by Love) "and" (Love) "extends to the whole of the faculties – the will, the understanding, the affections and all else." And this would be perfectly true.

But if you do what Calvinists do with sin and project this further, to come to the conclusion that, because this is so, **man is totally loving**, you are illogical.

This conclusion would leave out the factor of **sin** in man and like that of "Total Depravity", which leaves out the principle of love in man, would be completely divorced from actual reality and, although it contains an element of truth, it would therefore be erroneous.

WHY CAN'T CALVINISTS ARTICULATE ACCURATELY WHAT THEY MEAN?

I can't believe it was beyond their ability to use the resources of language, either French, Latin or Greek if it is beyond the scope of English, to replace the words "Total Depravity," with a few words to articulate accurately and clearly what they really mean, without confusion and double talk, if this indeed had been in their mind.

But I believe they must exaggerate and go beyond Biblical parameters to arrive at the extreme view, that man is totally dead to God spiritually, as a physical corpse is to the world.

When they give their explanation of what they mean by Total Depravity they are in fact admitting that the universally accepted meaning of those two words conveys the idea that man is completely wicked to the exclusion of any good, and they are contradicting themselves by the explanation, **for this is exactly the thought Calvinists wish to plant, that of the total depravity of man, which leads to the conclusion of the "total inability of man."**

Calvinists change the meaning of the words without changing the words, so that they can revert back to the true meaning, when it suits them.

Why use the words, "The Total Depravity of Man", if this does not accurately convey what you really mean - unless you wish to deceive or confuse or use it as a pretext?

The very idea Calvinists wish to establish, that of total spiritual deadness to God, like a carcass, they disestablish by their explanation! Man, if spiritually a corpse, could not give outward allegiance to the worship of God, or be able to recognize the will of God.

He would be completely oblivious to God, as a physical corpse is to its surroundings!

LIFE RECOGNISES AND CAN COMMUNICATE WITH LIFE

It takes a physically alive person to recognize and understand another person who is alive; and it takes a spiritually alive individual to be conscious of and understand the will of a Spiritual God.

Man is religious because of his awareness of God.

"God is a Spirit: and they that worship Him must worship Him in spirit and in truth." (JOHN 4:-24 K.J.V.)

THE LORD'S ASSESSMENT OF MAN'S STATE.

I would say that the accurate and the only dependable assessment of the true condition of man, is given by the one who is the Saviour of man, the Lord Jesus Christ; and who would know better than the Redeemer and Creator, the Great I AM?
To say that man is depraved or evil would be correct and Scriptural, but this does not exclude love and goodness, as the prefixed **'Total'** would before **'Depravity'** and we have the authority of our Lord to confirm this.
The Lord Jesus Christ in the articulation of the state of man, In Luke 11:-13, when He spoke to His disciples about their condition the Lord says: **"If ye then, being evil, know how to give good gifts unto your children:** how much more shall your heavenly Father give the Holy Spirit to them that ask Him?" K.J.V.
Why did He not say, If ye being Totally evil? After all it was only one small word more.
Did the Lord Jesus not know that every department of man's life was tainted by sin?
If total evil had been the actual condition of man, our Lord would most certainly have said so.
But the following words could not have been said, "Know how to give good gifts unto your children."

Even in this short statement of the Lord Jesus, explaining the state of man, He has a balanced assessment, which can be related to reality, with both evil and good in the text, unlike the Synod of Dort's pronouncement, "That man's natural **state is a state of Total Depravity."**
Note. The Greek word for good in Luke 11:-13, is **agatha** meaning good in a general sense. The other Greek word used in the New Testament for good in the sense of virtuous, is the word **kalos**.

CALVINISTS GO FAR BEYOND THE ASSESSMENT OF THE LORD JESUS

They go far beyond the assessment of our Lord Jesus Christ who is the Truth, and in so doing claim to know more than our Lord.
If total sinfulness were the genuine condition of man, it would be clearly evident in hell, where there is no restraining influence through the working of God's Word, or Christian witness.

EVEN IN HELL MAN HAS LOVE AND CONCERN FOR THOSE LEFT BEHIND

We have in Luke 16:-19, the story of the rich man and Lazarus and we find that the rich man was asking for Lazarus to be sent back from the dead to warn his five brothers, "Lest they also come into this place of torment".
So even in hell man has love and concern for those who were near and dear to him on earth.
This would be impossible if he were Totally Sinful.

W. J. SEATON REVERTS TO THE ACTUAL MEANING OF TOTAL DEPRAVITY

After explaining that total depravity doesn't mean total depravity, the writer reverts back to the actual meaning by quoting what is perhaps the nearest to a description of Total Wickedness you will find in the Old Testament Scriptures, then in the last part of his short chapter on Total Depravity he concludes by saying **"The depravity is total." (Of man).**

Pastor Seaton continues: **"By birth**: 'Behold, I was shapen in iniquity, and in sin did my mother conceive me.' [Ps 51.5]"
"By practice: 'And God saw that the wickedness of man was great upon the earth, and that every imagination of the thoughts of his heart was only evil continually.'" (Gen 6.5).
"**This then, is man's natural state**. We must ask, then: Can the **dead** raise themselves? Can the **bound** free themselves? Can the **blind** give themselves sight, or the **deaf** hearing? Can the **slaves** free themselves? Can the **uninstructable** teach themselves? Can the **naturally sinful** change themselves? Surely not! 'Who can bring a clean thing out of an unclean?' asks Job; and he answers, 'Not one!' [Job 14.4]. 'Can the Ethiopian change his skin, or the leopard his spots?' asks Jeremiah;
'If they can,' he concludes, 'then may ye also do good, that are accustomed to do evil.' [Jer 13:23].
Then he goes on to say, "Could the Word of God show more plainly than it does that **the depravity is total?** And that our inability to desire or procure salvation is also total?"

RELATING THE THEORY TO REALITY

"This then is man's natural state."
Take this kind of logic and apply it to the other group of people in Genesis destroyed because of their wickedness, Sodom and Gomorrah. Would he say that homosexuality is the natural state of man because God destroyed those cities for this particular sin?
Surely heterosexuality is man's natural state.
Let us move away from the generality of evil mentioned in Genesis 6:-5, and translate this into particular cases of evil in this contemporary age in which we live – happenings which I have no doubt would be reflected in similar forms of behaviour in those who lived before the flood, and also in Sodom and Gomorrah.

IS IT THE NATURAL STATE OF MOTHERS TO MURDER THEIR CHILDREN?

Recently I read in a daily paper of a woman in England who was convicted of suffocating two of her children, when they were infants, and the oldest child of about seven years of age she drowned in a bath.
The boy before he died, called out to his mother, **"Mummy please don't kill me."**
Is this the natural state and behaviour pattern of mothers in general?
Or take the Fred and Rosemary West case at Gloucester who were convicted of murdering a number of children, at least one being their own, among the 10 or more victims they murdered.
Is this the natural state and behaviour pattern of families in general?
Or the Dunblane killing of sixteen little children and their teacher by Thomas Hamilton?

Would pastor Seaton say that this is the natural behavioural pattern, and state of man? The very opposite is true.

THE REVULSION OF THE GENERAL PUBLIC TO SUCH EVIL

After the great revulsion of the general public the authorities have pulled down the house in Gloucester where these atrocities occurred, and ground down the bricks to powder and burned everything else.

The Gym Hall at Dunblane Primary school where the killing of the sixteen children and one teacher took place has also been destroyed and a new hall will be built on a different site at the tax payers' expense.
Great evil goes against the natural state of man, even although man is a sinner!
To take the statement of this text (Genesis 6:-5) out of context and to imply that God is saying that this is the natural state of man is wrong.

WAS IT NOT BECAUSE THEY HAD MOVED SO FAR AWAY FROM THEIR NATURAL STATE THAT GOD BROUGHT THE JUDGMENT OF THE FLOOD?
Pastor Seaton's statement is based on the findings of the Synod of Dort. But if the pronouncement that man's natural state is the condition of "Total Depravity" is to be taken at its face value, it is nonsense and divorced from actual reality. If people before the flood had been, as he has implied, Totally Depraved, God would not have needed to send the flood, they would have destroyed themselves.

BECAUSE EVIL IS DESTRUCTIVE, TOTAL EVIL WOULD BE TOTALLY DESTRUCTIVE!

COMPARING SCRIPTURE WITH SCRIPTURE

In the King James Version of Genesis 6:-5, it would appear to promote the idea that man became "Totally Depraved" before the flood, but when looked at in the light of other Scriptures you find that this could not possibly be so. This verse in the King James Version, cannot be taken literally, just as Exodus 3:-8, **"Unto a land following with milk and honey."** Were there rivers of milk and honey or were they ankle deep in milk and honey?
Or in Deu 1:-28, **"The cities are great and walled up to heaven."** K.J.V. Were the walls higher than the Empire State Building in New York?
Also in John 9:-2-3, "And his disciples asked Him, saying, master who did sin, this man, or his parents, that he was born blind? **Jesus answered, Neither hath this man sinned, nor his parents:** but that the works of God should be made manifest in him." K.J.V.
"And God saw that the wickedness of man was **great** in the earth, and that every imagination of the thoughts of his heart was only evil continually." Genesis 6:-5. K.J.V.

If the fall was **absolute and the depravity absolute,** why refer to the wickedness as **"Great"** when it was already known to be absolute if the Dortian idea is correct?
It is impossible for there to be a greater than total.

James Moffatt translates Genesis 6:-5-6, thus: "When the Eternal saw that the wickedness of man on the earth was great, and that man's mind was never bent on anything but evil, the Eternal was sorry that He had ever made man on the earth; it was a grief to Him."

The Living Bible interprets the same verses as follows, "When the Lord God saw the extent of human wickedness, and the trend and direction of men's lives were only towards evil, He was sorry He had made them. It broke His heart."

The Septuagint which is the principal Greek version of the Old Testament, translated by Jewish scholars, interprets the text as follows: "The Lord God, having seen that the wicked actions of men were multiplied upon the earth and that every one in his heart was brooding intently over evil continually."
Of the English translations, here, Moffatt's translation seems clearly to express the sense of the Hebrew text.

THE TEACHING OF CHRIST MAKES IT CLEAR

I believe that the answers to most theological problems are to be found in the gospels, and in the teaching of our Lord Jesus Christ. When I first considered Genesis 6:-5, in the King James Version, my thoughts were similar to the writer of the booklet, until I meditated upon this, especially after reading and considering what the Lord Jesus said in the gospel of Luke 17:-26-29, about the people before the flood, and I came to the conclusion that it would be an impossibility to go about the ordinary activities of life as the Lord Jesus clearly states they did, and only think evil continually.
Just as it would be impossible for a person to go about the ordinary activities of life, and be a total liar, which would mean 100% lies, and no truth, and it would be illogical, as well as extremely foolish, for it would mean telling lies when there was no reason to do so.

THE LORD SPOKE OF THE TWO GROUPS AS BEING SYNONYMOUS

The Lord Jesus when speaking about the people at the time of Noah links the cities of Sodom and Gomorrah as being in the same category and state as those of Noah's time and that is why the destruction came to both groups.

In Luke 17:-26-29, Jesus tells us: "And as it was in the days of Noah so shall it be also in the days of the Son of man. They did eat, they drank, they married wives, they were given in marriage, until the day Noah entered into the ark, and the flood came, and destroyed them all.

Likewise also as it was in the days of Lot; they did eat, they drank, they bought, they sold, they planted, they builded; But the same day that Lot went out of Sodom it rained fire and brimstone from heaven, and destroyed them all." K.J.V.

SODOM IN THE SAME MORAL STATE AS THE PEOPLE OF NOAH'S TIME

The people of Sodom were categorized by the Lord Jesus as being in the same state morally as those who lived before the flood, and therefore according to Calvinists "Totally Depraved" and would be considered to be without any vestige of spirituality and therefore dead to God as a Corpse is to its habitat. Yet the Lord Jesus in Matthew 11:-23, says: "And thou Capernaum which art exalted unto heaven, shalt be brought down to hell: **for if the mighty works, which have been done in thee, had been done in Sodom, it would have remained until this day." K.J.V.**

The Sodomites would have done what God's Chosen Jewish people did not do, they would have repented of their sins and believed that Jesus was who He said He was, **"The Christ the Son of the living God"**, and because of that fact the town of Sodom would have still existed at the time of Christ!

Note. It is interesting to see in Gen 14:-21, that the king of Sodom tries to thank Abram for what he has done for the Sodomites, it reads as follows: "And the king of Sodom said unto Abram, Give me the persons, and take the goods to thyself."

I would not have thought that the showing of gratitude could be classed as an act of a person who is "Totally Depraved".

IS IT CREDIBLE PEOPLE BEFORE THE FLOOD WERE TOTALLY DEPRAVED?

An architect has to apply his mind to the planning of a building, and a builder to building, and a teacher or lecturer to the subject he teaches, and the students to the learning of the subjects taught, and these are not evil activities, **but demand the expenditure of time in thought.**

We read in the newspapers and hear on the T.V. how evil men behave in order to fulfil their sexual lusts, they abduct women or children, and sexually abuse them and then murder their victims. The Lord Jesus tells us in the gospel, that the people before the flood, "Married, and were given in marriage". If the world at that time were Totally Immoral (which means 100%) - no moral standards at all - there would have been no marrying or giving in marriage.

But they did marry and that means that couples loved each other and loved and cared for their families. They might have been extremely depraved but they were not 100% evil, which is what total depravity means.

THE TOTAL SINLESSNESS OF THE LORD JESUS CHRIST: PERFECTION

For the Lord Jesus to remain perfect, and without sin, His thought-life had to be without one wrong thought or motive, and the same with His words and deeds. One unrighteous or sinful thought, word, or deed would have deprived Him of the title of being Totally Sinless.

Conversely one correct thought or motive, or truthful word or act of pity or unselfishness would deprive a person who is extremely wicked of the title of being totally evil, that is 100% wicked.

To put it in a different way, to be totally sinful (evil) or depraved, you would need to **think** 100% evil, **speak** 100% lies, and **act** 100% sinfully.

TOTAL EVIL IS THE EXACT OPPOSITE OF THE LIFE OF CHRIST AND WOULD MEAN SIN ABSOLUTE, WHICH IS WHAT TOTAL DEPRAVITY MEANS AND IN TURN THIS MEANS INFINITE SINFULNESS.

SOMETHING THAT CANNOT BE EXCEEDED.

AS THE LIFE OF CHRIST IS (100%) ABSOLUTE RIGHTEOUSNESS (HOLINESS) AND IS INFINITE, HIS RIGHTEOUSNESS, PERFECTION CANNOT BE EXCEEDED.

CHAPTER 8

IS MAN IN TOTAL DARKNESS?

It is true that men are in darkness, but not as the Calvinist would have us believe, in total darkness, (total depravity). Even a person who is not inherently blind is unable to see if he is in the dark.

But the Calvinists tell us that man is not only in Total darkness, **but that he is inherently blind spiritually** because he is spiritually dead and as far as God is concerned like a corpse. They put man in darkness with not even the illumination of a remote light to give direction.

The Wise men **travelled in the darkness**, at night, **guided only by a distant star, and they were brought to Christ.**

In the construction of Calvinism it is **Imperative** to make man out as being, within himself, in total darkness.

Sin, Evil, Wickedness, Iniquity and Darkness in God's Word are synonymous 1 John 1:-6, also chapter 2:-8-11. Romans 13:-12-13. Acts 26:-18. John 3:-19-20-21. 1 John:-1-5 "God is light and in Him is no darkness at all." K.J.V.

Total darkness is indispensable to arrive at the presumption that man is a spiritual carcass, and of **his Total Inability** to contribute or participate in his salvation. Corpse-like Spiritual deadness is not found in Scripture.

HAS MAN GOD-GIVEN LIGHT?

Although the Bible says nothing about an "Inner Receptive Spark" it does say a great deal about the Inner Light, which God has given man, as well as the light that comes from His Word.

Natural light is useless and of no value to a corpse. It would be absolutely meaningless to a physical carcass, as to whether it was in a dark room or one flooded with light, for it has not got Life to differentiate between the two, or to appreciate or use Light. So with the spiritual corpse, Light would be ineffective and useless to it, for it would be unable to use light.

So all references in God's Word about spiritual and moral light, are pointless if man is a spiritual corpse.

"And this is the condemnation, that Light has come into the world, and men loved darkness rather than light, because their deeds were evil." John 3:-19. K.J.V.

This text makes it clear that man can differentiate between light and darkness, so he is not inherently blind, like a corpse.

WHAT WE HAVE INHERITED FROM THE FALL

When Adam and Eve took of the "Tree of the Knowledge of Good and Evil", they Sinned against God, and they died that very moment as God had said spiritually. Their sin broke the intimate fellowship they had had with God and became a barrier between man and God, (this is spiritual death, separation). They did not become oblivious of God.
Adam and Eve passed their sin on to their children, but they also passed on the "Knowledge of Good and Evil", and with that the ability (conscience) to discern between Good and Evil - which is Light.

This is perhaps what Paul is referring to in Romans 2:-14-15.
God's Word tells us that, "Whatsoever doth make manifest is light"
Eph 5:-13. K.J.V.
"But everything exposed by the light becomes visible, for it is light that makes everything visible." Eph 5:-13-14. N.I.V.

In John's gospel chapter 1:-9 he says, **"That was the true Light, which lighteth every man that cometh into the world."** K.J.V.

"The true light that gives light to all was coming into the world!"
The same verse from the N.I.V.

In Proverbs 20:-27 we read, **"The spirit of man is the lamp of the Lord, Searching all the inner depths of his heart."** N.K.J.V.
Physical light enables man to move about and work in the material world, and he uses and enjoys light; and so with the spiritual light it enables him to understand and know the will of God, and enjoy the light of God's Word and His purpose for him in service. It also enables man to worship God in the Spirit.

THE OTHER SIDE OF THE COIN.

The Bible tells us, "All have sinned, and come short of the glory of God." And Jesus tells us that man is Evil. He is capable of great wickedness, and without a doubt is a sinner by nature.
But there is another side to the coin, which some theologians ignore, or to which they pay little attention.

It is the communication God gives within man as well as what theologians call general revelation.

This would be impossible if man were a spiritual carcass, as it is a spiritual revelation given by a Spiritual God.
Sinning is not the only thing man does **by nature**.
God tells us that Man does something else by nature, which reveals that he **has light within himself and, because of this, life to receive and sight to use the light.**

THE LAW WRITTEN IN MAN'S HEART

Romans 2:-14-15, "For when the Gentiles, which have not the Law, do by nature the things contained in the Law, these, having not the Law, are a law unto themselves: Which shew **the work of the law written in their hearts**, their conscience also bearing witness, and their thoughts the mean while accusing or else excusing one another." K.J.V.
This is what the Scriptures say man does by nature. **They "Do by nature the things contained in the Law," "because the work of the Law is written in their hearts."**

In Romans 7:-12 we read, **"Wherefore the law is holy, and the commandment holy, and just and good." K.J.V.**

In Romans 7:-14, it says, "For we know that the Law is spiritual." K.J.V.
This would be impossible if man were "Totally Depraved" and therefore spiritually dead to God. Because of this you have to have spiritual awareness to understand it, (the moral law) and apply it to daily living.
Out of the different translations I looked up, six use the same phrase as the King James Bible, **"Do by nature the things contained in the law,"**

The others use words with similar meaning.
"Obey by instinct the commands of the law."
Weymouth's translation.

"Carry out its precepts by the light of nature."
The New English Bible.

"Obey instinctively the Law's requirements."
James Moffatt translation.

All agree that the Works of the Law are written on men's Hearts. One uses the word **"Inscribed"** (The New English Bible) and two others **"Engraven on their hearts."** (Weymouth's and The Jerusalem Bible.)

Knox translates it. **"And this shews that the obligations of the law are written in their hearts."**
The conscience bears witness to the law written in the heart of man.
The conscience is apart from, and not the written **Law** in man's heart.

As J. B. Phillips' version puts it, **"They show that they have a law in themselves, for they demonstrate the effect of the law operating in their own hearts, Their own consciences endorse the existence of such a law, for there is something which condemns or commends their actions."**
The Scripture also tells us, in Romans 1:-19, "Because that which may be known of God is manifest" (revealed) "in them; for God hath shewed it unto them." K.J.V.
Not only is it revealed in them, by God, but we are told it is also made visible around them. Romans 1:-20 "For the invisible things of Him from the Creation of the world are clearly seen, being understood by the things that are made, even His eternal power and Godhead; **so that they are without excuse."** K.J.V.
GOD WILL HOLD EVERY MAN ACCOUNTABLE, BECAUSE OF THE LIGHT (REVELATION) HE HAS GIVEN HIM, BOTH WITHIN AND AROUND HIM.

To sum this subject up: **The purpose of light is to reveal.** So man is not inherently blind spiritually, but is blind because he chooses to walk in darkness (sin), but is without excuse through the inner light given to him by God, (the moral law written in their hearts and the law is spiritual Romans 7:-14) as well as the Word of God.
To know that which may be known of a Spiritual God, one must have spiritual existence, sight and hearing in order to understand this spiritual knowledge.
It is Light and there must be Life, and Sight (spiritual) in order to receive this and use it.
So the concept of man being a Spiritual Corpse and therefore inherently blind in a spiritual sense, is certainly not found in Scripture, but is produced to try to back up an erroneous theological theory.

CHAPTER 9.

IS THE SINNER DEAF AND BLIND SPIRITUALLY?

Pastor Seaton also says, while still thinking of the dead body of Lazarus, "Can the blind give themselves sight, or the deaf hearing?" And the text he quotes to substantiate his claim that man is Blind and Deaf, is Mark 4:-11.

"But unto them that are without, all these things are done in parables; That seeing they may see and not perceive; and hearing they may hear and not understand;" K.J.V.

The Scripture he quotes does not say that those without were Blind and Deaf, in fact it says the opposite, **"that seeing they may see** and not perceive, **and hearing they may hear** and not understand."

In the old Testament there are comparable verses, in Isaiah 42:-18-20, "Oh, how blind and deaf you are towards God! Why won't you **Listen?** Why won't you **See**?" "Who in all the world is as blind as my own people." "You see and understand what is right but won't heed nor do it; **You hear but you won't listen."** T.L.B.

Speaking to the Pharisees In John 9:-41, "Jesus said unto them: **'If ye were blind, ye should have no sin:** but now ye say, We see; therefore your sin remaineth.'" K.J.V.

"Jesus said, 'if you were blind, you would not be guilty of sin. But since you keep saying you see, your guilt remains.'"

The same text from the N.C.V.

The Lord Jesus makes it clear that if people were genuinely blind spiritually they would be free from all guilt of sin.

This is equally true if a person is dead spiritually like a corpse, which would mean they most assuredly would be deaf and blind and they would have no sin.

The Calvinists tell us that man is completely blind to spiritual things, and yet they still hold man responsible for his sin.

But people are not blind spiritually.

The context makes it clear that they would have seen and heard clearly if they had paid proper attention to what was said. But they did not, so Jesus spoke to them in parables.

The truth is we hear, but we do not pay proper attention.

HEARING BUT NOT LISTENING

Some time ago I was in a friend's house, and the lady of the house said to her husband, as she was going out to visit her mother, "Your meals are laid out on the table, and all you have to do is make the tea when you are ready."

The husband heard his wife, as I did, but his interests were on other things and he paid no attention to what she said.

As time went on he was waiting for his wife to return and make the tea, and wondered what had hindered her return.

Then he happened to go into the kitchen for something and discovered, to his surprise our tea all laid out on the table wrapped in cling film and all ready for us, and then it dawned on him what she had said.

He was not deaf, he heard what his wife said, but did not listen.

Things or people we are too familiar with or consider not important enough, or perhaps because of preoccupation with something else, we do not give our whole attention to; they are listened to, we hear them, yet we don't hear, simply because we do not pay enough attention to what is being said, or we see, but we don't really see, because we do not think they are important enough to give them our full attention.

This is the kind of thing I believe Jesus was referring to.

In Mark 4:-24, we read, "If you have ears, listen! And be sure to put into practice what you hear. The more you do this the more you will understand what I tell you. To him who has shall be given; from him who has not shall be taken away even what he has." T.L.B.

If we look at the same incident in Matthew 13:- from verse 9, and read the context, "He who has ears [to hear], let him be listening and consider and perceive and comprehend by hearing . Then the disciples came to Him and said, Why do You speak to them in parables?" Verse 12, "For whoever has [spiritual knowledge], to him will more be given and he will be furnished richly, so that he will have abundance; but from him who has not, even what he has will be taken away." The Amplified New Testament.

What the Lord Jesus is saying is I have given them the clear simple message, and they will not receive it, or pay enough attention in order to grasp what I am teaching them, so I now teach them in parables.

Acceptance of God's truth as we hear it is the imperative prerequisite for perceiving and receiving additional truth.
You only have what you are prepared to receive and, if you accept it, more will be given.

"This is the reason that I speak to them in parables, because having the power of seeing they do not see, and having the power of hearing they do not hear, nor do they grasp and understand." Matthew 13:-13.
The Amplified New Testament.
This same translation of the latter part of Mark 4:-12, uses the words, "Lest haply they should turn again, and it [their wilful rejection of the truth] should be forgiven them."

Those capricious people were hearing the clearly communicated teaching of the Kingdom without genuinely responding, because they were not paying proper attention to what was being said, and their own guilt was accumulating, and at the same time, they were diminishing their ability to respond.

So the Lord Jesus, because of His Love for them, did not want to add to their guilt, (and the penalty at the judgment day), although at the same time, their lethargy in not paying proper attention to the teaching of Christ merited the automatic forfeiture they brought upon themselves.

What we will not use we will therefore lose.

CHAPTER 10

THE CALVINIST BELIEF OF SPIRIPTUAL DEATH AS CORPSE-LIKE AND THE WRONG VIEWS OF THOSE WHO DO NOT FOLLOW CALVIN

I again quote from the Pastor Seaton and his article on the five points:
"Wrong views of the corruption of human nature will always carry with them wrong views of the grand antidote and cure of that corruption." He goes on to say that what is, "Fundamental in the matter of salvation is a correct assessment of the condition of the one to be saved." "If we have deficient and light views about sin, then we are liable to have defective views regarding the means necessary for the salvation of the sinner."

We would agree with these sentiments, but would like to point out that the same is true if you go to the other extreme and exaggerate the condition of man beyond what is factual and Scriptural, as the Calvinists do.

THE CALVINISTS' EXPLANATION OF MAN'S SPIRITUAL STATE

Pastor Seaton goes on to say: "The Synod of Dort, basing their findings firmly on Scripture, pronounced that **man's natural state is a state of total depravity** and therefore, there was a **total inability** on the part of man to gain, or contribute to, his own salvation."
"The picture is that of **Death – Spiritual Death** we are like Lazarus in the tomb; we are bound hand and foot; corruption has taken hold of us. Just as there was no glimmer of life in the dead body of Lazarus, so there is no inner receptive spark in our hearts."
"But the Lord performs a miracle – both with the physically dead, and the spiritually dead; 'For you hath He quickened' – made alive – 'who were dead in trespasses and sins.' (Eph 2:-1)
Salvation, by its very nature, must be of the Lord."
This is what they call a correct assessment of the natural state of man, "Total Depravity" and the conclusion, man is a Spiritual Corpse. What they mean by, "Salvation, by its very nature, must be of the Lord" is that **God must do everything** because, in the spiritual sense, man is **corpse-like**.

Because of their insistence that man is dead spiritually, in the same sense as a corpse, and because they say that a carcass cannot do anything, hear, understand, see, recognize, move, respond, speak or communicate, so man before he is born again is the same spiritually.

THE MISBELIEF THAT BELIEVING FOLLOWS REGENERATION

Dr. Hodge says in Evangelical Theology page 121: "If God begins the work, if our believing follows His quickening, then it is God, not man, who makes the difference between the quickened and the unquickened.
If we believe, it is because we have been first quickened." (Regenerated).

Note. "And you hath He quickened who were dead in trespasses and sins." K.J.V. Ephesians 2:-1.
"Hath He quickened" is in Italics and is not in the original Greek and has been inserted by the translators.

To quicken, you have to have life, because it means to Reinvigorate, Speed up or Energize.
Regeneration according to the dictionary means: "To undergo or cause to undergo moral, spiritual or physical renewal or invigoration."
The conjecture is that there must first be life, if there is to be Regeneration whether that is spiritual, moral or physical.

Mainstream Calvinism believes that man is spiritually dead like a corpse and that God* Arbitrarily, regenerates a person first, so that He can give that individual faith and repentance to believe in the Lord Jesus and be Saved.
*They claim the selection has nothing to do with anything in, or any action of, the Chosen.

This conclusion is not something that the Calvinists shout from the housetops, simply because it is so diametrically opposed to the whole tenor of the Gospel and sound Scriptural teaching, and rejected because of this by the majority of Bible believing Christians.

WHAT THE BIBLE TEACHES ON REGENERATION

The Bible teaches that if we are regenerated - born again we are saved from condemnation, and are cleansed and have the forgiveness of our sins, through the very means of regeneration.

"He saved us, by the washing of regeneration, and renewing of the Holy Ghost." Titus 3:-5. K.J.V.

"He saved us, by means of the bath of regeneration and renewal by the Holy Spirit." Titus 3:-5. R. F. Weymouth.

The Jerusalem Bible interprets the same verse thus:
"He saved us, by means of the cleansing water of rebirth and by renewing us with the Holy Spirit."

Scripture teaches beyond doubt that a regenerated - born again person is saved as a result of the regeneration.
But in order to be born again, one must first of all believe in Christ. It is not the reverse as the Calvinists affirm.

"For an example to [encourage] those who would thereafter believe on Him for [the gaining of] eternal life."
The latter part of 1 Tim 1:-16, in The Amplified New Testament.

"As a pattern to those who are going to believe on Him for everlasting life." 1 Tim 1:-16. N.K.J.V.

"Those here written have been recorded in order that you may hold the faith that Jesus is the Christ, the Son of God, **and that through this faith you may possess eternal life by His name."** John 20:-31. N.E.B.

"But these are written so that you may believe that Jesus is the Christ, the Son of God. **Then, by believing, you may have life through His name."** John 20:-31. N.C.V.

FAITH IN CHRIST AND REPENTANCE COMES BEFORE REGENERATION

Why should anyone need the means, Faith and Repentance to bring him to a destination he has already reached, if he has obtained the new birth without it? If I were in London and found myself miraculously conveyed to Edinburgh, would I need means of transport to bring me to Edinburgh, when I have already arrived without transport?
Believing in Christ and repenting is the conveyance that transports men to eternal life and salvation - not the reverse.

WE ARE REGENERATED AND CLEANSED BY GOD'S WORD

God uses the Word of God to regenerate and cleanse individuals and this is

done through believing the gospel message. The Bible tells us that, "Christ also loved the Church, and gave Himself for it; That He might sanctify and cleanse it with the washing of water by the word."
Ephesians 5:-25-26. K.J.V.
So to say that God gives the sinner regeneration - new birth first in order that He can give the sinner faith and repentance is nonsense.
As Jesus, in John 5:-24, says: "Verily, verily, I say unto you, He that heareth my word, and believeth on him that sent me, hath everlasting life, and shall not come into condemnation; but is passed from death unto life." K.J.V. Believing comes before eternal life and salvation is resultant from this and not the opposite way round.

CAN YOU GO ANY FURTHER THAN THE OPPOSITE OF WHAT THE LORD JESUS TAUGHT?

FAITH AND REPENTANCE: GIFTS FROM GOD TO THE SPIRITUALLY DEAD

Many who profess to be Calvinists would not admit to believing that God gives the new birth first, without the sinner exercising faith, and by so doing prove that they are not true Calvinists, but they do believe that God gives faith and repentance as a gift before anyone can be saved.
This also has no Scriptural basis.
How can a spiritual carcass receive, let alone exercise faith?

To quote: **"There is no inner receptive spark in our hearts."**
"Or glimmer of life."
You could give a physical carcass gifts, but it could neither receive, nor use them!
So with the spiritual corpse, if you could give it faith and repentance, there would be no life either to receive or exercise faith! So you would have first to give life!
So if one believes that men are spiritually dead like a physical carcass, such a belief leads to insurmountable problems in the reconciliation of this view with Scripture.

THE CALVINIST SAYS, "HOW CAN THE SPIRITUALLY DEAD BELIEVE?"

Arthur Pink in his book "The Sovereignty of God" (Page 55) says "How can those who are 'Dead in trespasses and sins,' believe in Christ? How could God foreknow some men as believers **when belief was impossible to them?"**

An Evangelist at one of his meetings was exhorting his congregation to believe in Christ and repent of their sins, and when he was shaking hands with the people at the door one man said, "How can a person who is 'dead in trespasses and sins' believe and repent, when he is dead?"
The Evangelist answered, "How can a dead man sin?" Of course there was no answer to the Evangelist's question.

HOW CAN THE SPIRITUALLY DEAD SIN?

How can, a person who is dead to God, that is oblivious of His existence, as a corpse is to its surroundings, sin against God?
If a corpse is incapable of sinning, and not held responsible in law, so also are the spiritually dead if they are corpse-like.

Romans 6:-7, **"For he that is dead is freed from sin."** K.J.V.

"Anyone who has died is made free from sin's control."
The same verse in the N.C.V.

The Evangelist was following the Lord Jesus, (Mark 1:-15.)
"The kingdom of God is at hand: repent ye, and believe the gospel." K.J.V.
John the Baptist, (Matt 3:-2) **"Repent ye: for the kingdom of heaven is at hand."** K.J.V.
Peter, (Acts 3:-19.) **"Repent ye therefore, and be converted, that your sins may be blotted out."** K.J.V.

And Paul in (Acts 17:-30) **"Truly, these times of ignorance God overlooked, but now He commands all men everywhere to repent."** N.K.J.V.

Do they really believe that they have superior knowledge to the Lord Jesus Christ and the Apostles?

THE TWO CALLINGS OF CALVINISM

Calvin in his “Institutes” expounds his doctrine of the two calls, without giving any convincing Scriptural evidence. In fact he contradicts what the Lord Jesus and the Bible teach.
Calvin’s teaching is as follows: “There is the General call, by which God invites all equally to Himself through the outward preaching of the word – even those to whom He intends it as a savour of death (2 Cor 2:-16.) and as the occasion for severer condemnation. The other kind of call is special, which He designs for the most part to give to the believers alone, while by the inward illumination of His Spirit He causes the preached Word to dwell in their hearts. Yet sometimes He also causes those whom He illumines for a time to partake of it; then he justly forsakes them on account of their ingratitude and strikes them with even greater blindness.”

A DISTORTED PICTURE OF THE CHARACTER OF GOD

Reader, can you read that paragraph without a feeling of revulsion? Can you honestly imagine the Holy Spirit deceiving people by inviting “all equally to Himself,” and then playing cat-and-mouse with them, resulting in “severer condemnation” and “even greater blindness?” The most despicable action in warfare is to invite emissaries to advance under a flag of truce, and then shoot them down. Is that the way the Holy Spirit operates? I think not!
Calvin makes God out to be deceptive, unjust, hypocritical and partial.

GOD’S REVEALED WILL AND DISPOSITION TOWARDS MANKIND IS CLEAR

For the Word of God states: “For this is good and acceptable in the sight of God our Saviour; **who will have all men to be saved, and come unto the knowledge of the truth.”** 1 Timothy 2:-3-4. K.J.V.

“For the Son of man is not come to destroy men’s lives but to save them.” Luke 9:-56. K.J.V.
“The Lord is not slack concerning His promise, as some men count slackness; but is longsuffering to us-ward, **not willing that any should perish, but that all should come to repentance.”** 2 Peter 3:-9. K.J.V.

“But if you treat one person as being more important than another, you are sinning. You are guilty of breaking God’s law.” James 2:-9. N.C.V.
Whom should we believe Calvin or the Word of God?

What in fact Calvin is saying is that the Lord gives a general hypocritical call and pretends to want all men to be saved, but only selects those He Loves and wants to save, by giving them "An Effectual Call", and rejects the rest and destines them for hell.

HOW CAN THE DEAD HEAR OR SEE?

But if they are spiritually dead, like a physical carcass, as Calvinists constantly insist all sinners are, then all are Deaf, and Totally Blind spiritually just as a corpse would be to the world, then neither group would hear God speaking to them through His Word, or see any illumination from the Word, unless God first gave them regeneration - new birth; and then the call would become a nonsense and completely unnecessary, for the purpose of God calling and speaking, through His Word, is to make the sinner aware of his sin, and bring him to repentance so that he can believe and receive Eternal Life and Salvation.

How can the Calvinist's so-called spiritual corpse or non-existent spiritual life receive "inward illumination" or have "ingratitude" or be struck with "even greater blindness?"
HOW DO YOU GO ABOUT GIVING A CORPSE EVEN GREATER BLINDNESS THAN TOTAL BLINDNESS?

CAN THE SPIRITUALLY DEAD BRING THEMSELVES BACK TO LIFE?

Pastor Seaton says, "Can the dead raise themselves? and the answer must inevitably be: of course not."
In his picture of spiritual death, Pastor Seaton uses Lazarus as an illustration. It is true that there would be no "Inner receptive spark" or "Glimmer of life" in the body of Lazarus, and the assumption is that the Lord Jesus brought new life into the carcass of Lazarus, but this is not so.

IT WAS NOT NEW LIFE JESUS BROUGHT INTO LAZARUS'S CORPSE

Jesus did not bring New Life into the carcass of Lazarus, **He brought Lazarus back into his body.**
Whatever physical problem was the means of Lazarus leaving his body, the Lord Jesus put that right, and this allowed him to be reunited with his body, when Jesus called him to.

The Lord did not just call to the carcass of Lazarus but to his soul and spirit, and reunited the Person of Lazarus with his body. In other words He resolved the problem of the separation of Lazarus from his body. Physical death is when the soul and spirit vacate the body. Just as our Lord has resolved the problem of our separation from God (spiritual death) through sin, by taking our sin's punishment and reconciling us to God, making it possible for Christ the Lord to come into our life, when we believe in Him. It is when God is brought into our lives that Man is regenerated - born again, and becomes united with the Lord, and has Eternal Life.

"But now in Christ Jesus, you who were far away from God are brought near through the blood of Christ's death." Ephesians 2:-13, N.C.V.
Psalm 73:-27. "For, lo, they that are far from Thee shall perish." K.J.V.

DEATH IS FAR-AWAY-NESS

When Lazarus left his body he was no longer near his loved ones, he was **"Far away."**

Was it not **his far-away-ness** that was death, and the corpse just the result of this? This was certainly the judgment of the Lord Jesus. We shall look at this later.

THE SPIRITUAL CORPSE WHICH, CAN UNDERSTAND GOD'S WILL!

Although Pastor Seaton asks the question, "Can the dead raise themselves?" and gives the answer as, "No."
What this Calvinist's spiritual corpse can't do they can, for they will persist in resurrecting this carcass and explaining what it can do and how, while still maintaining it is a corpse.
When explaining what he means by "Total Depravity," the picture given is not that of a spiritual carcass, with no "Glimmer of life," but that of spiritual life and awareness.

He writes as follows: "When Calvinists speak about total depravity, however, they do not mean that every man is as evil as he could possibly be, nor that man is unable to recognize the will of God, or even give outward allegiance to the worship of God." See Note 1.
Have you ever known a physical corpse recognize someone, let alone understand his will? If it did it wouldn't be a corpse.

But here is a spiritual carcass which is dead to God, and which is not only

aware of a Spiritual God, but can know and understand His will, and also worships this same God.
The evidence of life is awareness and activity and it is this that leads to the worship of God.

MAN IS RELIGIOUS BECAUSE HE IS GOD CONSCIOUS!

This is the spiritual carcass which, **"Has no inner receptive spark, or Glimmer of life."**

Note 1. The same kind of explanation is given by other Calvinist apologists in their works on systematic theology and their explanation of "Total Depravity", and this would be a commonly held view among Calvinists.

THE PUBLISHER OF "THE SOVEREIGNTY OF GOD" THEIR NOTES AND COMMENTS

The publisher of "The Sovereignty of God" by A.W. Pink, in a note at the foot of one of the pages, in order perhaps to confirm but also correct omissions that Pink has made, (as quoted previously): "The work of the Spirit in 'quickening' the one dead in sins, precedes faith in Christ, just as cause ever precedes effect."
"This is not to deny that the Spirit does work in a certain sense on those who remain unbelievers and finally perish."
"The Spirit may "Strive" with the impenitent (Gen.6:-3) **and men may resist His operations**. (Acts 7:-51-52.)"
"There is a general work of the Holy Spirit upon those who hear the truth and which in some cases seems to be saving (Matt.13:-5-6-20-21.) and yet because of the unremoved enmity of the natural heart this work is ineffectual in all if He did not work in a special and regenerating manner in the elect, enabling them to believe those saving truths which, "The Natural Man Receiveth Not" (1 Cor 2:-14.)
What in fact they are saying sounds rather like: **"What is isn't and yet at the same time what isn't is."**

CAN YOU NUMBER THAT WHICH IS WANTING?

Ecclesiastes 1:-15,
"That which is wanting cannot be numbered." K.J.V.

The same verse in the New Century Bible,
"If something is missing you can't say it is there."

But the Calvinists do this continually, by creating a want that does not exist, that is, saying that something is missing in man when it is there, and by maintaining that man is spiritually dead, so man is wanting spiritual awareness, ability to act in response to God, and then because Scripture is continually referring to man's ability to respond to God, they say that God works with and on this non-existent spiritual life, or spiritual corpse.

"IF SOMETHING IS MISSING YOU CAN'T SAY IT IS THERE."

They say **"The Spirit of God does work in a certain sense, on unbelievers, and "Strives" with the impenitent."**

I would ask how, and in what sense?

Why would any person want to "Strive" or fight with a physical corpse, let alone a spiritual one?

A corpse does not fight or strive!

How do you "Strive" with the non-existent spiritual life, or the dead spiritual carcass of lost man?

Can you give it, or give to it a spiritual revelation of truth?

They affirm that the lost are blind to spiritual things!

Can you speak to this non-life and convey the truth of the gospel?

They tell us the lost are spiritually deaf!

How can the non-existent spiritual awareness of lost man "resist" the operations of the Holy Spirit? **Pink tells us, that so far as lost man is concerned, that, "It is Utterly Impossible for him" to "Form a spiritual concept" to "Think a spiritual thought," or "Understand spiritual things!"**

They have lengthy and dogmatic explanations telling us that nothing short of a spiritual resurrection is needed, "A RE-ANIMATION OF A DEAD SPIRITUAL LIFE," to bring about life in this Corpse, and at the same time tell us what God the Spirit does to and in this non-existent spiritual life, or spiritual corpse.

"There is a General work of the Holy Spirit upon those who hear the truth." If you believe what Calvinists say, I would ask, **how can there be?**

"IF SOMETHING IS MISSING YOU CAN'T SAY IT IS THERE"

The very Foundation building block of their thesis, is the Total Depravity of man, and the inability of man because of this to respond in any way because he is spiritually dead to God (like a corpse).
Yet they refer to Scriptures again and again which take it for granted that man is **not** a spiritual corpse, and can and does respond to God.

WHO ARE THEY TRYING TO DECEIVE AND LEAD ASTRAY?

They deceive themselves and those who are foolish enough to accept without question a thesis that is so erroneous and bankrupt of any Scriptural evidence. "Prove all things; hold fast that which is good." 1 Thess 5:-21 K.J.V.

"But test and prove all things [until you can recognize] what is good; [to that] hold fast." The same verse in the Amplified New Testament.

THE BIBLE UNNECESSARY IN CALVIN'S THEOLOGY

Theology is the study of the Bible, but Calvinism is the study of what a man and his followers have said about the Bible, God and salvation!
A minister friend of mine who, when he was studying in a Calvinist College in Northern Ireland, told me that on one occasion, as the students were between lectures, he asked the other students, "What is the subject of the next lecture," another student replied, "Theology".
My friend said that he took his large Bible and threw it to the one side and said, "We won't be needing this then."
He told me that the one thing they never used at theology classes was the Bible.

THE STUDY OF SUBJECT MATTER NEVER MENTIONED IN SCRIPTURE

This is understandable when many of the subject matters and themes they expound are not mentioned in Scripture.

When reading in Hodge's Systematic Theology on the subject of "Free Will" and "Free Agency", there was not one Scriptural reference in the pages dealing with these subjects.
Whatever this might be called, in truth it could not be called the study of the Bible (Theology).

Theology is literally a combination of two words (Theos) – God and (Logos) – Word.
"Free Will" or "Free Agency" are never mentioned in Scripture but like the Fact of God the Will of man is always assumed as being a Fact in man's ability to accept God's way or not.

"If it seem evil unto you to serve the Lord, **choose you this day whom ye Will serve**...But as for me and my house, **we Will serve the Lord."** Joshua 24:-15. K.J.V.
"And the people said unto Joshua, Nay; **but we Will serve the Lord."** Joshua 24:-21. K.J.V.
"And the people said unto Joshua, The Lord our God **Will We Serve, and His voice Will we obey."** Joshua 24:-24. K.J.V.

WHAT IS PHYSICAL AND SPIRITUAL DEATH?

Calvinists have a misconception of what spiritual death is, just as the Sadducees had with understanding physical death.
It would appear from what Jesus said that they believed that once a person died that was the finish of him, and also that the soul and spirit was non existent, and failed to realize that a carcass was a vacated house. Both physical and spiritual death is caused through separation, and the **spirit** of **man** did not become corpse-like or cease to exist when God left man after he had sinned in the Garden of Eden.

Note. The belief of the Sadducees i.e., that man has no soul or spirit, is held by the modern day Jehovah's Witnesses, and the Calvinists believe that (unregenerate) man has a soul but not a spirit.
Spiritual death was caused in man when God vacated man because of man's sin!
The spirit of man is part of the soul, Hebrews 4:-12, **"Even to the dividing asunder of soul and spirit"**. K.J.V.

1 Thess 5:-23, "Your whole spirit and soul and body be preserved blameless," K.J.V.

NO SUCH THING AS A SPIRITUAL CORPSE OR NON EXISTENT SPIRIT

There cannot be such a thing as an non-existent spirit which man once had, or spirit corpse, simply because unlike the physical body spirit is everlasting and deathless! Scripture testifies to this.

"For the things which are seen are temporal; but the things which are not seen are eternal." The latter part of 2 Cor 4:-18. K.J.V.

"For the things that are visible are temporal (brief and fleeting), but the things that are invisible are deathless and everlasting."
The same verse from The Amplified New Testament.

AS THE SPIRIT AND SOUL OF MAN ARE UNSEEN, THIS CLEARLY MEANS THAT MAN DID NOT CEASE TO EXIST SPIRITUALLY, OR BECOME A SPIRITUAL CORPSE, WHEN GOD DEPARTED FROM HIM, and the Bible undeniably corroborates this fact.

Jesus rebuked the Sadducees because of their lack of understanding about what Scripture taught about the soul and spirit of man, when they questioned Him about the resurrection by saying, "Your trouble is that you don't know the Scriptures, and don't know the power of God." "God said to Moses, 'I am the God of Abraham, and I am the God of Isaac, and I am the God of Jacob.' God was telling Moses that these men, though dead for hundreds of years, were still very much alive, **for He would not have said, 'I am the God' of those who don't exist!** You have made a serious error." Mark 12:-24-26-27. T.L.B.

GOD IS NOT THE GOD OF A WORLD GRAVEYARD OF SPIRITUAL CORPSES!

Numbers 27:-16, says, **"The Lord the God of the spirits of all flesh." K.J.V.**

"The Lord is the God of the spirits of all people." The same verse in N.C.V.

THE LORD JESUS TEACHES US WHAT DEATH IS: IN LUKE 15

The Lord Jesus in Luke 15, clearly explains the meaning of death in the story of the prodigal son.

When the father said of his son, **"This my son was dead and is alive again; was lost and is found."** K.J.V.

Twice the father uses this phrase, once to his servants, and again to his other son.

Was the boy a corpse? Certainly not!

It was the son's returning that brought alive (quickened) Eph 2:-1, the relationship with his father, which before was dead, because of the son's separation.

The Prodigal son was not oblivious of his father, in the far country, nor was he incapable of repenting, (changing his mind and returning to his father).

No, and neither is man in his awareness of God, or his ability to repent.

The Lord is saying that it was the son's far-away-ness that was death, his separation.

Psalm 73:-27: "For lo, those who are far from You shall perish."
The Amplified Bible.

THE PRODIGAL'S SELFISHNESS SEPARATED HIM FROM HIS FATHER

It was his selfishness that separated him from his Father.

When the prodigal son asked for his inheritance it was like saying to his father, I wish you were dead!

People turn their back on God and live as if He were dead.

They don't need to say it, **they live it**.

At the heart of sin is selfishness and, as all men are at heart selfish, all men are sinners. It was also his selfishness or sense of self-preservation that brought him back to his father – his need to be saved and not to perish in the far country.

There was nothing meritorious about his faith in his father or his repentance; it was his selfish desire not to perish that brought him home, not his love for his father. **The same is true of the repentant sinner.**

JESUS CLEARLY TAUGHT THAT DEATH IS SEPARATION!

SPIRITUAL DEADNESS MENTIONED IN THE EPISTLES

Paul in 1 Timothy 5:-6, describes spiritual deadness, in the text: "But she that liveth in pleasure is dead while she liveth." K.J.V.

"That we, being dead to sins, should live unto righteousness."1 Peter 2:-24. Does this mean that we are unconscious of sin, and therefore unable to be tempted by sin, (just like a physical carcass). If one follows the logic of the Calvinist argument that is what one must be led to believe.

But what I believe the text means is, we are to separate ourselves from the environment of sin, and live righteously for God.
As 2 Corinthians 6:-17-18 puts it: "Wherefore come out from among them, and be ye separate, saith the Lord, and touch not the unclean thing; and I will receive you, And will be a Father unto you, and ye shall be My sons and daughters, saith the Lord Almighty." K.J.V.

MAN MADE IN THE IMAGE OF GOD

As God is a trinity and yet one, so also is man. "And God said, Let us make man in our image, after our likeness." (Genesis 1:-26) and in 1 Thessalonians 5:-23, Paul says: "And I pray God your whole **spirit** and **soul** and **body** be preserved blameless unto the coming of our Lord Jesus Christ." K.J.V.
The soul is ghost-like and similar to the spirit but with an entirely different function.
John 20:-22: "And when He had said this, He breathed on them, and saith unto them, Receive ye the Holy Ghost:" K.J.V.

In Ecclesiastes 12:-6 the writer describes his understanding of a person departing this life in the words: **"Or ever the silver cord be loosed."** K.J.V
"Before the silver cord of life is snapped apart." The Amplified Bible.
The hymn writer paraphrases it thus.
"Some day the silver cord will break and I no more as now shall sing; but oh, the joy when I shall wake within the palace of the King."
There is a connection between the soul and spirit and the body, which is broken at death. Although the soul and spirit have separate functions they too are joined or connected.

In Hebrews 4:-12, we read: "For the word of God is quick, and powerful, sharper than any two-edged sword, piercing even to the dividing asunder of **soul** and **spirit**, and of the joints and marrow, and is a discerner of the thoughts and intents of the heart." K.J.V.

So the word of God has the power to divide asunder the soul and spirit. So they must be joined.
"God's word is alive and working and is sharper than a double-edged sword. **It cuts all the way into us, where the soul and spirit are joined,** to the centre of our joints and bones." Hebrews 4:-12. N.C.V.

ANIMALS HAVE SOULS AND *SPIRITS*

Animals have souls. They are aware of the world around them through their bodies. Job 12:-10, **"In whose hand is the soul of every living thing."** K.J.V.
Also according to Ecclesiastes 3:-21 a spirit ,"Who knoweth the spirit of man that goeth upward, and the spirit of the beast that goeth downward to the earth?" K.J.V.
"Who can be sure that the human spirit goes up to God and that the spirit of an animal goes down into the ground?" Ecclesiastes 3:-21. N.C.V.
The inference of the above verse is that the spirit of man and that of animals are different and that the direction of the spirit after death of men and animals may very well be the opposite and therefore diverse. Although we are told Man's "Spirit will return unto God who gave it." Eccl 12:-7, N.C.V.
But there is no place in Scripture, which would indicate the destination of the soul and spirit of the animal kingdom after death.

MAN CREATED FOR A DIFFERENT PURPOSE THAN ANIMALS

That animals have spirits would perhaps explain the fact that Baalam's ass was able to see the angel (a spiritual being) barring the way, and it would appear it was more sensitive to the spiritual than the prophet. God spoke to the whale that swallowed Jonah, presumably to the spirit of the animal.
But man was created specifically for fellowship with God, and made in His Image, unlike animals.

GOD IS LIGHT

If Moses after being in communion with God on mount Sinai for forty days, had to veil his face, because of the brightness of the light that shone from him, how much more Adam and Eve, before they had sinned.

They would most likely have been clothed with light, because God dwelt in this sinless couple, and "God is light." 1 John 1:-5.

"Who covereth Thyself with light as with a garment:" Psalm 104:-2. K.J.V.

This would mean that Adam and Eve could have walked in the Garden of Eden at night and would have had the light to do so, because they were sinless and there was nothing (no sin) to hinder the fulness of the glory of the Lord dwelling in them, and showing itself through them.
But when Adam and Eve sinned, God departed, and left, as someone has put it, **"A God shaped vacuum in man, which only God can fill."**
"God is Love" and "Perfect Love casteth out fear". This was most likely the reason for their great Fear! The Lord departing from them.

Not only did the first created couple pass their sin on to their descendants, they also passed on the knowledge of good and evil, and that vacuum in man that only God can fill - that sense of incompleteness.
When we lose someone very close to us, we have a sense that part of us has died (departed or separated from us) and we have a feeling of not being complete, because that person is no longer with us. This is the experience I believe that Adam and Eve had, but far more acute, when God departed from them. It is the spirit of man that makes him aware and alive to the fact of God. But there is also another powerful element in man, the fact of that God shaped vacuum; or, to put it a different way, a God active principle, which can only be satisfied with God.
"Also He has put eternity in their hearts." Ecc 3:-11. N.K.J.V.

"He also has planted eternity in men's heart and mind."
The same verse from The Amplified Bible.

ANIMALS HAVE NO SUCH PRINCIPLE AS FAR AS WE KNOW.

SALVATION IS MORE THAN BEING SAVED FROM HELL

In William Tyndale's translation of the New Testament he translates the word Salvation, in Hebrews 2:-3: "How shall we escape, if we neglect so great salvation," as "SO GREAT HEALTH," which means wholeness, or unimpaired, which I believe is correct.
Salvation is not only the deliverance from the consequences of our sin, but the restoration of spiritual and moral health which means wholeness and completeness.

Because man was made specifically for fellowship with God, he is lost and incomplete without the Lord in his life.

The completeness comes when the Lord Jesus comes into our lives. He is Eternal Life. John 17:-3 "And this is Life Eternal that they may know Thee the only true God, and Jesus Christ, whom Thou hast sent." K.J.V.
Salvation is the restoration in our lives of the relationship and communion with God, that our original parents lost and which we inherited.
This I believe is what is meant by being born again. **Bringing the Lord into our lives.**
"And this is the record that God hath given us eternal life, **and this life is in His Son**. He that hath the Son hath Life, and he that hath not the Son of God hath not Life." 1 John 5:-11-12. K.J.V.

Colossians 2:-9-10: "For in Him dwelleth all the Fulness of the Godhead bodily. **And ye are complete in Him**, which is the head of all principality and power." K.J.V.

THERE ARE NO RELIGIOUS ANIMALS

You find no religious groups among animals, because they were not created for the purpose of fellowship with God.
Apart from the fact that I believe the theory of Evolution to be complete nonsense and devoid of any real scientific basis, this is perhaps the greatest argument against Evolution, they have no noticeable GOD AWARENESS, simply because they were not brought into being for the same purpose as man, although I believe they can be made aware of God's wishes, if He so desires, because they have a spirit.

Man is aware of God, animals so far as we know, are not.
So the nearest understanding you could get to the Calvinist's spiritual death, is perhaps that, of the kingdom of animals, where there is an inability to know and commune with God, and an incapability of any kind of worship of the Lord of Glory, and an apparent unawareness of God.

Animals are not moral beings, and left to themselves are limited to and locked into instinctive behavioural patterns.

BUT THIS IS MOST CERTAINLY NOT TRUE OF MANKIND!

See notes and comments on this chapter in the Appendix.

CHAPTER 11

THE CENTRAL POINT OF THE FIVE: LIMITED ATONEMENT

The question is asked by Pastor W. J. Seaton when referring to the death of Christ: **"Whose punishment did He bear, and whose Salvation did He procure?"**
"There are three avenues we can travel with regards to this:

1.Christ died to **save all men without distinction.**

2.Christ died to **save no one in particular.**

3.Christ died to **save a certain number."**

The third is the Calvinist's point of view.
In order to hold this view they must change the meaning of the word "World" to convey something other than what is universally accepted.

THE PASTOR'S WAY OF COMPARING SCRIPTURE WITH SCRIPTURE

So Pastor Seaton says:
"We do not overlook the fact that there are some Scriptures which refer to the "world", and many have taken these as their starting point in the question of redemption. However, when we compare Scripture with Scripture, we see that the use of the word "world" need not imply "every man and woman in the world." "Behold, the world has gone after Him" they said of Jesus; every person, however, had not "gone after" Christ.
The expression means " every kind of person - and normally Gentile as well as Jew."
Pastor Seaton's conjecture being that the same word in John 3:-16, and other passages which refer to the redemption of the "world", should be explained in the same way, in order to accommodate the doctrine of "Limited Atonement!"

This is an unacceptable exegesis, and a defective assumption.
One must differentiate between the hyperbolic remarks of man and the categorical statements of God.

THE BASIC MEANING OF THE WORD WORLD

The Greek word for world, in the phrase, "The world has gone after Him" is "Kosmos" from which we get our English equivalent Cosmos, which means "The universe considered as an ordered system". This word is used to express the created universe, all things in heaven and earth and which includes all mankind. To use it in a limited sense so far as mankind is concerned is accordingly an incorrect use of that word.

The basic meaning of the ancient Greek word doesn't change because of its inappropriate use, as the writer seems to think.

JOHN 3:-16 IS GOD'S WORD: WHAT THE PHARISEES SAID IS NOT

Any text should be examined in the light of its context; and who said it is as important as why it was said! By doing this we can get an idea of what the user means, even if the words are misused.

It is fallacious to put the Lord Jesus Christ in the same category as the Pharisees and to think that their words are as trustworthy as the Lord's. What the Lord Jesus said in John 3:-14-17 IS THE WORD OF GOD, and what he quotes "Behold, the world has gone after Him." **is the word of unbelieving men.**

Dr. A. T. Pierson correctly said: "When the Bible narrates human events, or records human utterances, in which God is not represented either as acting or speaking through man, inspiration covers only the essential accuracy of the narrative."

Consequently it is inappropriate to use the words of the unbelieving Jewish leaders, and the personal interpretation of them, as a measuring stick in assessing what the Lord meant when He spoke of the atonement for the sin of the world.

The announcement that "The world has gone after Him" was clearly a hyperbolic statement, and should be treated as such.

The nation has gone after Him, would have been nearer the truth.

THEY CHANGE MEANINGS OF WORDS TO FIT IN WITH THEIR DOCTRINE

Pastor Seaton, along with many other apologists of Calvin, attempts to undermine the generally accepted understanding of "world", from universe, which would include all mankind, to something very much narrower in scope, in an endeavour to achieve for Calvin's theology, the impossible

reconciliation with the Bible.
Pastor Seaton here is following his teacher, Calvin, whose comment on 1 Timothy 2:-4, **"Who will have all men to be saved, and come unto the knowledge of the truth,"** is as follows: "The apostle simply means that there is no people and no rank in the world that is excluded from salvation; because God wishes that the gospel should be proclaimed to all without exception." Calvin conveniently changes the revealed will of God in willing all men to be saved **into wanting all men to hear the gospel**, in order to suit his Thesis. The apostle simply means what he says, and does not need any so-called correction from Calvin.
The words of the apostles to the Sadducees are just as applicable to Calvin. **Acts 4:-19, "Whether it be right in the sight of God to hearken unto you more than unto God, judge ye." K.J.V.**

DID ALL MANKIND BENEFIT FROM THE JEWISH REJECTION OF CHRIST?

Another apologist of Calvin, a Professor of Systematic Theology, attempting to do the same with the word "world", writes as follows: "Such words as 'world' and 'all' and such expressions as 'every one' and 'all men' do not always in Scripture mean every member of the human race."

"For Example, when Paul says with reference to the unbelief of Israel, 'If their trespass is the riches of the world***how much more their fulness' (Romans 11:-12), are we to suppose that he meant that the trespass of Israel brought the riches of which he was speaking to every person who had been, is now, and ever will be in the 'world'? Such an interpretation would make nonsense."
"The word 'world' would then have to include Israel, which is here contrasted with the world. And it is not true that every member of the human race was enriched by the fall of Israel. When Paul used the word 'world' here he meant the Gentile world as contrasted with Israel. The context makes this abundantly plain."
"So we have an example of the word 'world' used in a restricted sense and does not mean all men distributively."

JEWS ARE CONTRASTED WITH THE WORLD BUT INCLUDED IN THE WORLD

In Romans 11:-15 we read, "When God turned away from the Jews, He became friends with other people in the world. So when God accepts the Jews, surely that will bring them life after death." From the N.C.V.

"When God turned away from them **it meant that He turned to the rest of the world to offer His salvation;** and now it is even more wonderful when the Jews come to Christ. It will be like dead people coming back to life." The same verse in T.L.B.

"For God hath concluded them all in unbelief, that He might have mercy upon all." Romans 11:-32. K.J.V.

"For in making all mankind prisoners to disobedience, God's purpose was to show mercy to all mankind." Romans 11:-32. N.E.B.
The Jews are contrasted with the rest of the world but they are also included in the world.

THE WHOLE OF THE CREATED UNIVERSE BENIFITS FROM CHRIST'S DEATH

The rejection of Christ by the Jews and His crucifixion and resurrection benefits all mankind, literally and practically, **"To every person who had been, is now and ever will be in the 'world,'"** from the Immediate judgment of their sins and God's Grace (His loving kindness) is experienced by all mankind and enriches the lives of all, solely because of Christ's atonement.
To be more accurate the judgment of God would have been placed on our first parents Adam and Eve, but instead was put on Christ.
"The Lord is good to all: and His tender mercies are over all His works." Psalm 145:-9. K.J.V.

WHAT CAUSED THE FALL OF THE JEWISH NATION?

The repudiation of Christ by the nation of Israel and their fall was in two parts. They rejected Christ as the Messiah, and the Son of God, and crucified Him, and then they rejected the resurrected Christ in the gospel as the Saviour and Son of God.
"It was necessary that the word of God should first be spoken to you: but seeing you put it from you, **and judge yourselves unworthy of everlasting life, lo, we turn to the Gentiles."** Acts 13:-46. K.J.V.
The misconception of this professor and many other apologists of Calvin in their insatiable desire and ingenious arguments in their search to

circumscribe the word "world" in an attempt to justify their erroneous doctrine of "Limited Atonement", is the inherent assumption that if they can establish a framework to diminish the meaning of the word "world" from including all mankind they would be at liberty to impose this understanding and interpretation on all other passages in which the word "world" occurs, as and when they desire.

WHAT CALVINISTS' "LIMITED ATONEMENT" TEACHES US

As previously quoted. 2. **"That Christ Jesus hath not suffered for any other than for the elect only, having neither had any intent nor commandment of the Father to make satisfaction for the SINS OF THE WHOLE WORLD."**

WHAT IS THE WORTH OF THE INFINITE SON OF GOD'S SACRIFICE?

They contradict the words of our Lord Jesus Christ in John 3:-16-17, and also in 1 John 2:-2. "And He is the propitiation for our sins: and not for ours only, but also for the sins of the whole world." K.J.V.

Also Titus 2:-11. "God's readiness to give and forgive is now public. Salvation's available for everyone!" The Message.
The death of the infinite Son of God cannot have procured less than an infinite atonement. (An atonement, which cannot be exceeded or surpassed). The availability of that atonement is free to, but not accepted by, all mankind.

THE CONCLUSION OF LIMITED ATONEMENT

Limited Atonement, the central point, brings about diametrically opposed conflict with Scripture, and the very words of the Lord Jesus Himself, which the Calvinists seem willing to try to explain away, or argue around the categorical statements of the Bible, in order to accommodate their false premise.
Calvin tells us: "All are not created on equal terms, but some are preordained to eternal life, others to eternal damnation; and, accordingly as each has been created for one or other of these ends, we say that he has been predestinated to life or to death."
What a monster of a God they depict in their theology.

Where in Scripture does it tell us that God predestinated people to damnation?

This doctrine is without any Biblical basis.
The Scottish poet Robert Burns, sums up the Calvinistic doctrine in the first verse of his satirical poem, "Holy Willie."

"O Thou, that in the heavens does dwell,
Wha, as it pleases best Thysel,
Sends ane tae heaven an' ten tae hell,
A' for Thy glory,
And no for onie guid or ill
They've done afore Thee!"

WHO ARE THE TRUE FOLLOWERS OF CALVIN?

It is because of their doctrine on "Unconditional Election" that they must insist on "Limited Atonement", and they inevitably come to the opinion that God does not love all men, but only the elect.
Many Calvinists would deny this, but it is an unavoidable conclusion of their five-point dogma. There are also those who are aggressively outspoken in expressing themselves in this appalling conclusion. They would also insist that those who do not hold this opinion cannot be Calvinists, which is correct, if you take what Calvin himself has said, and follow their theological argument to its logical conclusion.
The only people who are true to the teaching of Calvin are those who are termed Hyper-Calvinists. Hyper-Calvinism only comes into being as one Calvinist theologian says, when the five points are FIRMLY BELIEVED. In other words those who are not Hyper are those who hold lightly to the doctrine of Calvinism, because they see the folly of working out those beliefs, and the obvious contradiction this would bring from Scripture.
It has nothing to do with going beyond what Calvin taught, as the word Hyper would suggest. It is really like comparing the belief of nominal Christians with those who are real Christians. **So many who go under the name of Calvinists are not Calvinists at all.**

THE CONTRADICTION OF THE VERY WORDS OF OUR LORD

One American professor and reformed author, Homer C. Hoeksema who I will from now on refer to as the "Professor" when quoting from his writings, speaking about election, in the preface of his booklet, "GOD SO LOVED THE WORLD," writes as follows:

"John 3:-16 is probably the most frequently misinterpreted and misused verse in all Holy Scripture. I refer to the fact, of course, that so often it is explained as meaning that God loves all men. **Nothing could be further from the truth!"** It is inescapable that their logic takes them down this road, because of the central Point, "Limited Atonement," which is the natural outcome of the first two points.

Might I remind the "Professor" that the Scriptures tell us in Proverbs 30:-5. **"Every Word of God is true."**
And also adds a warning in Proverbs 30:-6. **"Do not add to His Words, or He will correct you and prove you a liar."** N.C.V.

THE "PROFESSOR" GIVES US THE ARMINIAN GOSPEL

The "Professor" goes on to say, "When the gospel is preached, the question, 'Whom does God love' must be answered. And again, the answer must be that of the Scriptures. Only that answer may be proclaimed as the Gospel of Jesus Christ."
"The text says that God loved the world. And by far the most common explanation which is given of this expression 'the world', is that this means that God loves **all men**, every individual member of the human race."
"This is the open teaching of all Arminians, freewill pulpits. We have all heard this kind of preaching many times, if not in our church then via radio or television. According to this position God loves all men."

"Because He loved all men, God gave His only begotten Son. God's only begotten Son died for the whole world, that is, for all men, thus making provision for all men to be saved."
"The gospel is for all sinners. And now it is up to the sinner to believe or not believe, to embrace the love of God or not to embrace it, to be saved and to have eternal life, or to perish."

THE PROFESSOR'S CALVINIST GOSPEL

He goes on to say: "The opposite is that of the Reformed faith, sometimes called Calvinism. It holds that as far as men are concerned, **God does not love all, but only His elect,** that is, those whom He has chosen in Christ Jesus from before the foundation of the world."

"It teaches, further, that Christ died only for His own sheep, that is those whom the Father gave Him. He continues: "Furthermore, the Reformed faith maintains that when the gospel of Christ crucified is proclaimed, the gift of faith is sovereignly bestowed, only upon the elect through regeneration and the efficacious calling, that then the Elect repent and believe and have everlasting life."

All the points mentioned in the latter part of the above paragraph, and the misconceptions issuing from them, I have refuted, in other chapters of this book. I would remind the Professor of Isaiah 53:-6, which tells us: **"All we like sheep have gone astray; we have turned everyone to his own way; and the Lord hath laid on Him the iniquity of us all." K.J.V.**

We all go astray, and all our iniquities have been laid upon Christ our redeemer.

THE REDUNDANT GOSPEL

He implies that God acts solely and purely out of His sovereign will, to bring about the new birth and salvation in men and for no other reason, and man is completely passive and divorced from any participation in this whatsoever.

As with babies who die in infancy according to Calvinism and who are elected, they are sovereignly regenerated and taken to Glory and the un-elected sent to hell. Note(3)

This reduces men to nothing more than robots, and makes the Gospel redundant or merely incidental.

Consequently, the Almighty can achieve the salvation of the elect adults as He does with babies, without the preaching of the gospel, if the sole factor is His sovereignty, and man has no active part in his regeneration - new birth.

SO WHY BOTHER TO PREACH THE GOSPEL?

CALVINISTS' VIEW ON THE ELECTION OF BABIES WHO DIE IN INFANCY

Note 3. In the Westminster Confession it states, "Elect infants, dying in infancy, are regenerated and saved by Christ through the Spirit, who worketh where, and when, and how He pleaseth. So also are all other elect persons who are incapable of being outwardly called by the ministry of the word." The inference is that those who are not elect are damned to hell. Calvin, as previously quoted tells us:

"All are not created on equal terms, but some are preordained to eternal life, others to eternal damnation."

JESUS SAID: "LET THE LITTLE CHILDREN COME TO ME" N.C.V.

King David said of the first child Bathsheba the wife of Uriah the Hittite bore to him, when God took the child.
"I shall go to him, but he shall not return to me." 2 Sam 12:-23, K.J.V.
David had no doubt that he would meet the child in Glory.
So far as infants are concerned the only sin they have is what is inherited through their parents from Adam and Eve and Scripture tells us that the child shall not be punished for the sins of the father.
Deu 24:-16, "The fathers shall not be put to death for their children, nor shall the children be put to death for their fathers; a person shall be put to death for his own sin." N.K.J.V.
There is no one poorer than an infant. It comes into the world with no resources and is absolutely dependent upon adults to care for it, if it is going to live and survive. Perhaps this is one of the particular groups of the poor that the Lord Jesus Christ had in mind when he said in Luke 6:-20: **"Blessed be ye poor: for yours is the kingdom of God." K.J.V.**
What The Lord Jesus said about Little Children will also be applicable to infants.
Jesus said, "Except ye be converted and become as little children, ye shall not enter into the kingdom of heaven. Whosoever therefore shall humble himself as this little child, the same is greatest in the kingdom of heaven." Matthew 18:-3-4. K.J.V.
"Jesus said, "Let the little children come to me. Don't stop them, because the kingdom of heaven belongs to people who are like these children." Matthew 19:-14. N.C.V.
I believe Christ will welcome all infants and little children into The Kingdom of Heaven, because it "belongs to people like these children."
If they die in infancy or as children He will not be less gracious in Glory than He was on earth.

SCRIPTURAL WARRANT TO BELIEVE ALL INFANTS IN DEATH ARE SAVED

Unlike the Calvinist's thesis which has no Scriptural warrant there is a Scriptural basis for believing that all babies and young children who die are

saved by virtue of the death of Christ.
Romans 5:-18-19. "We see, then, as one act of sin exposed the whole race of men to God's judgment and condemnation, **so one act of perfect righteousness presents all men freely acquitted in the sight of God.** 19, One man's disobedience placed all men under the threat of condemnation, but one man's obedience has the power to present all men righteous before God." J. B. Phillips, translation.

"No distinction is made; for all alike have sinned, and consciously fall short of the glory of God, **but are acquitted freely by His Grace through the ransom given in Christ Jesus."** Romans 3:-23-24. The Weymouth Version. It is clear from these texts that not some but all infants and young children would be covered by the Blood of Christ and are safe in Christ's care!

JESUS PRAYS FOR THE DISCIPLES BUT NOT THE WORLD

The "Professor", goes on to say, "In the high priestly prayer of the Lord Jesus, preserved for us in this same gospel narrative of John, chapter 17, verses 8 and 9, we read: 'For I have given unto them the words which thou gavest me; and they have received them, and have known surely that I came out from Thee, and they have believed that thou didst send me.'" "I pray for them: I pray not for the world, but for them which thou hast given me; for they are thine."
"From this passage, in comparison with John 3:-16, it is evident, in the first place, that the term "world" here in John 17 is not the same as in John 3. This is evident from the simple point that Jesus does not pray for this "world."
"And certainly it would be blasphemous to assume that our Lord Jesus Christ does not pray for the world which God loved."
How could it be blasphemous, for Jesus not to pray directly for the world, that God Loved? The Lord Jesus and God the Father are one, so Their will, plan, and purpose are one.

JESUS PRAYS FOR ONENESS SO THAT THE WORLD WILL BELIEVE

In verse 21, of the same chapter, speaking about the disciples we read: "That they may be one; as thou, Father, art in Me, and I in Thee, that they also may be one in US: **that the world may believe that thou hast sent Me"**. K.J.V. Jesus prays for the oneness of believers with the Godhead, so that the "world may believe that thou hast sent Me".

So the prayer for the disciples was in order that the world would believe in Christ. Although not a direct prayer for the world, the outcome of the prayer included the blessing of the world, through the disciples. So the prayer was not as exclusive as he makes out, for it was for the ultimate advantage, and betterment of the "world" that God loves. To use the term "blasphemous" in this context is nonsense.

The "Professor" infers that as Jesus did not pray for the "world", in John 17, that God therefore did not love and Christ did not "Die for the world".

WE ARE EXHORTED TO PRAY FOR THE WORLD

Jesus in John 17, divides the inhabitants of the earth into only two groups, the Believers in Christ, and the world (unbelievers). Did not the Lord Jesus pray from the cross, **"Father, forgive them; for they know not what they do?"** He was not in that prayer, praying for the believers (the disciples) but for the "world," (the unbelievers) those who were crucifying Him.

The Church is exhorted to pray for the "world". In 1 Timothy 2:-1-6, we read: "I exhort therefore, that first of all, supplications, prayers, intercessions, and the giving of thanks, be made for all men;" "For kings, and for all that are in authority; that we may lead a quiet and peaceable life in all godliness and honesty."

"For this is good and acceptable in the sight of God our Saviour; Who will have all men to be saved, and come unto the knowledge of the truth." "For there is one God, and one mediator between God and men, the man Christ Jesus. Who gave Himself a ransom for all, to be testified in due time." K.J.V.

IN THE ABOVE TEXTS <u>ALL MEANS EVERYONE</u>

Note 4. The word all is an all-embracing word. The phrase in the Greek is *"PANTON ANTHROPON"* "Meaning all mankind". All is a word of totality. It is an adjective and qualifies the noun to which it is related. For example, if I use the phrase, "all red cars," that would mean "every red car." If I did not intend it to embrace every red car I would have to introduce another qualifying phrase such as "which have sun roofs."

"Clearly this would not mean every red car, but only red cars with sun roofs. This would be a limiting phrase, **but no such phrase is used in the Scriptures regarding God's desire that all men should be saved.**

In 1 Timothy 2; verse 6 we have the phrase: **"A ransom for all"**

(Antilutron uper panton) Antilutron comes from two Greek words, "*anti*" and "*lutron*" ("*anti*" means "in place of" and "*lutron*" means a "ransom" **The above phrase means** "A RANSOM IN PLACE OF ALL MEN."

WORLD (KOSMOS) MEANS UNIVERSE BUT IN JOHN 3:-16 IT MEANS ELECT

I quote from page 11 of the "Professor's" article, "John 3:16 answers: God loved the world, the cosmos. The general meaning of that term is that of harmony, orderly arrangement, beauty. Our word "cosmetics" is derived from it. And the term is used to denote the created universe, all creatures in heaven and earth, as an organic whole, from the viewpoint of its order and harmony."
"And while that same term "world" is used in Scripture to denote the whole of reprobate, wicked men, as they are in darkness, and as they subject all things in their universe to their own sinful mind and will, and use all things in the service of sin, **it is used in John 3:-16 to denote the sum total of the Elect as an organic whole, the body of Christ, the Church**, again in connection with the whole universe."
"We must always remember that in His elect God does not merely save a number of individual men. God saves an organism, a whole world!"
There is no place in Scripture where it tells us that God saves an organism. He saves people!

He explains what the word "Kosmos" means, and then tells us that in John 3:-16, **its meaning is entirely different**, and instead of being all embracing, it becomes narrow and exclusive, it means "The sum total of the elect, the body of Christ, the Church."

So the fundamental meaning of the original Greek word is changed to accommodate the false doctrine of "Limited Atonement"! Where is his authority for this statement? It is certainly not from Scripture! The "Professor" is not the only Calvinist apologist to put forward this idea.

LET US PUT HIS EXPOSITION TO THE TEST

Let us change the word world in John 3:-16 to what the "Professor" says it means, and see what results.
"For God so loved the world" (The elect, The body of Christ, The church) "that He gave His only Begotten Son that whosoever" (of the elect, the body of Christ, the Church) "believeth in Him should not perish but have everlasting life."

So this would mean that the elect, the body of Christ, the Church is perishing and needs to be saved!

HIS EXPOSITION IS AN ABSURDITY

Take his exposition of what the word "world" means, "The sum total of the elect, the body of Christ, the Church," and try to explain just a few of the verses, with the word "world" (Kosmos) in them! So let us insert the words "The elect, the body of Christ, the Church" into passages where the word "world" appears and see how this completely alters their meaning.
"Know ye not that the friendship of the world" (The elect, The body of Christ, The Church), "is enmity with God? whosoever therefore will be a friend of the world" (The elect, The body of Christ, The Church,) "is the enemy of God." K.J.V. James 4:-4.

"Even the Spirit of Truth; whom the world" (The elect, The body of Christ, The Church,) "cannot receive." John-14:-17. K.J.V.

"Lord, how is it that thou wilt manifest Thyself unto us, and not unto the world?" "(The elect, The body of Christ, The Church)." John 14:-22. K.J.V.

"That we should not be condemned with the world." "(The elect, The body of Christ, the Church)". 1 Cor 11:-32. K.J.V.
It is the same word, "KOSMOS" in the above texts as in John 3:-16, and chapter 17.

HOW WILL THE CALVINIST EXPLAIN THIS CRAZY EXEGESIS?

So what elaborate labyrinth of explanation have they got for reconciling the exegesis given of "world" in John 3:-16, and the same Greek word used for "world" in John 17:-25, and in these other texts.
It is a devious, and Scripturally unsubstantiated assumption.
Where in Scripture are the Believers (The Church) ever referred to as the world?
Paul tells believers to: "Come out from among them," (the world) "and be ye separate, saith the Lord, and touch not the unclean thing; and I will receive you, And will be a Father unto you, and ye shall be My sons and daughters, saith the Lord Almighty." 2 Corinthians 6:-17-18. K.J.V. Believers are the called out ones, from the sinfulness of the world, and although they are in the "world" physically they are not of the "world." John 17 Verse, 14. Believers, have the Spirit of Christ and not the spirit of the "world."

"The spirit that now worketh in the children of disobedience." Ephesians 2:-2.

THE UNLIMITED ATONEMENT OF CHRIST

The "Professor" goes to considerable trouble to try to reduce the meaning of the word "world" from universe, to the "Sum total of the elect," but fails to take into account the many verses in the Bible that corroborate, and give conclusive proof, that the word "world" means all creation and includes ALL MANKIND. He also asks the question, which is also put forward by a number of other Calvinist writers, in an effort to justify his theory: "Could it possibly be that the gift of God's Son was either wholly or partially in vain?"

Asking questions does not refute, nor does it in any way disprove the categorical statements of Scripture.

The question could be asked of those who believe in limited atonement, **could it possibly be that the death of the infinite Son of God was insufficient payment for the sins of all mankind, but sufficient only for the few?**

THE ATONEMENT WAS PRINCIPALLY TO SATISFY GOD'S JUSTICE AND RIGHTEOUSNESS, ENABLING HIM TO SHOW GRACE TO ALL MANKIND.

THE ATONEMENET WAS GOD-WARD AND NOT MAN-WARD

The Atonement was intrinsically God-ward and not man-ward.

Its worth or legitimacy does not depend on the acceptance or rejection of any man, but rather the opposite, on its approval by God and His justice and righteousness.

If the atonement of Christ were limited it would necessitate, because of the justice of God, **the immediate destruction of all who had not been atoned for. The Grace of God shown to all mankind is solely based upon the satisfaction of God's justice through the work of Christ on the cross, that is, the propitiation for the sins of the whole world and on no other basis. 1 John 2:-2.**

"Grace and truth came by Jesus Christ." God could not show Grace towards sinful man without justification for doing so and this is found only in Christ's atonement.

Abraham said "Shall not the judge of all the earth do right?"

Genesis 18:-25. Indeed He will show Himself to be just and righteous, beyond any shadow of a doubt!

It is inconceivable that God who is Love, would allow all men to be partakers

of the sin of the first man, through no fault of their own, just because they are identified with Adam by birth, but extend the salvation that Christ (the last Adam 1 Cor 15:-45.) purchased through His sacrifice, only to a limited number and not to all.
As sin has affected the whole "world" so the life, death and resurrection of Christ is for the whole sin-affected "Kosmos."

THE SCRIPTURES STATE THAT CHRIST DIED FOR ALL HUMANITY!

Arthur Pink, putting his case for limited atonement says, "He bears whose legal obligations He discharges. Furthermore, if the lawgiver accepts the satisfaction which is made by the substitute acts, **whose place He takes, must necessarily be acquitted." "If it was offered for all mankind then the debt incurred by every man has been cancelled."**
This is exactly what God tells us in Scripture has taken place because of Christ's sacrifice for the world, not just for the Calvinist's so-called elect but for all those for whom Christ died, (The whole world) and the word 'acquitted' is used in a number of translations.

A LIFE-GIVING AQUITTAL FOR ALL MANKIND

We find in Romans 5:-18-19, (see note.)
"Well then, as one man's trespass issued in doom for all, so one man's act of redress ***issued in acquittal and life for all.*** Just as one man's disobedience made all the rest sinners, so one man's obedience will make all the rest righteous." J.M.V.

"Well then, just as the result of a single transgression is condemnation for all mankind, so also the result of a single deed of righteousness **is a life-giving acquittal for all mankind.** For as through the disobedience of one individual the mass of mankind were made sinners, so also through the obedience of One the mass of mankind will be made righteous." The same verses from R. F. Weymouth.

"No distinction is made; for all alike have sinned, and consciously fall short of the glory of God, **but are acquitted freely by His grace through the ransom given by Christ Jesus,** whom God put forward as a propitiation available to faith in virtue of His blood." Romans 3:-23-25. R.F. Weymouth.

"Since all have sinned and are falling short of the honor and glory which God bestows and receives. [All] are justified and made upright and in right standing with God, freely and gratuitously by His grace (His unmerited favor and mercy), through the redemption which is [provided] in Christ Jesus."

Romans 3:-23-24. The Amplified New Testament

In other words a pardon, acquittal, has been granted for all humanity, it is there for the taking or rejecting.

Man is a moral being and has a free will.

If he had not, he would be nothing more than an automaton with no freedom of choice and consequently it would be unjust and immoral to condemn him to hell. These verses underline the Truth and confirm the full scope of the Atonement of John 3:-16, and make it unequivocal, that as Adam's sin brought condemnation, not to some but to all, so the life, death and resurrection of Christ (The second Adam) Brought Salvation, not to some, but to all.

Titus 2:-11. The Jerusalem Bible. **"You see, God's grace has been revealed, and it has made salvation possible for the whole human race."** So the Grace of God is extended to all mankind.

See note in the appendix to this book.

THE BIBLE REMOVES ANY UNCERTAINTY ABOUT THE ATONEMENT

There is no doubt in most peoples' minds as to what is meant by "world" in John 3:-16.

"Thou too, art part of the "World", so that thine heart cannot deceive itself and think. The Lord died for Peter and Paul, but not for me." Martin Luther.

Both John and Titus make an unequivocal statement (in 1 John 2:-2, and Titus 2:-11,) that dissipates any vestige of a doubt and confirms again what Jesus meant in John 3:-16 as to the scope of the atonement and the focus and object of God's Love.

"And He is the propitiation for our sins: and not for ours only, but also for the sins of the whole world ". K.J.V.

Limited atonement, says, "and He is the propitiation for our" (the believers) "sins."

But God says, "not for ours" (believers) "only, but for the sins of the whole world".

"The Lord is not slow in keeping His promise, as some understand slowness. He is patient with you, **not wanting anyone to perish,** but everyone to come to repentance." 2 Peter 3:-9. N.I.V.

These texts (and there are more in Scripture) remove any uncertainty regarding the compass of the Atonement in the many texts referring to Christ's death on the cross for the "world".

1 John 4:-14, "The Father sent the Son to be the Saviour of the world." K.J.V.
John the Baptist called out **"Behold the Lamb of God, which taketh away the sin of the world."** John 1:-29 K.J.V.
The word sin is in the singular indicating that the whole principle (Tree, root and branch) of sin had been dealt with and not just the sins of the Calvinist's so-called elect.
The Lord Jesus Christ and John the Baptist meant the whole world, that is the whole of humanity and not, as the Calvinists say the world of the elect.

COMMON GRACE AT WHAT PRICE?

We often hear Calvinist preachers preach about what they term, "Common Grace" but this universal grace, shown by God to all men, would not be possible if Christ had not satisfied the justice of God the Father by appeasing his wrath, and taking sin's punishment, for the whole world, upon himself.

2 Corinthians 5:-19, "To wit, that God was in Christ, reconciling the world to Himself, <u>not imputing their trespasses unto them;</u> and hath committed unto us the word of reconciliation." K.J.V.

In 2 Peter 2:-1, Peter, when speaking about the False Prophets, says, "even denying the Lord that bought them." K.J.V.
It is obvious that Christ died for those lost, so-called "unelected" false prophets, otherwise they could not have denied the Lord that bought them!

IF THE ATONEMENT IS LIMITED TO THE "ELECT" THEN THOSE WHO ARE "NOT OF THE ELECT" CANNOT BE BLAMED FOR THE FACT OF THEIR INABILITY TO BE SAVED.

The "Professor" does not so much use the Word of God, in justifying his argument, (I believe that with his premise, that would be impossible), but rather depends on his unsubstantiated statements with elaborate and presumptuous explanation of Scripture texts, to establish his adopted theological theory. I quote his own words:
"'Whom does God love' must be answered. And again, the answer must be that of the Scriptures. Only that answer may be proclaimed as the Gospel of Jesus Christ."

Page 5, I quote: "The sole question is: What does the Word of God say? And let every earnest-minded Christian, who wants to walk in obedience to the will of Christ, and who wants the Church to be faithful to its calling to preach the Gospel, BOW BEFORE THAT WORD."

I WOULD SAY AMEN TO THAT.

THERE IS NO GOOD NEWS IN THE CALVINISTIC MESSAGE

But it is not the "Professor's" so-called Calvinistic gospel, but Christ's in John 3:-16. He is presuming that what the Calvinists teach about election and atonement is true to Scripture and should be preached as the "gospel".
But there is no Gospel, "Good News" in the Calvinistic message.
A summary of their so-called gospel is:
God does not love everybody; in fact He hates most people, because they are not elected, and is going to condemn them to hell for ever, and there is nothing the sinful unelected can do.
If you are saved don't bother to pray for your lost loved ones, because if they are not among the elect, you can pray as earnestly as you like, they won't be saved if God hates them, and if they are elected they will be saved anyway.
And they have the audacity to call that "The Gospel", Good News for sinners.

THE INHIBITING INFLUENCE OF CALVINISM IN GOSPEL PREACHING

No Calvinist can honestly say to a sinner with any degree of assurance, "God truly loves you and is concerned about you and sent His only begotten Son to die for your sins that you might be saved". If he does express such sentiments he is being deceptive, because such a view is contrary to his doctrine of "Limited Atonement."
As a result there must always be by the very nature of the doctrine a considerable degree of reservation, and uncertainty and lack of freedom in the proclamation of the gospel by the Calvinist, especially on a one-to-one basis, because of the belief that God does not love everyone and Christ only died for a few they call the elect.
The five points of Calvinism is another gospel, so-called, but it is not the Gospel of the Bible. There is nothing more inhibiting to the preaching of the

gospel than believing the five point doctrine of Calvinism.
So far as freedom in evangelism is concerned, it is like being in a straitjacket with five tight knots preventing any possibility of movement. It is a doctrine that spawns lethargy and takes all motivation out of the need to reach people with the gospel.

CHAPTER 12

THE HATRED OF GOD FOR THE WICKED

The "Professor" goes on to say, "Let us not forget that the same Scriptures which speak of the love of God also speak of the very opposite of His love, namely, His divine hatred. Now if it is true that God loves all men, then it must be true that He hates no man."
"But if the Scriptures cannot be broken, and if then it can be shown that by those very Scriptures that God hates so much as even one man, then it also follows that God does not love all men, and that the term "world" in John 3:-16 cannot possibly mean **"all men."**
" Let us examine the Scriptures with a view to this question. In Psalm 5:-4-5, we read: "For thou art not a God that hath pleasure in wickedness: neither shall evil dwell with Thee. The foolish shall not stand in Thy sight: **Thou hatest all workers of iniquity."** K.J.V.
In Psalm 11:-5-6 we read: "The Lord trieth the righteous: **but the wicked and him that loveth violence His soul hateth."** K.J.V.
"And in Romans 9, a chapter that is very significant for this whole question, we read in verses 10-13, "And not only this; but when Rebekah also had conceived by one, even by our father Isaac; For the children being not yet born, neither having done any good or evil that the purpose of God according to election might stand, not of works, but of Him that calleth; It was said unto her, The elder shall serve the younger. As it is written, Jacob have I loved, but Esau have I hated."
"But if the Scriptures cannot be broken, and if then it can be shown that by those very Scriptures that God hates so much as even one man, then it also follows that God does not love all men, and that the term "world" in John 3:-16 cannot possibly mean all men."
He quotes Psalm 5:-4-5, and the latter part of verse 5 says, **"Thou hatest all the workers of iniquity."**

Also the latter part of verse 6, in Psalm 11, reads, **"But the wicked and him that loveth violence His soul hateth."**

In Psalm 5:-5, The word "workers" used in the King James Version, and "work" are from the same root in the Hebrew and can be used for ACHIEVEMENTS, or MIGHTY DEEDS, and not necessarily for the perpetrator of the deeds, so the Living Bible's rendering of the verse, is accordingly a good interpretation of the text, which is as follows, **"Therefore proud sinners will not survive Your searching gaze, for how you hate their evil deeds."**

The N.I.V. interprets the last part of verse 5 of Psalm 5:-5: **"You hate all who do wrong."**

If God Hates **"All who do wrong"**, and all the wicked and those who love violence, He hates all mankind, "For all have sinned and come short of the glory of God." Romans 3:-23, K.J.V.

According to the writer's own doctrine and there can be little doubt that he believes in the five points of Calvinism and the first is that man's natural state, is that of, "The Total Depravity (wickedness) of Man."

Calvinists are quick to point out, "The heart is deceitful above all things and desperately wicked: who can know it?" Jeremiah 17:-9. K.J.V.

And Psalm 51:-5. "Behold, I was shapen in iniquity; and in sin did my mother conceive me." K.J.V.

So it would not be just "one man" or a few persons, but humanity in its entirety that would come under the scope of God's hatred!

His own adopted theology makes nonsense of his hypothesis.

Whatever those Scriptures mean, they do not mean that God hates the person who is a wrongdoer, or who is wicked, or is a lover of violence; otherwise they could not be reconciled with the teaching of Christ or the rest of Scripture.

AN UNFAIR EXCHANGE

But no matter how strong the word hate is in the Hebrew or Greek, it would make no difference, because the focus of that hate is on the sin and not the sinner, or more correctly on the sin bearer, (2 Corinthians 5:-21). *"For He hath made Him to be sin for us, who new no sin; that we might be made the righteousness of God in Him." K.J.V.*

This literally means that God made the Lord Jesus Christ our sinfulness, and all God's hatred for our sin was poured upon Christ and God punished Him instead of us. The Lord Jesus voluntarily went to the cross knowing exactly

what would happen there.
Isaiah 53:-6 "All we like sheep have gone astray; we have turned everyone to his own way; and the Lord hath laid on Him the iniquity of us all." K.J.V. (Hath made the iniquities of us all to meet on Him)
Note.
The word in the Greek for love, in the verse, "Jacob have I loved" is the highest form of love, "AGAPE", and the Greek for hated, in, "Esau have I hated" is the word "MISEO" which is also a strong word, and means to hate in the sense of "detesting".
It is the same verb which is used in, "They hated me without a cause," in John 15:-25. From "MISOS" – meaning "hatred" John 15:25 (emisesan) – They hated. Romans 9:13 (emisesa) – I hated.
In Malachi 1:-2-3, "Esau have I hated" the Hebrew word "Sawnay" is used and means to detest or to hate utterly.

SURELY GOD'S HATRED FOR SIN IS WITHOUT COMPROMISE!

FOCUSED HATRED ON THE SIN BEARER

If Jehovah's hatred had been focused on the sinner, it would have resulted in the immediate destruction of Adam and Eve in the Garden of Eden, instead of the killing of the animals and the clothing of our first parents with the skins of animals, thus teaching them substitution. God's hatred for and punishment of sin was placed on **"The Lamb slain from the foundation of the world."** Rev 13:-8. K.J.V.
The Scriptures clearly state that God does not hold men's sins against them, which would not be the case if God hated Esau, "All those who do wrong" and "The wicked and those who love violence". 2 Cor 5:-19, says: "To wit, that God was in Christ, reconciling the world unto Himself, **not imputing their trespasses unto them;** and hath committed unto us the word of reconciliation." K.J.V.

"In Christ God was reconciling the world to Himself, **not charging men's transgressions to their account,** and how He has deposited with us the message of this reconciliation." The same text from R. F. WEYMOUTH .

Also in Romans 5:-18, "So as one sin of Adam brought punishment of death to all people, one good act that Christ did makes all people right with God. And that brings true life for all." N.C.V.

DID GOD HATE ESAU?

Speaking about Romans 9:-13, and God's disposition towards Jacob and Esau, the great preacher C. H. Spurgeon said in one of his messages: "Before you begin to argue upon the doctrine, just recollect, that whatever you may think about it, you cannot alter it; and however much you may object to it, it is actually true that God did love Jacob, and did not love Esau. **Why did God hate Esau? Why does God hate any man?"**

See note in the appendix.

Calvinists depict this word Hate and rigorously apply it to the individual, which is incorrect. The reference in Romans 9:-13 to Jacob and Esau are generic, and not of the individuals. If this were specifically referring to the two brothers, and applied as the five point Calvinists apply it, this would mean, God loving and blessing Jacob and hating and bringing evil on Esau. But this would not be correct, and could not be borne out by Scriptural evidence.

Calvinists by linking up verse 11 with verse 13 of Romans 9, make out that God hated Esau; He settled His hatred on the little unborn baby boy. Poor little fellow! Hated by God before he ever saw the light of day!

However, his father loved him, for we are told in Genesis 25:-28, **"And Isaac loved Esau."** K.J.V. So he was evidently kinder than God and Isaac is thereby made out to be more righteous than the Lord.

"Shall mortal man be more just than God? shall a man be more pure than his maker?" Job 4:-17. K.J.V.

ISAAC WISHED GOD TO BLESS BOTH HIS SONS AND HE DID

According to the Calvinist teaching Isaac should have blessed Jacob and cursed Esau. **But Isaac most certainly wanted the Lord to bless both his sons,** and God concurred with the desires and wishes of Isaac in this matter. We read in Hebrews 11:-20, "By faith Isaac Blessed Jacob and Esau concerning things to come." K.J.V.

"It was by faith that Isaac knew God would give future blessings to his two sons, Jacob and Esau." T.L.B.

A verse completely ignored by Calvinist commentaries on Romans 9. The blessing of God was the result of His love for both of them.

Both of the sons of Isaac were blessed by God.

One was not blessed and the other cursed, as the Calvinists imply.

WHAT THE BIBLE ACTUALLY SAYS ABOUT JACOB AND ESAU

In the book of Genesis 25:-23, God told Rebekah: *"Two nations are in thy womb, and two manner of people shall be separated from thy bowels; and the one people shall be stronger than the other people; and the elder shall serve the younger". K.J.V.*

This was a prophetic statement, and deals Specifically with the issue of the two brothers and not with the individuals. The verse starts with the words "Two Nations", and speaks about "Peoples," and not individuals, but the descendants of the two children.

There is no Scriptural evidence that Esau ever served Jacob but the very reverse is true.

This is outlined in Genesis chapters 32-33, and in the first part of verse 4 of chapter 32 we are told that Jacob instructed his servants as follows: "And he commanded them, saying, Thus shall ye speak unto my lord Esau; Thy Servant Jacob saith thus,..."K.J.V.

Jacob sends gifts in order as he thought, to appease the wrath of Esau, and find favour with his brother, and calls Esau his lord **and refers to himself as his (Esau's) servant.**

THE EVIDENT BLESSING AND PROSPERITY OF ESAU BY GOD

It seems evident that the Lord had prospered Esau materially even more than Jacob, because Jacob was terrified at the large company of men (400) Esau brought with him, and another factor was Esau's intention to kill Jacob, made known 20 years before. Genesis, 27:-41-42.

It would appear the prosperity given to Esau was even greater than He gave Abraham who recaptured Lot and his family as well as the people of Sodom with 318 men born in his household. Genesis14:-14.

What appeased the wrath of Esau against his brother over the years of absence was the blessing and material prosperity the Lord had given him.

During the lifetime of the two brothers, the descendants of Esau were more numerous because of the blessing of the Lord and stronger, (they were warrior type people,) than those of Jacob, but this changed after Jacob's sojourn in Egypt.

The N.C.V. interprets Genesis 25:-23, as follows:

"Two nations are in your body, and two groups of people will be taken from you. One group will be stronger than the other, and the older will serve the younger."

THE OLDER ESAU SERVING THE YOUNGER JACOB WAS GENERIC

Although it cannot be proved from Scripture that Esau ever served Jacob, there is distinct Biblical evidence that the descendants of Esau served the house of Jacob, as the Lord reveals clearly to Rebekah, but not until David becomes king.

In 1 Chronicles 18:-12-13, we read: "Moreover *Abishai the son of Zeruiah slew of the Edomites in the valley of salt eighteen thousand. And he put garrisons in Edom and all the Edomites became David's servants." K.J.V.
*Abishai was a nephew of king David, he was the son of David's sister Zeruiah, as were Joab and Asahel. 1 Chronicles 2:-16.
Genesis 36:-9 says **"Esau the father of the Edomites in mount Seir."** K.J.V.
This subjection of the Edomites continued until king Jehoram.
2 Kings 8:-20, "In Jehoram's time Edom broke away from Judah's rule and chose their own king." N.C.V.
This rebellion was prophesied by Isaac when he blessed Esau, in Genesis 27:-40, and he was speaking Generically, "And by thy sword shalt thou live, and shalt serve thy brother; and it shall come to pass when thou shalt have dominion, that thou shalt break his yoke from of thy neck." K.J.V.

GOD'S CHOICE AS TO WHO WILL BE HIS WITNESS TO THE WORLD

The "Purpose of God according to election," deals generically with the choice of Jacob as the father of the nation Israel, being served by the descendants of Esau, and the replacing of Israel with the Church, and this has to do with the choice of God, and not Jehovah hating one and loving the other.
See note on next page.

ROMANS 9 HAS NOTHING TO DO WITH THE SALVATION OF JACOB OR ESAU

It should be emphasized that Romans 9 has nothing whatsoever to do with the personal salvation of either Jacob or Esau, and if this was the main focus of the chapter it would be referred to, but Paul argues that God has exercised His right to choose whom He would have as His witness to the world.

GOD REPLACES ISRAEL WITH HIS CHURCH AS WITNESS TO THE WORLD

The Lord Jesus in Matthew 21:-43, speaking to the Jewish leaders said, "Therefore say I unto you, The Kingdom of God shall be taken from you, and given to a nation bringing forth the fruits thereof." K.J.V.
The Lord Jesus makes this clear also in the parable of the vineyard and the husbandmen in (Matt 21:-33-46; Mark 12:-1-12; Luke 20:-9-18.)
The nation replacing Israel being the Church of Christ: "But you are a chosen people, royal priests, **a holy nation**, a people for God's own possession. You were chosen to tell about the wonderful acts of God, who called you out of darkness into His wonderful light." 1 Peter 2:-9. N.C.V.
See note.
The Calvinists infer through Romans nine that Jehovah chooses in an arbitrary way those who are going to be saved and those He is going to condemn to hell. In other words the people He loves and those He hates.
When the passage deals with one nation serving another, and the Church taking the place of Israel, as a witness to the world.

THE LORD CORRECTS ALL NATIONS BECAUSE HE LOVES THEM

When we read through the Old Testament we find a good deal of it taken up with God chastening and punishing His people, by the sword, famine and pestilence, and on some occasions vast numbers are slain, not because the Lord hated them, but because of their sin against God, and the Lord trying to get them back in line.
We are also told in Psalm 94:-10: **"He that chastiseth the heathen, shall He not correct?"** K.J.V.

"Won't the one who corrects nations punish you?" The same text from the N.C.V.
In Hebrews 12:-6, we are told also: **"For whom the Lord loveth He chasteneth."** K.J.V.

"The Lord corrects those He loves." The same verse in the N.C.V.
Note. In my reference to the Church of Christ replacing Israel, I would not accept what the reformers taught regarding this, or the modern day replacement theology, which I believe to be erroneous.

So His love and chastisement was not only of His own chosen people!
The slaughter was so great against the house of Jacob, that the question was asked in **Ezekiel 11:-13: "Ah Lord God! wilt thou make a full end of the remnant of Israel?"** K.J.V.
"I will not utterly destroy the house of Jacob, saith the Lord." Amos 9:-8. K.J.V.
But He always spares a remnant, because of the promises given to Abraham, Isaac, Jacob, and David and the line from Abraham through David to the birth of The Christ was intact.

THERE WAS NO HATRED SHOWN TO ESAU OR HIS DESCENDANTS

God loved the nation that issued from Esau. This I believe is clear from Scripture.
Nor did He want the house of Jacob to hate their brothers, the Edomites. Deuteronomy 23:-7: **"Thou shalt not abhor" (hate) "an Edomite for he is thy brother:" K.J.V.**
"Don't hate Edomites; they are your close relatives." The same verse from the N.C.V.

Before Jacob went down to Egypt the Edomites, that is the descendants of Esau, were a much more numerous and a stronger (Warrior type) people than the descendants of Jacob, but this situation is reversed, when Jacob comes out of Egypt four hundred years later.

GOD SHOWS HIS LOVE FOR ESAU WHEN HE GIVES ORDERS TO ISRAEL

When the children of Israel came out of Egypt and eventually came back to Canaan, God showed clearly His continued love and care for the house of Esau.
In Deuteronomy 2:-4-5, God commands the Israelites: "And command thou the people, saying, Ye are to pass through the coast of your brethren the children of Esau, which dwell in Seir; and they shall be afraid of you: take ye good heed unto yourselves therefore: **meddle not with them; for I will not give you their land, no, not so much as a foot breadth; because I have given mount Seir unto Esau for a possession."** K.J.V.

This is not the language of hatred, but God's care and love in looking after the interests of the house of Esau.
No promises were ever made to Esau or his issue, and we find the Lord does not spare any remnant when He punishes them for their sins.

THE REASON FOR GOD'S JUDGMENT ON ESAU: THEIR SIN AGAINST ISRAEL

Their sin, was a great hatred for, and barbarous acts against the Israelites (The house of Jacob). The smallest book in the Old Testament, Obadiah, is given over completely to an explanation of the sin that brought the punishment and why the judgment is so great.

THE MESSAGE OF JUDGMENT FROM OBADIAH TO ESAU (Edomites)

Obadiah from verse 9, says: "Then, city of Teman, your best warriors will be afraid and everyone from the mountains of Edom will be killed."
"You did violence to your relatives, the Israelites, so you will be covered with shame and destroyed for ever. You stood aside without helping while strangers carried Israel's treasures away."
"When foreigners entered Israel's gate and threw lots to decide what part of Jerusalem they would take, you were like one of them."
Obadiah verses 9 to 11. N.C.V.

Verse 15 of Obadiah says: **"The same evil things you did to other people will happen to you; they will come back upon your own head."** N.C.V.

WHAT ROMANS 9 ACTUALLY SAYS OF JACOB AND ESAU IS GENERIC

The Calvinists combine verse 11, of Romans 9, **"Not yet born, neither having done any good or evil" with verse 13 "Jacob have I loved, but Esau have I hated"** and instead of looking at verse 13 as referring to the two nations of the brothers, imply that God's love and hatred were towards these individuals, and that it was predetermined long before they were born, before they had done any good or evil. THIS IS NOT SO.

The declaration about God loving Jacob and hating Esau, was given to the nation of Israel in the book of Malachi and was not made before the brothers were born, but probably about 1,300 years or more after their deaths.

THE SUBJECT HAS TO DO WITH TWO NATIONS AND NOT INDIVIDUALS

The whole matter has to do with the two Nations, which issue from Jacob and Esau. This is clearly explained to Rebekah, and also to the house of Jacob through the prophet Malachi.

The word to Rebekah was prophetic and the statement by Malachi was historical.

Malachi 1:-1-2-3. (To the nation Israel)

"The word of the Lord to Israel by Malachi – (My messenger)."

"I have loved you, says the Lord. Yet you say, In what and how have You loved us? Was not Esau Jacob's brother? says the Lord; yet I loved Jacob (Israel), But [in comparison with the degree of love I have for Jacob] I have hated Esau [Edom], and have laid waste his mountains, and his heritage I have given to the jackals of the wilderness." [Romans 9:-13-16] The Amplified Bible.

GOD'S ARGUMENT PUT FORWARD IN MALACHI

The argument in the above verses God puts forward to convince the Israelites that He loves them (and it is evident that they doubted and questioned His Love, because of His harsh dealings with them on account of their sins), was to make a comparison in the severity of the punishment He had dealt out to the house of Esau in contrast with His punishment of the house of Jacob.

In Obadiah verse 18 it says: **"There will be no one left of the people of Esau. This will happen because the Lord has said it."** N.C.V.

God would most certainly have totally destroyed Jacob, but for the promises made to, Abraham, Isaac, Jacob and David.

"I will not cast them away, neither will I abhor them, **to destroy them utterly,** and to break My covenant with them: for I am the Lord their God." Leviticus 26:- 44. K.J.V.

WHEN GOD PUNISHED ISRAEL FOR THEIR SINS HE SPARED A FEW,

BUT WHEN HE PUNISHED ESAU (THE EDOMITES) HE SPARED NONE.

THE DESTRUCTION OF THE EDOMITES WAS TO BE COMPLETE.

Note. This was not done all at the one time, as the Hebrew would indicate that it was to be completed in the future. First the Edomites where destroyed as a nation and their land made desolate and the judgment was to continue thereafter until there was no survivor of Esau.

The Amplified New Testement interprets, Romans 9:-13 as follows,

"As it is written, Jacob have I loved, but Esau have I hated [held in relative disregard in comparison with My feeling for Jacob]. [Mal. 1:2,3]" This is also speaking generically.

CALVINISTS BELIEVE GOD IS SELECTIVE IN SHOWING MERCY

The Calvinists would quote verse 15, of Romans chapter 9:

"I will have mercy on whom I will have mercy, and I will have compassion on whom I will have compassion," in order to justify their belief that the Lord hates some and shows them no mercy and loves others and shows compassion and mercy to them.

The word "mercy" here is not Hilaskomai, as in Luke 18:-13, "God be merciful to me a sinner," but Eleeo, which means showing kindness or favour, as in Matthew 17:-15: "Lord, have mercy on my son; for he is a lunatick, and sore vexed." Bartimeus used the same word in Mark 10:- 46 - 52. Its meaning is even more obvious in Romans 12:- 8: "He that sheweth mercy, with cheerfulness." K.J.V.

"And those who do works of mercy do them cheerfully."

The same text from the Jerusalem bible.

ON WHOM WILL GOD HAVE MERCY?

But in the eleventh chapter of the book of Romans in verse 32, we are told whom God Will have mercy upon, and the extent and scope of His Mercy.

"For God hath concluded them all in unbelief, that He might have mercy on all." K.J.V.

"God has given all people over to their stubborn ways so that He can show mercy to all." N.C.V.

J. B. Phillips interprets the same verse, "God has all men penned up together in the prison of disobedience, that He may have mercy upon them all."
"The Lord is good to all; He has compassion on all He has made."
Psalm 145:-9. N.I V.

GOD'S HATRED FOR JACOB IS ALSO GENERIC

Calvinists seem to ignore or are ignorant of the fact that God's Word states that God hated Jacob also. This must be taken into consideration when trying to understand Romans 9.
In Jeremiah 12:-8, God speaking of Israel says: **"Mine heritage is unto me as a lion in the forest; it crieth out against Me: therefore have I hated it."** K.J.V.

"My people have become to me like a lion in the forest. They roar at me, so I hate them." The same text from the N.C.V.

Also in Psalm 78:-59, "When God heard this, He was wroth, and greatly abhorred" (hated) "Israel." K.J.V.

Also in Psalm 106:-40, we read:
"Therefore was the wrath of the Lord kindled against his people, insomuch that he abhorred" (hated) "His own inheritance." K.J.V.

"So the Lord became angry with His people and hated His own children." The same text from the N.C.V.

SO IT WOULD APPEAR FROM SCRIPTURE THAT IT WAS NOT ONLY ESAU THAT WAS HATED, HE ALSO HATED JACOB.

GOD'S JUDGMENTS ARE NOT PARTIAL

The judgment that came on Esau's and on Jacob's issue, was not the result of God hating them, but the result of their sin, and the difference was in the extent of the judgment; in the one case almost total destruction, and in the other total.
God does not show partiality towards individuals, or nations when dealing with their sinfulness. This is made very clear when reading through the Old and New Testaments.

"For there is no respect of persons with God." (Romans 2:-11) K.J.V.

"For God judges all people in the same way." Rom 2:-11. N.C.V.

James 2:- 9, says, **"But if you show partiality you commit sin, and are convicted by the law as offenders."** R. F. Weymouth version.

BELIEVE THE TEACHING OF CHRIST RATHER THAN TRADITIONS OF MEN.

It is much better to believe and obey the Word of God, than to follow the theological dogmas of men, and be led into error. As the Lord Jesus said to the Pharisees:
"Making the Word of God of none effect through your tradition."
Mark 7:-13. K.J.V.
"By your own rules, which you teach people, you are rejecting what God has said." The same verse in the N.C.V.

Our beliefs guide us in the way we should go and the disposition we assume. The right belief produces good fruit and is a benefit and blessing to others as well as to ourselves, and can help the furtherance of His work. If our belief is wrong it can obstruct and frustrate the blessing of God in our lives and, through us, in the lives of others also, as the following story illustrates.

A HORRIFIC EXPERIENCE OF ONE WOMAN TURNED TO GOOD FOR OTHERS

I heard a story of a lady in America, whose only child, a lovely daughter of twenty three years of age, who had trained to be a missionary and who, when she was about to leave home for service in the mission field, was brutally raped and murdered. The police caught the perpetrator, and he received a prison sentence. Some time later this lady was at a meeting where the "Gideons" were speaking about their work of placing Bibles in schools, hotels and prisons. After the meeting finished she asked if they did any work in a particular prison in another state, and was told they did. She then asked, if payment was made for a Bible, would they be able to give it to a certain prisoner.
The answer was yes. So she paid for the Scriptures to be given to the man

who had raped and murdered her only daughter.

A comment was made that, "he will not likely accept the Book from your representative, but tell him my name and that I have been praying for him every day for the past year, and I would like him to accept the Bible and read it." The prisoner refused the Scriptures as the lady had said.

But after being told who sent it and that she had been praying for him each day for the past year, he took it.

The prisoner read the Bible and was gloriously saved, and because of the great transformation in his life other prisoners were saved and also some of the warders.

That mother turned the tragic death of her daughter from a disaster into a victory, and her daughter's death was not in vain, because of her trust in God's Word and her prayers.

She believed that God loves, even violent and wicked men and that Christ died for them.

She also was obedient to Christ's command to "love your enemies," and the person who had brought her the greatest amount of anguish and misery became the focus of her prayers that he would be saved.

How inhibiting it is to prayer and evangelism of the lost to believe that God hates wicked men and that Jesus died for only the respectable sinners, and only a limited number of them. AND HOW UNTRUE!

If she had believed that God hated the wicked, she would not have seen the miracle of an appalling and horrific experience turned into a glorious victory in the salvation of a wicked and violent man, and the results that followed in others who, seeing such a person transformed, were converted to Christ as the result of what God had done in that man's life.

If God hates wicked and violent men, that man would never have been saved and neither would millions of others.

This story and many others only confirm the Bible's teaching, that God loves all men and our Lord died for every individual on earth.

What "The Professor" is trying to do is to persuade his readers, that if God hates some men "then it also follows that God does not love all men and that the term "World" in John 3;-16 cannot possibly mean all men. In other words Christ's atonement was not for all men, thus proving the theory of "Limited Atonement."

IN ISRAEL THE ATONEMENT WAS NOT PARTICULAR BUT COVERED ALL THE ISRAELITES

"To make an atonement for the children of Israel for all their sins once a

year." Leviticus 16:-34 K.J.V.
"To make Atonement for the children of Israel [to cleanse them] from all their sins once a year." The same verse from the J. N. Darby.

"And the priests killed them;" (animals) "and they presented the blood on the altar as a sin offering to make atonement for all Israel."
2 Chron 29:-24. N.K.J.V.
"And the priests slaughtered them," (animals) "and they made purification for sin with their blood upon the altar, **to make atonement for all Israel, because for all Israel, said the king, is the burnt-offering and the sin offering."** 2 Chron 29:-24. From the J. N. Darby Version.

The Atonement covered the whole Nation not just those who believed and were obedient. All Israel was Elected or Chosen through the atonement. Likewise in John 3:-16, Christ sets out God's plan of atonement for the whole world.
The hymn writer was correct when he wrote:
"Blind unbelief is sure to err and scan His work in vain, God is His own interpreter and He will make it plain."

SCRIPTURE VERSUS THE "PROFESSOR"

But Scripture proves the "Professor" wrong, because of the texts that tell us that God loves and Christ died for all the inhabitants of the world, which would include those who are wicked and love violence, and Esau as well as Jacob. So the Professor's claim is invalid.
Christ did not die for good people, but for sinners, that is the gospel, good news. **"Christ Jesus came into the world to save sinners."**
1 Timothy 1:15. K.J.V.
"For I am not come to call the righteous, but sinners to repentance." Matthew 9:-13. K.J.V.
The following verses confirm the Truth in the Gospel of John 3:-16. Immaterial to what some men believe the disposition of God is towards men. God loves and Christ died for all men without exception, as the subsequent verses make crystal clear. In 1 Timothy 4:-10 we read: "For therefore we both labour and suffer reproach, because we trust in the Living God, **Who is the Saviour of all men, specially of those that believe."** K.J.V.
"This is why we work and struggle: we hope in the living God **who is the Saviour of all people, especially of those who believe."**

1 Timothy 4:-10 N.C.V.
Similar confirmation of the extent of the atonement is found in the Old Testament.
In Isaiah 53:- 6, we read: "All we like sheep have gone astray; we have turned everyone to his own way; and the Lord has laid on Him the iniquity of us all." K.J.V.
The verse begins with all going astray, and finishes with the iniquity of all, being laid on Him, Jesus atoning for the sins of everyone.

ATONING FOR THE SINS OF ALL MEN MEANS GOD ELECTING ALL MEN.

In Hebrews 2:- 9, the latter part of the verse: **"Crowned with glory and honour; that He by the grace of God should taste death for every man."** K.J.V.

"Crowned with glory and honor because of His having suffered death, in order that by the grace (unmerited favor) of God [to us sinners] He might experience death for every individual person."
The same verse in The Amplified New Testament.
It is the Disposition of God that is the motivation in sending His Son who **"Tasted death for everyone in all the world."** Hebrews 2:-9. T.L.B.

This authenticates the emphasis of John 3:-16.
"For the grace of God, which can save every man, has now become known." Titus 2:-11. J. B. Phillips version.

"For the grace of God - His unmerited favor and blessing - has come forward (appeared) for the deliverance from sin and the eternal salvation for all mankind." Titus 2:-11 The Amplified New Testament.

THE SECOND PART OF CHAPTER TWELVE

HATE IN MANY PARTS OF SCRIPTURE MEANS ONLY A LESSER LOVE

Many Calvinist writers and preachers quote Romans 9:-10-13, as a proof that God does not love all men, and through this try to prove the theory of "Unconditional Election", and " Limited Atonement."

Bible students know that the word hate in Scripture is not always to be understood rigorously. It customarily signifies no more than a lesser degree of love, e.g. In Deuteronomy 21:-15. "If a man have two wives, one beloved, and another hated." (That is less beloved). K.J.V.

In Proverbs 13:-24, we read: "He who spares his rod hates his son. But he who loves him disciplines him promptly." N.K.J.V.

Genesis 29:-31, "And when the Lord saw that Leah was hated," (loved less) "he opened her womb: but Rachel was barren." K.J.V.

"When the Lord saw that Jacob loved Rachel more than Leah, He made it possible for Leah to have children, but not Rachel." The same verse in the N.C.V.

There are times when the word Hate in Scripture can be interpreted rigorously and this is usually fairly obvious, as in, 1 John 3:-15: **"Whosoever hateth his brother is a murderer: and ye know that no murderer hath eternal life abiding in him."** K.J.V.

In Luke 14:-26 we read: **"If any man come to Me, and hate not his father, and mother, and wife, and children, and brethren, and sisters, yea, and his own life also, he cannot be My disciple."** K.J.V.

No one who knows the Scriptures would suggest that the word hate in the above text could be taken and applied rigorously.

In the Ten Commandments we are told **"Honour thy father and thy mother."** Jesus commands us to love one another and in Ephesians 5:-25, God's Word speaks about the kind of love a man should have for his wife when it says, "Husbands, love your wives, even as Christ also loved the Church, and gave himself for it." What Jesus is saying is that we have to love the Lord with all our heart, body and soul and our love for others will be in comparison like hate, at least to the onlooker, it can look like hate, as they see the outcome of this greater and lesser love.

In Matthew 10:-37, we read: "He that loveth father or mother more than Me is not worthy of Me: and he that loveth son or daughter more than Me is not worthy of Me." K.J.V.

ABRAHAM'S LOVE FOR HIS SON ISAAC LOOKED MORE LIKE HATRED

Was this not true when Abraham offered up Isaac, as he lifted up the knife to kill his son? Anyone observing this would have considered that he hated his son, but this was far from true. Having waited twenty-five years for God to fulfil His promise of a son through Sarah, and having fathered the child when he was 100 years old, Isaac was the apple of his father's eye. He would gladly have changed places with his son.

But God wanted to see how much Abraham loved Him.

His love for God was greater than that for his son Isaac, which would have appeared to any observer more like hate.

GOD SHOWS US BY EXAMPLE

The Lord shows us by example how to love Him. He gave His only begotten Son, to die for us. He put us first! Did not the Lord Jesus call out when He was on the cross:

"MY GOD, MY GOD, WHY HAST THOU FORSAKEN ME?"

The one that God the Father loved the most He sacrificed for us. Most of us would rather take the place of a suffering loved one than watch that person suffer. There is a cost to loving. The god in anyone's life is the person or the thing that comes first, and for which we would sacrifice most. To put it another way it is the person or thing that is the pre-eminent and central focus of our lives.

THE LORD OUR CREATOR AND SAVIOUR, WANTS TO BE GOD IN OUR LIVES.

AN ILLUSTATION FROM SCOTTISH HISTORY

During the Covenanting times, which was a little more than one hundred years after the Reformation in Scotland. King Charles II, decreed, that he was the head of the Church and wanted to unify the Churches of England and Scotland and force the people of Scotland to accept him as head of the Church.

He introduced Episcopal worship and bishops into Church government in Scotland, which to the Presbyterians was anathema. Gilbert Wilson a farmer and his wife conformed to the wishes of the king in the matter of religion but their three children, Margaret aged 18, Agnes aged 13 and Thomas aged 15,

were among those who declined to conform.
They refused to attend the Episcopal worship, which was forced on all congregations and would meet with the Covenanters in the hills for their services, which were called "Coventicles". Because their children were Covenanters and non attendance at Episcopal services was punishable with fines, Gilbert Wilson was made to appear in court and fined a great deal of money and from being a fairly well-off farmer he was brought to poverty.

CAPTURED BY THEIR ENEMIES

Margaret and Agnes went into the town of Wigtown to visit a godly old Covenanter called Margaret MacLaughlan. Their brother Thomas did not go because he believed it was too dangerous. His fears proved to be correct for during this visit they were captured by the soldiers. The two Margarets and little Agnes refused to swear what was called the 'Abjuration Oath', which acknowledged the king as head of the Church, because they believed the Bible, * that Christ alone was the head of the Church and not any king or pope. They were all sentenced to death, but because Agnes was so young, Gilbert Wilson was able with great difficulty to save her from the death penalty by paying £100 for her release, which was in those days a fortune.
*Ephesians 5:-23. **"Even as Christ is the head of the Church."** K.J.V.
Colossians 1:-18 **"And He" (Christ) "is the head of the body, the Church."** K.J.V.

THE PRICE PAID FOR TRUSTING CHRIST ALONE

On the 11th May 1685 the two Margarets were taken to the Solway Firth where the tide comes in very rapidly and the older woman was tied to a post farther out in the Firth and the younger Margaret much nearer the shore. They thought that Margaret Wilson when she saw her friend die would recant and swear the 'Abjuration Oath'. When the water came up to Margaret MacLaughlan's mouth she struggled and one of the soldiers said to the young Margaret, 'what do you think of the old bitch now?' Her answer was 'I think I see Christ struggling in her.'
People from the crowd shouted to Margaret "Just say the words Margaret and they will set you free." But she would not.
So she died for the Biblical principle of truth, that CHRIST ALONE IS THE HEAD OF THE CHURCH AND NO ONE ELSE.
A Scriptural truth that many appear to ignore today.

Comment. We, as believers, should follow young Margaret's example and instead of focusing on the faults in other believers, look for Christ struggling in them.

THEY MADE THE LORD, GOD IN THEIR LIVES

These three young people were hunted as fugitives and had to survive on the moors and hills during the Scottish winters and brought a great deal of persecution and hardship not only to themselves, but to their parents and we are told that years later when Gilbert Wilson died his widow had to depend on the kindness and help of her friends in order to live. It was not that these young people hated their parents, although to some it would look like that. It was that their love for Christ eclipsed the love for parents and, in young Margaret's case, for her own life.

There is such a thing as a greater and lesser love in Christian living as Christ clearly taught.

This story illustrates what Jesus said in Luke 14:-26, where we read:

"If any man come to Me, and hate not his father and mother, and wife, and children, and brethren, and sisters, yea and his own life also, he cannot be My disciple." K.J.V.

THIS TEXT PUT INTO PRACTICE IN RECENT TIMES

An Evangelist and a very dear friend of mine, who has, as he himself would have said, gone to Heaven for the good of his health, was once holding a mission on one of the islands in the north of Scotland, and was experiencing what he described as a time of revival. A telegram came informing him of his mother's death and the time of the funeral. It would, in those days, have taken him about a week to have attended the funeral and return to his mission. He felt, as souls were being wonderfully saved every night that if he broke off the campaign for a few days, the whole momentum of the mission would be lost, and so also would souls. So he decided that he would not go to his mother's funeral, but carry on with the campaign. It was a heart-rending decision for him, for he loved his mother dearly. But Jesus was first and Lord in his life. He was misunderstood by his family and friends who thought he had no feeling of love for his mother at all. Note. A Calvinist would not have this problem because they believe that God will save all the elect immaterial of what his servants do or do not do. But then it would be unlikely that they would trouble themselves with an evangelistic campaign, for that very reason.

THE OUTWORKING OF GOD'S LOVE FOR BELIEVERS AND UNBELIEVERS

It is also true with regard to the outworking of the Lord's love for those who believe, love and obey Him and for those who don't. It is not that God loves them less, it is because His love cannot be fully implemented in their lives. This is also true among believers. Jude verse 21, "Keep yourselves in the love of God, looking for the mercy of our Lord Jesus Christ unto eternal life." K.J.V.

"Stay always within the boundaries where God's love can reach and bless you." Jude 21, T.L.B.

The story of the prodigal son in Luke 15, illustrates this.

The Love of the father for his prodigal son was the same when his son was in the far country as it was when he came home.

The difference was it could not be implemented (or realized) until his son's attitude and position changed.

THE LORD JESUS' LOVE FOR THE VIOLENT AND WICKED IN JERUSALEM

When texts appear like Psalm 5:- 4 - 5, and 11:- 5 - 6, and a phrase like "As it is written Jacob have I loved and Esau have I Hated", (Although Generic), they must be interpreted in the light and teaching of Scripture as a whole and, in particular, in the light of the life and teaching of Christ. In Christ we have the revealed character of God, which is in Essence, "God is Love."

THE LORD JESUS REVEALS THE CHARACTER OF GOD

There are many instances where Christ displays this in His dealings with men, which manifests the character of God, in Christ. In John 14:- 9, we read: "He that hath seen Me hath seen the Father". K.J.V.

"The Son reflects the glory of God and shows exactly what God is like." Hebrews 1:- 3. N.C.V.

In Matthew 23:- 37, we read: "O Jerusalem, Jerusalem, thou that killest the prophets, and stonest them that are sent unto thee, how often would I have gathered thy children together, even as a hen gathereth her chickens under her wings, AND YE WOULD NOT!" K.J.V.

Is this the Language of Hate towards those who are violent, and wicked murderers? Luke tells us in chapter 19:- 41, that Jesus wept over the city.

Surely His concern and tears were the result of His love **for those lost people of Jerusalem who had rejected Him.**

A WEEPING GOD CONCERNED FOR THE LOST

The great preacher Dr. Joseph Parker, said of this verse, "Take it as a sentiment: is there anything deeper in human pathos? **Take it as a revelation of God, and surely to the weeping God, even a little child may go."**
When the Lord was on the cross He called out **"Father forgive them for they know not what they do."** K.J.V. The prayer was for the WICKED AND VIOLENT MEN who were crucifying Him--the same class of men that Psalm 5:-4-5 and Psalm 11:-5-6 speak about. The prayer was said out of love, for the wicked men who were so violently cruel to Him.
Forgiveness is not just words, but rather an attitude of heart, and Jesus, when He prayed that prayer, was revealing His DISPOSITION OF LOVE FOR SINNERS. **The prayer from the cross was not the phrase of hate for violent and wicked men, as depicted in Psalm 11:-5-6.**

GOD'S COMMANDMENT TO LOVE OUR ENEMIES.

The Gospels display the life of Christ, and His teaching to the disciples was to love one another; and in Matthew 5:-43-48. He exhorts them to love their enemies.
"Ye have heard that it hath been said, Thou shalt love thy neighbour, and hate thine enemy. But I say unto you, Love your enemies, bless them that curse you, do good to them that hate you, and pray for them which dispitefully use you; and persecute you, That ye may be the children of your Father which is in heaven: for He maketh His sun to shine on the evil and on the good, and sendeth rain on the just and on the unjust." K.J.V. Verse 48, **"Be ye therefore perfect, as your Father which is in heaven is perfect." K.J.V.**
The reason Jesus gives for obeying these injunctions is so that we will be like God our Father and display our Father's Disposition and Attitudes.

THE CLEAR TEACHING OF CHRIST'S EXHORTATION

The inference is that we will be imperfect without obeying His exhortation to love and do good to our enemies, as God does.
It also infers that God would be imperfect if He did not love all men!

We are to love the perpetrator, not his deeds! There is a distinct separation between the two. The Bible clearly makes that distinction. In Romans 12:9, we are told to "Abhor that which is evil; cleave to that which is good." K.J.V. The Living Bible, interprets the verse: "Don't just pretend that you love others: really love them. Hate what is wrong. Stand on the side of good." See Note.

The natural thing is for man to hate the evildoer as well as the evil deed.

It is clear from Scripture that God loves humanity, and that Christ died for each and every individual! And that God hates sin, and the focus of His hatred is on the principle and not on the perpetrator! Although it is also clear that God punishes those who are persistent and unrepentant in their sin, and it is this that is seen and interpreted by many as God's hatred.

While in "the land of the living" man has been granted pardon and acquittal from the punishment of his sin through Christ, it is there for the taking. The judgment of God on the offender is suspended, solely because of Christ's sacrifice on the sinner's behalf, and Jehovah has given men space to repent, before this happens. And in 1 Thessalonians 5:-15: "See that none render evil for evil unto any man; but ever follow that which is good, both among yourselves, and to all men." K.J.V.

Note
CHRIST SPEAKS ABOUT LOVE AS A PRINCIPLE

In the present age in which we live, love is linked with the sensual and changes with circumstances. It has more to do with the way individuals feel than with the moral code of love, which Christ expects His followers to obey. The love Christ is speaking about is a principle and disposition, which believers should cultivate and this is brought into being by an act of the will rather than an act motivated by feelings or whims.

We are never told in Scripture to feel love for other people; but to love them. We should act in love towards others whether we like or dislike these individuals, this certainly is what Christ would have us do.

Love in the Biblical sense is **"A desire and a working for the advancement and prosperity of others."**

This is a reflection of the disposition and attitude of God Himself towards mankind.

CHAPTER 13

CALVINISTS ON BEING BORN AGAIN AND THE WIND OF THE SPIRIT

The book, "The Sovereignty of God," from which I am about to quote comes from a prominent Calvinist apologist and Biblical commentator, Arthur W. Pink whose books I have heard quoted many times from the pulpit and of whom a Calvinist preacher friend of mine said, that this particular book (which has sold 160,000 copies since it was first printed), in his opinion was a classic, but a classic of what, he did not say.
John 3:- 8 "The wind bloweth where it listeth, and thou hearest the sound thereof, but canst not tell whence it cometh, and whither it goeth: so is everyone that is born of the Spirit."

PINK'S COMMENTS ON THIS VERSE ARE AS FOLLOWS

"The first point of the analogy is seen in the words "Where it listeth" or "pleaseth" "The wind blows where it pleaseth so is everyone that is "Born of the Spirit". This wind is an element which man can neither harness nor hinder. "The wind blows when it pleases, where it pleases, as it pleases. So it is with the Spirit. The wind is regulated by divine wisdom yet so far as man is concerned, **it is absolutely sovereign in its operations. So it is with the Spirit."**
"Sometimes the wind blows so soft it scarcely rustles a leaf; at other times it blows so loudly that its roar can be heard for miles. So it is with the matter of the New birth...born of the Spirit." (John 3:-6)"

"THE NEW BIRTH IS SOLELY THE WORK OF GOD THE SPIRIT AND MAN HAS NO PART OR LOT IN CAUSING IT."

My question is: If man has no part or lot in causing the new birth, how many members were in the Church at Corinth, or Ephesus before Paul the apostle preached the Gospel in these two towns?
How many were born again of the Spirit by the wind of the Spirit moving through Corinth or Ephesus before Paul went to them with the "Glad Tidings?"

THE ANSWER IS? *** NONE!

How many cannibals in the New Hebrides were members of a Christian Church and were born again through the wind of the Spirit moving through the islands of the New Hebrides before John Paton and the other missionaries went with the Gospel?

THE ANSWER IS? *** NONE!

Note. A similar phrase to that of Pink's is used in the Westminster Confession regarding the working of the Holy Spirit when it speaks about, "elect infants dying in infancy, are regenerated and saved by Christ, through the Spirit, Who worketh where, and when, and how He pleaseth."

THE WIND IS NOT SELECTIVE

(John 3:-8) This is often referred to by Calvinists as "The selective ministry of the Holy Spirit," but has anyone known the wind to be selective? Have you ever gone for a walk with friends, and found that the wind blew on some of you and avoided the others?

This is a text taken completely out of context in order to fit in with their belief that regeneration comes before Faith in Christ.

The expression "where it listeth" or "where it wants to" N.C.V. obviously does not mean that the wind has the power of choice.

We have all heard, and used, such expressions as: "The sun is trying to break through", or "The weather cannot make up its mind what to do." A B.B.C. weather forecaster said: "The cold front has decided to come south again." Such statements are obviously not meant to be understood literally.

All will agree that the verse consists of an illustration - **"The Wind"** - and an application - **"So Is." So Is What? The Holy Spirit?** The verse does not say so.

The wind is not likened to the Holy Spirit, but to the regenerated person. "SO IS EVERY ONE THAT IS BORN OF THE SPIRIT."

MAN AND THE WORD OF GOD ARE INVOLVED IN THE NEW BIRTH

The New Birth is not solely the work of the Spirit of God, which selects some individuals, when, and where, and as He pleases, with man having no part or lot in causing it. To say that man has no part or lot in the second birth is as ridiculous and untrue as it would be to say that man takes no part in physical birth; it is just not true.

But in Pink's and many other Calvinists' understanding of the new birth, because of their belief in "Total Depravity" and "Unconditional Election," **God the Holy Spirit, and only God the Holy Spirit is involved.**

What utter nonsense this Monergistic thesis produces.

The Lord Jesus Christ said these words in John 6:-63,
"It is the spirit that quickeneth; the flesh profiteth nothing: the words that I speak unto you, they are spirit, and they are life." K.J.V.

1 John 5:-6, says, **"And it is the Spirit that beareth witness, because the Spirit is truth."** K.J.V.
"And the Spirit says that this is true, because the Spirit is truth." 1 John 5:-6. N.C.V.
What Jesus is saying is that it is His Word (The Truth) that is spirit and which quickens, and which brings life (Spiritual and Eternal).

The Psalmist says, "For Thy Word hath quickened me." Psalm 119:-50, K.J.V. Also in Psalm 119:-93, "I will never forget thy precepts, **for with them thou hast quickened me."** K.J.V.

"I will never forget Your precepts; [how can I?] for it is by them You have quickened me – granted me life."
The Amplified Bible interpretation of the same verse.

So even in the Old Testament we have the age-old truth that regeneration, new birth, comes through belief in the Truth of God's Word.

Note: Just as the Lord Jesus brought the spirit and soul of Lazarus back into his body and raised him from the dead, so man is given eternal life (the life forfeited by Adam and Eve when they sinned and God departed from them) when he welcomes the Lord into his life, and this is done through believing the Truth, His Word. "For Thy Word hath quickened me." I refer to the chapter on spiritual death in this book.
It is believers who convey the Lord through the Gospel to other people, and with it the Spirit, which is the Word, who works in and through the Word. "The Sword of the Spirit, which is the Word of God." Eph 6:-17. K.J.V.

PERSUADED TO BELIEVE THROUGH REASONING FROM THE SCRIPTURES

Paul, the apostle, reasoned with the unregenerate Jews in the Synagogues from the Scriptures so that they would believe in Christ and be saved. None of the Jews were converted to Christ without understanding the Gospel message, and

believing it. Paul and Silas preached in Berea to the unregenerate Jews. "These were more noble than those in Thessalonica, in that they received the Word with all readiness of mind, and searched the Scriptures daily, whether those things were so. Therefore many of them believed; also of honourable women which were Greeks, and of men, not a few." Acts 17:-11-12. K.J.V.
They were not at that time, followers of Christ but they were able to understand the Gospel in relationship to the Old Testament Scriptures, and assess from this that Jesus was the Christ the Son of God.

UNDERSTANDING IS NOT IMPERATIVE BUT BELIEVING IS

It is not imperative that one needs to understand the Gospel and all that it means to be saved, one only needs to believe in the Lord Jesus Christ, that He died on the cross for one's sins and rose again from the dead. There are many children and adults who are regenerated because they believe in Christ wholeheartedly but only come to a full understanding of the Gospel later.
Note. The Greek for "word" is Logos from which we get our English word logic and it is through the logic or understanding of the Word or message that people believe in Christ and are regenerated.

THE GODHEAD WORK TOGETHER AND NOT AS SEPARATE UNITS

2 Corinthians 3:-17, says: **"Now the Lord is the Spirit**, and where the Spirit of the Lord is, there is freedom." N.I.V.
John 1:-1, "In the beginning was the Word, and the Word was with God, and the Word was God." K.J.V.
Logos, could be translated Message, and it is in some translations, for it means any kind of communication.
In Genesis 1:-2-3, "And the earth was without form, and void; and darkness was upon the face of the deep. And the Spirit of God moved upon the face of the waters. And God said let there be light and there was light." K.J.V.
"By The Word of the Lord were the heavens made; and all the host of them by the breath of His mouth." Psalm 33:-6. K.J.V.
The Holy Spirit in the creation of the world was not acting independently of God the Father or the Lord Jesus, but rather in and through the Word (Message) Christ from God the Father, because all things were created by Him. For **"The Lord is the Spirit."** 2 Cor 3:-17.
God planned creation, and this was defined in the Word (Message) Christ and the Holy Spirit through the Message (Christ) brings it into being.

THE PRINCIPLE IS THE SAME IN THE NEW CREATION

In the New Creation it is the same. God planned salvation, and Christ, the defining Word, expounded it, and made it reality by His atonement on the cross, and the Holy Spirit through the Word, Message, Christ, brings it into being, in those who believe. John 6:-63.
It was the Word (the communication from God) that created all things. "All things were made by Him;" (The Word, Christ) "and without Him was not anything made that was made." John 1:-3. K.J.V.
In the New Creation (The Second Birth) it is also the Word (Message), which brings about regeneration in those who believe.
When Jesus said "I will build my church; and the gates of hell shall not prevail against it." Matthew 16:-18 K.J.V, **His meaning was precisely that.**
When the Lord Jesus spoke to Saul on the road to Damascus, He did not say why are you persecuting my people, but, **"Saul, Saul, why persecutest thou Me?"** K.J.V. **He meant exactly that.**

Christ dwelt in and was working through His people, and was active in the communication of the Gospel, and building His Church; for Christ is the Word (Message), and the New Birth is brought about in all who accept the Message, WHICH MEANS CHRIST.

WE ARE BORN AGAIN BY BELIEVING THE WORD OF GOD

James says in his epistle, **"God decided to give us life through the Word of truth."** James 1:-18. N.C.V.

"By His own choice He made us His children by the Message of the Truth." The same verse in The Jerusalem Bible.

Peter tells us, "Whereby are given unto us exceeding great and precious promises: **that by these ye might be partakers of the divine nature."**
2 Peter 1:-4. K.J.V. We use the promises of God in order to be born-again.

Peter also tells us "Being born again, not of corruptible seed, **but of incorruptible, by the Word of God, which liveth and abideth forever."**
1 Peter 1:-23. K.J.V.

"You have been regenerated – born again – not from a mortal origin (seed, sperm) but from one that is immortal by the ever living and lasting Word of God." The same verses from The Amplified New Testament.

PAUL WAS INVOLVED IN THE NEW BIRTH OF OTHERS - AS WE SHOULD BE

Paul said in 1 Corinthians 4;-15. "For though you have ten thousand instructors in Christ, yet have ye not many fathers: **for in Christ Jesus I have begotten you through the gospel." K.J.V.**

What Paul is saying is, I have given birth to you (spiritually) through the message of the gospel. They were regenerated through believing the message of the Good News.
This is in agreement with what the Lord Jesus, The Psalmist, James and Peter say. The word Begotten is the same word that is used in John 3:-16 in the King James Bible, and has the meaning of **"Issuing from."**
The Lord Jesus confirms this in John 8:-42. **"For I proceeded forth and came from God."** (K.J.V.) As would be the case when a woman gives birth, which is reproduction or an extension of oneself. But in the spiritual sense the reproducing of one's spiritual life, which is by faith in Christ; in others, is done by the conveying or preaching of the Gospel Message, as Paul Tells us in 1 Cor 4:-15.
So Paul was very **profoundly involved** in the New Birth of those who became Christians at Corinth, and at all the other Churches He founded.
"You have been born again, and this new life did not come from something that dies, but from something that cannot die. You were born again through God's living Message that continues for ever."
1 Peter 1:-23. N.C.V.
"You may have ten thousand tutors in Christ, but you have only one father. For in Christ Jesus you are my offspring, and mine alone, through the preaching of the Gospel." 1 Corinthians 4:-15. N.E.B.
PAUL DID NOT SAY I HAVE BEGOTTEN YOU BY THE WIND OF THE SPIRIT!

PARTICIPATE IN THE NEW BIRTH OF OTHERS BY PREACHING THE GOSPEL

Wherever we take the Gospel Message, we take the dynamic of God the Spirit, so man has a great deal to do with people being born again.
"I am proud of the Good News, **because it is the power God uses to save everyone who believes."** Romans 1:-16. N.C.V.
For where we take the News of the Lord Jesus Christ the wind of the Spirit will blow, (when people believe the message), and where we don't take the "Glad Tidings," it will not blow.

IT IS THE SHEEP WHICH GIVE BIRTH AND REPRODUCE

An analogy in both the Old and New Testaments is that we (believers) are His sheep (Psalm 23 and John 10). The flock does not increase in number in any other way than by **the sheep reproducing.**

Christians give birth to others because they convey the Gospel Message to them, and they believe and are regenerated - born again.

As Paul said to the Corinthians, **"For in Christ Jesus you are my offspring, and mine alone, through the preaching of the Gospel."** 1 Cor 4:-15. N.E.B.

THE FRUIT COMES THROUGH THE BRANCHES AS WE ABIDE IN CHRIST

There is also the analogy of the Vine and the branches in John 15, and it is the branches that bare the fruit, as they abide in the Vine which is Christ, and the life of Christ moves through the branches in order to produce the fruit. **But the fruit comes through the branches.**

The new birth comes through the message and not by the Holy Spirit working independently **"When He pleases, where He pleases, as He pleases,"** But by the Spirit operating through the message, and the Spirit is already in the Word, for the Word of Christ is Spirit.

Without the gospel there is no regeneration – no new birth!

A VAIN ATTEMPT TO PROVE THE NEW BIRTH COMES BEFORE BELIEVING

Arthur W. Pink in a desperate attempt to try to justify the erroneous Calvinist doctrine from Scripture, that regeneration comes before believing and is given by God arbitrarily and only to those He loves. He informs us that the person who is the recipient of the new birth has nothing to do with it. His Scriptural proof is as follows:

"That the work of the Holy Spirit precedes our believing is unequivocally established by 2 Thess 2:-13 "God hath from the beginning chosen you to salvation through sanctification of the Spirit and belief of the truth." K.J.V.

PINK'S ARGUMENT

"Note that 'sanctification of the Spirit' comes before and makes possible 'belief of the truth'. What then is the 'sanctification of the Spirit'? We answer,

the new birth. In Scripture 'sanctification' always means 'separation,' separation from something and unto something or someone. Let us now amplify our assertion that the 'sanctification of the Spirit' corresponds to the new birth and points to the positional effect of it."
This may be what is believed by Calvinists but it has no Biblical basis, and contradicts Christ's teaching. It is Theological Nonsense.

In 1 Thessalonians 4:-3-4, we read, "For this is the will of God even your sanctification, that ye should abstain from fornication: That every one of you should know how to possess his vessel in sanctification and honour." K.J.V.

"For this is the will of God, that you should be consecrated – separated and set apart for pure and holy living: that you should abstain and shrink from all sexual vice." 1 Thess 4:-3-4. The Amplified New Testament.

This Letter was written to the same Church, a group of born-again believers, and God's will was that they should be sanctified and it is quite clear from this text that sanctification is not the new birth.

THE NEW BIRTH IS NOT POSITIONAL: IT IS PRACTICAL

The new birth is not positional but a spiritual experience that in a practical way radically changes our whole life.
Unlike justification, imputed righteousness, sanctification, and ultimate Glorification which are positional in Christ and which are the promised benefits which come from the new birth which is brought about by believing in Christ.
Four times in John chapter 3 does the Lord Jesus tell us how to be saved and receive eternal life in verses 15-16-18 and 36, and it is by believing and this could not be clearer, and also, in Acts 26:-18, when the word sanctified is used. When the Lord Jesus spoke to Paul and told him what he had to do for Him, He said, "To open their eyes, and to turn them from darkness to light, and from the power of Satan unto God, that they may receive forgiveness of sins, **and inheritance among them which are sanctified by faith that is in Me."** K.J.V.

"To open their eyes so that they may turn away from darkness to the light, away from the power of Satan and to God. Then their sins can be forgiven, **and they can have a place with those people who have been made holy" (sanctified) "BY BELIEVING IN ME."** Acts 26:-18. N.C.V.

THERE CAN BE NO MIRACLE OF REGENERATION –
NO NEW BIRTH – WITHOUT THE RECIPIENT BELIEVING FIRST!

CHAPTER 14

LOST MAN'S CARNAL LIFE IS "ENMITY AGAINST GOD" AND MAN HATES GOD

Another reason Arthur W. Pink gives for lost man not being able to receive Christ is:
"Because he has a mind that is **"Enmity against" Him. (Rom 8:-7)**
"Because the carnal mind is enmity against God."
"Because he has a heart that hates Him" (God). John 15:-18.
"If the world hate you, ye know that it hated me before it hated you."
"But the natural man receiveth not the things of the Spirit of God: for they are foolishness unto him: neither can he know them, because they are spiritually discerned." 1 Cor 2:-14. K.J.V.
From this the Calvinist concludes that **"The natural man"** means all mankind who are not born again; but this is not so.

ARE ALL CHRISTIANS FREE FROM CARNAL ACTIVITY?

Are all born again people free from the carnal activities associated with "The natural man," envy, pride, strife, division and the party spirit, which is the following of men? **I think not!**

The same text 1 Cor 2:-14, from two other translations.
"The unspiritual man rejects these truths of the Spirit of God; to him they are 'sheer folly,' he cannot understand them. And the reason is, that they must be read with the spiritual eye." James Moffatt Translation.

"The unspiritual man rejects the teachings of the Spirit of God; to him they are folly, and he cannot learn them, because they are spiritually measured." R.F.Weymouth version.

PAUL THE APOSTLE'S LETTER TO THE CORINTHIAN CHURCH

When Paul wrote to the church at Corinth he was writing to a congregation of Christian believers, and not to lost souls, and he said in chapter three, verse one, of his first letter:
"And I, brethren, could not speak unto you as unto spiritual, but as unto carnal, even as unto babes in Christ." K.J.V.
"Brothers and sisters, in the past I could not talk to you as I talk to spiritual people. **I had to talk to you as I would to people without the Spirit - babies in Christ."** 1 Cor 3:-1 N.C.V.

The New English Bible interprets verses one, three and four as follows: “For my part, my brothers, I could not speak to you as I should speak to people who have the Spirit. **I had to deal with you on a merely natural plane, as infants in Christ.”**
In other words Paul had to speak to them in the same way as he would have spoken to the unregenerate, carnal, lost souls.

“For you are still on the merely natural plane.
Can you not see that while there is jealousy and strife among you, you are living on the purely human level of your lower nature? When one says ‘I am Paul’s man,’ and another, ‘I am for Appolos,’ are you not all too human?”
1 Cor 3:-3 N.E.B.

Did the Corinthian Church by reason of Envy, Strife and Divisions among its members, because of their carnal living, hate God?
Were they unable to receive Christ because they were carnal? (natural men).
Were they not saved and born again and still carnal, (Living as natural men)?
That was exactly what Paul was saying to them, although he had doubts whether all of them were born again, (1 Cor 15:-34) and he wanted them to become Spiritual!
There are churches throughout the world unfortunately, where there is Jealousy, Envy, Strife, and the Party spirit, which is the following of men (and Calvin is one) instead of Christ. But it would be unwise and Scripturally incorrect to say that they are not born again, because they are carnal, that is, **“Living on the purely human level of your lower nature.”** 1 Cor 3:-4. N.E.B.
They are carnal, although believers in Christ.

FOLLOWING CALVIN IS DOING WHAT PAUL CONDEMNED AS CARNAL

Those who follow and preach and teach Calvinism, fall into the same carnal grouping that Paul is speaking about, which existed in the Church at Corinth. Because they follow a man, and because it is carnal it is “Enmity Against God.” Is not one of the doctrines, which cause strife and division in Churches today, the teaching of Calvinism?

IS THE PERSON WHO IS BORN AGAIN FREE FROM CARNAL THINKING ?

Pink takes Romans 8:-7, Because the carnally minded are at “Enmity with God” and John 15:-18, and interprets this to mean that the thinking of every

person in the world is Carnal and that such persons also hate God, which is nonsense.
The clear inference that he makes is that if a person is born again then he is not carnal, **and he is super-spiritual and above carnal things, which is just not so.**

THERE ARE CARNAL CHRISTIANS WHO COMMIT SPIRITUAL ADULTERY

Was James not writing to Christians when he wrote:
"Ye adulterers and adulteresses, know ye not that the friendship of the world is enmity with God? whosoever therefore will be a friend of the world is the enemy of God." James 4:-4 K.J.V.

ALL THE WORLD DID NOT HATE JESUS

The verse in John 15:-18, starts with the word "IF the world hate you," but Pink turns the word IF into ALL, which is incorrect and untrue. All the world did not hate Jesus, for we are told **"The common people heard Him gladly"** Mark 12:-37, and in Luke 19:-48 **"For all the people were very attentive to hear Him."** K.J.V.
And the Pharisees said of Jesus, "Behold the world is gone after Him"
John 12:-19. K.J.V.
In John 7:-7, Jesus speaking to His disciples says: "The world cannot hate you, but it hates Me, because I tell it the evil things it does." N.C.V.
There were and still are in the world a great many who do not hate the Lord Jesus.

PINK TELLS US NO ONE WOULD HAVE ACCEPTED CHRIST IF GOD HAD NOT GIVEN THEM NEW BIRTH FIRST, BECAUSE ALL SINNERS HATE GOD

He goes on to say, "Had God done nothing more than given Christ to die for sinners and then sent forth his servants to proclaim salvation through Christ, leaving sinners entirely to themselves to accept or reject as they pleased, **then every sinner would have rejected, because at heart every man hates God and is at enmity with Him** (Rom 8:-7)."
"Therefore the work of the Holy Spirit is needed to bring sinners to Christ, to overcome their innate opposition, and bring them to accept the provision God has made."

No one would disagree that the Holy Spirit is needed to work in the hearts of sinners **Through the Gospel**, in order to draw them to Christ.

But what Pink means is that regeneration is given to individuals who hate God (To the so-called elect) first, in spite of the innate opposition they have to God and without their believing, so that **faith and repentance** may be gifted by God in order that they can be saved.
A quote from the publisher of A.W. Pink's writings.
"The work of the Spirit in 'quickening' the one dead in sins, precedes faith in Christ, just as cause ever precedes effect."

THIS IS THE VERY OPPOSITE OF WHAT CHRIST TAUGHT.

PINK APPEALS TO THE ACTUAL EXPERIENCE OF HIS READERS

Pink also says: "Let us appeal to the actual experience of the Christian reader. Was there not a time (may the remembrance of it bow each of us into the dust) when you were unwilling to come to Christ? There was. Since then you have come to Him. Are you now prepared to give Him all the glory for that? (Ps 115:-1)."
"Do you not acknowledge you came to Christ because the Holy Spirit brought you from unwillingness to willingness? You do.
Then is it not also a patent fact that the Holy Spirit has not done in many others what he has in you?"
"At heart every man hates God, and is at enmity with Him, and they are unwilling to come to Christ."
Making sweeping statements and generalizing is one of the traits of Calvinism.

It is not true, and neither does Scripture teach, that every person who is not a Christian hates Christ and His people, or that all the lost are carnal in their thinking and living. In fact they are very often less carnal and lead better moral, and more prayerful lives than some believers.

WHAT THE BIBLE SAYS IN ANSWER TO PINK'S STATEMENT

In Acts 10:-1-2, it says: "There was a certain man in Caesarea called Cornelius, a Centurion of the band called the Italian band. **A devout man**, and one that **feared God** with all his house, which gave much alms to the people, and prayed to God always." K.J.V.

The Amplified New Testament interprets verse two as follows:
"A devout man who venerated God and treated Him with reverential obedience, as did all his household, and he gave much alms to the people, and prayed continually to God."

OF HOW MANY CHRISTIANS COULD THE SAME BE SAID?

"Cornelius, thy prayer is heard, and thine alms are had in remembrance in the sight of God." Acts 10:-31. K.J.V.

God was going to help and bless Cornelius through the **"Glad Tidings,"** so that he could **believe** and be born again, with his whole household.
Cornelius was not at that time born again, although like most of the Jews who were saved at the day of Pentecost he was a very good living, prayerful, religious person who feared God.
The Psalmist said: "Surely His salvation is near to those who fear Him." Psalm 85:-9. N.K.J.V.
It was not until after Peter preached the Gospel to him and his household, **and they believed that they were regenerated.**

THEY WERE TO BE REGENERATED AND SAVED THROUGH THE MESSAGE !

"He" (Peter) "will teach you truths by which you and all your household will be saved." Acts 11:-14. R. F. Weymouth.

"Peter, who will tell you words by which you and your household will be saved." Acts 11:-14. N.K.J.V.

"He saved us, by the washing of regeneration and renewing of the Holy Ghost." Titus 3:-5, K.J.V.
Part of the message that Peter brought them was in verse 43 of Acts chapter 10, which is, "To him give all the Prophets witness, that through His name whosoever believeth in Him shall receive remission of sins." K.J.V.

WHY DID THE HOLY SPIRIT NOT DO THE WORK WITHOUT PETER ?

If man has no part or lot in bringing about the new birth, why did the wind of the Spirit not blow over Cornelius and his household with the new birth experience, without Peter being involved?

Simply because the second birth comes, **as Jesus taught, only through the Gospel Message, and belief in it!**

DID CORNELIUS AND HIS HOUSEHOLD HATE GOD BEFORE THEY WERE BORN AGAIN?

DID THEY OPPOSE THE GOSPEL OF CHRIST AND HIS PEOPLE?

WERE THEY UNWILLING TO HAVE GOD SAVE THEM?

DID CORNELIUS AND HIS HOUSEHOLD NEED TO BE BORN AGAIN, BEFORE THEY FEARED GOD, AND SOUGHT HIM?

DID HE NEED TO BE REGENERATED TO ENTER INTO THE SPIRITUAL WORK OF PRAYER?

DID HE NEED THE NEW BIRTH BEFORE HE HAD REVERENTIAL OBEDIENCE TO GOD?
The answer to all these questions is NO, NO, NO, NO, NO, NO!

PINK TELLS US THE EXPERIENCE OF CORNELIUS WAS IMPOSSIBLE

Pink tells us: "Apart from this Divine and holy nature which is imparted to us at the new birth, **it is utterly impossible for any man to generate a spiritual impulse, form a spiritual concept, think a spiritual thought, understand spiritual things, still less engage in spiritual work."**

Cornelius had reverential obedience to God, and served God in fasting and prayer and his prayers were heard and answered by the Lord and what work is there more spiritual than the work of prayer? He had to have spiritual impulse, spiritual thought, spiritual concept, and understanding to do these things! We are told, in Luke 2:-37, that Anna "Departed not from the Temple, but served God with fastings and prayers night and day." K.J.V.

THE DOCTRINE OF MAN'S LOST FREE WILL EXPOUNDED

Pink again from his book "The Sovereignty of God" also says, "Man chooses that which is according to his nature, therefore before he will ever choose or prefer that which is divine and spiritual, a new nature must be imparted to him, in other words he must be born again."

Cornelius and his household prove this statement to be complete nonsense and unscriptural **because man can and does choose the divine and spiritual without the new birth!** Did not the Lord Jesus say, **"If any man will** come after me, let him deny himself, and take up his cross, and follow Me." Matthew 16:-24. K.J.V. **"If any man"** means exactly what the Lord Jesus says, and not as Pink would have us believe any man who is born again! So man has a will and can deny himself and follow Christ, and is not inescapably locked into doing "that which is according to his nature," even before he is regenerated as the story of Cornelius shows us. It would appear that this Italian Gentile Centurion, Cornelius, and his household did all the things that Calvinists tell us the **unregenerate man cannot do.**

SO WHO IS RIGHT, SCRIPTURE OR THE CALVINISTS?

Note: On a television programme a Hindu, a former Indian Prime minister, testified that he spent the first two and a half hours of each day in prayer and meditation, before he started his daily tasks as Prime Minister of India. This Hindu was **denying himself** each day for two and a half hours to pray and meditate! How many born again Christians **deny themselves** and spend two and a half hours in prayer and meditation on the Scriptures each day, before they go to work?

It would take a great deal of self-denial to do such a thing.

If this were the common practice among Christians, there would be far less strife and more vibrant spiritual life in the churches and the divorce rate among Christians would plummet. Revival would be a common experience in our fellowships and not as it is at present such a very, very rare occurrence.

THE CONFLICT BETWEEN THE "NATURAL MAN" AND THE "SPIRIT OF MAN"

It is the spirit of man that makes him aware of God, and the soul that makes him conscious of the world around him.

The spirit of man is the deepest part of his being and cannot but express itself through the body and soul, in acts of worship, or superstition.

It is to the spirit of man that God speaks. Romans 8:-16.

In the "natural man" the "spirit of man" is dominated and in subjection to the carnal nature which is the flesh with its desires and lusts, simply because of the individual's **Focus of attention and living being on carnal things,** so "the spirit of man" becomes inactive, or its propensities put to the one side and is in abeyance because of the assertiveness of the animal soul. So much is that so, that very often there is little evidence of **"The spirit of man."**

While the Carnal life is prominent and dominant there is little or no real spiritual activity, although to salve the conscience there may be religious or ritualized worship, and the more ritualization in worship the less will be the spiritual content, and it can be likened to equivocation in speech instead of meaningful and reasoned communication, so ritualization is a substitute for the spiritual.

"The true worshippers shall worship the Father in spirit and in Truth: for the Father seeketh such to worship Him." John 4:-23. K.J.V.
"Thy Law is the Truth." Psalm 119:-142. "All Thy commandments are Truth." Psalm 119:-151. K.J.V. "By the Word of Truth". "The Word of the Truth of the Gospel." 2 Cor 6:-7 and Col 1:-5. K.J.V.

THE REASON FOR THE PROPHETS' FASTINGS ?

Was this not the main reason for the prophets' fasting, (for as long as forty days in some cases), to focus their attention on God and spiritual things, and to reverse this situation and subdue the flesh (body and animal soul) so that the spiritual life could be asserted ?

It is significant that the Lord Jesus Christ fasted for forty days before His earthly ministry.

"CAN A PERSON BE PROUD AND BE A CHRISTIAN?"

A question was asked at a conference, "Can a person be proud and be a Christian." The answer to that question was given by Professor Finlayson of the Free Church of Scotland as follows: "If you want to walk with God you have to come down to His level."
The Professor was correct in his answer, because Jesus said, "Take my yoke upon you, and learn of me; **for I am meek and lowly in heart**: and ye shall find rest unto your souls." Matthew 11:-29. K.J.V.

"For thus saith the high and lofty One that inhabiteth eternity, whose name is Holy; **I dwell in the high and holy place, with him also that is of a contrite and humble spirit**, to revive the spirit of the humble, and to revive the heart of the contrite ones." Isaiah 57:-15. K.J.V.

"But If any one of you lack wisdom, let him ask of God, who gives to all

freely and reproaches not, and it shall be given to him: but let him ask in faith, nothing doubting." James 1:-5. J.N. Darby version..
Lack of wisdom covers also the understanding of the Scriptures and it is much better to have God's help than to trust in the opinions of fallible men.

FOCUSING OUR LIVES ON THE SPIRITUAL

Every week I get a magazine, which has in it a picture with another hidden three-dimensional picture contained in it. The picture is often a mass of leaves or what looks like a rather meaningless pattern of colour. But if you take the trouble to focus your eyes on the picture in a certain way, you are able to see clearly the hidden three-dimensional picture.
The Lord Jesus informs us how to see spiritual things clearly by telling us: "Then Jesus said to His disciples, If any one desires to be My disciple, let him deny himself - that is, disregard, lose sight of and forget himself and his own interests - and take up his cross and follow Me [cleave steadily to Me, conform wholly to My example in living and if need be in dying, also]." Matthew 16:-24. The Amplified New Testament.

We must give our wholehearted attention and focus to the Lord and to spiritual things.

OUR OWN SELF LIFE MUST BE CRUCIFIED SO WE LIVE FOR CHRIST

It is not that man is dead to God (like a physical carcass) but the natural life has to be kept under, in order for the spiritual life to thrive. The Bible to the natural man may look like a meaningless pattern of colourful words, but if we adjust our focus and give our whole attention to spiritual thoughts and the things of God, we will see clearly. Cornelius is an excellent example of this. But this means a complete change of mind and direction, which is repentance. We walk in the flesh or in the spirit.

"For the grace of God, which can save every man, has now become known, and it teaches us to have no more to do with godlessness or the desires of this world but to live, here and now, responsible, honourable and God-fearing lives." Titus 2:-11. J.B. Phillips translation.

WE MUST LOSE OUR LOWER LIFE TO GAIN THE HIGHER SPIRITUAL LIFE

This is not something we do once and never again, but we do this every day by choosing His way instead of our own, in the decisions we make daily in our lives. In Matthew 10:-39, Jesus said, "Whoever finds his [lower] life will lose [the higher life], and whoever loses his [lower] life on My account will find [the higher life]." The Amplified New Testament.

Romans 8:-verses-5-6. "If men comply with their lower nature, their thoughts are shaped by the lower nature; if with their spiritual nature, by the spiritual. Thoughts shaped by the lower nature mean death; thoughts shaped by the spiritual mean life and peace. For the thoughts shaped by the lower nature mean a state of enmity to God." R.F.Weymouth version.

"Those who live on the level of our lower nature have their outlook formed by it, and that spells death; but those who live on the level of the spirit have the spiritual outlook, and that is life and peace. For the outlook of the lower nature is enmity with God." Romans 8:-5-6, From the New English Bible.

We choose to believe in the Lord Jesus, or not. We also choose how spiritual we are going to be, whether we are going to be carnal Christians, or through the Spirit, mortify the deeds of the body and be Spiritually minded Christians. WE ARE AS GODLY AND AS SPIRITUAL AS WE WANT TO BE.

THINGS WE CAN LEARN FROM THE STORY OF CORNELIUS

Centurions were, as a rule, men of great wealth and mostly from among the Roman aristocracy, although not exclusively so.
Cornelius and his household (which would inevitably include numbers of slaves) had not become Jews, although it is evident from Acts 10 that they had heard about the true God, the God of Israel, and had repented and changed their way of living.
It is most likely Cornelius and his household, were converted from serving Roman gods (idols) to serving the true God, The God of Israel.

"Then Peter opened his mouth and said, 'In truth I perceive that God shows no partiality. But in every nation whoever fears Him and works righteousness is accepted by Him.'" Acts 10:-34-35. N.K.J.V.
Cornelius, (as well as his household), had a real faith in the true God of Israel before he and his household became born again, and this was expressed in his fasting and his continual prayer to Him.

"But without Faith it is impossible to please Him: for he that cometh to God must believe that He is, and that He is a rewarder of them that diligently seek Him." Hebrews 11:-6. K.J.V. How did he come by this faith? Calvinists say **God gifts a special faith**, in order to be saved.

WHAT DIFFERENCE BETWEEN FAITH IN GOD AND FAITH IN CHRIST?

Was there any difference between the faith Cornelius had in the true God, which changed his whole life, and the faith he placed in the Lord Jesus Christ in order to be saved?

Cornelius had repented of his sins and was converted to the True and living God (The God of Israel) **before he was born again.**

The Lord Jesus tells us in John 14:-1 **"Ye believe in God, believe also in Me."** K.J.V. The Lord Jesus equates believing in Him as being the same as believing in God.

Scripture gives the answer, "So then Faith cometh by hearing, and hearing by the Word of God." Romans 10:-17. K.J.V.

He and his household worshipped **"God in spirit and in Truth,"** and they were not born again.

So he was not dead in the Calvinistic sense, to God spiritually like a physical carcass! John 4:-24.

"God is Spirit: and they that worship Him must worship Him in spirit and in truth." K.J.V.

As previously quoted.

Pink tells us: "Do you not acknowledge you came to Christ because the Holy Spirit brought you from unwillingness to willingness? You do.

Then is it not also a patent fact that the Holy Spirit has not done in many others what he has in you?"

"AT HEART EVERY MAN HATES GOD AND IS AT ENMITY WITH HIM, AND THEY ARE UNWILLING TO COME TO CHRIST."

MY OWN EXPERIENCE OF COMING TO CHRIST

Although I was brought up in a nominal Christian home, my mother made sure that all her children went to Sunday School, and I am eternally thankful to her for this, and because of this my own experience is that I cannot ever remember a time when I did not believe the Bible to be God's Word and that

Christ died on the cross for my sins and rose again from the dead. Nor do I remember a time when I did not want to follow Christ, although I was not saved until I was seventeen, through a Gospel open air meeting at the Mound in Princes Street, Edinburgh.

Like the Psalmist I can say, "I call to remembrance my song in the night: I commune with mine own heart: and my spirit made diligent search."
Psalm 77:-6. K.J.V.

Even as a child, with the hymn writer I could also say:
"I sometimes think about the cross, and close my eyes and try to see the cruel nails and crown of thorns and Jesus crucified for me."
When I was a small boy of seven or eight I can remember a number of times singing myself to sleep, singing a hymn I knew off by heart, "There is a green hill far away without a city wall, where the dear Lord was crucified who died to save us all." As I sang the hymn, I would in my mind picture Christ going to Calvary, and I asked myself the question, what does it mean to be saved? I came to the conclusion that that meant to be saved from hell and the punishment of our sins.
When it came to the third verse "He died that we might be forgiven, He died to make us good, That we might go at last to heaven saved by His precious blood," I remember asking myself, what has the blood of CHRIST TO DO WITH BEING SAVED, and how could Jesus who died all these years ago pay for my sins when I had not yet been born?
These questions did not in any way deter me from believing that Christ died for me.
As a youngster I remember being in St. Cuthberts Church in Edinburgh's West End at a morning service with our scout troop and as I looked up at the minister and listened to what he had to say, the thought came to me that God seemed to be as far away from me as the moon, and how I longed for Him to be near me, and to know Him.
When I became a teenager, I recall praying to God in bed with the tears streaming down my face "Lord save me or take my life", and in that prayer I asked the Lord that I might get to know Him, as my life was so meaningless and without purpose and I wanted to know God, and find the purpose in life He had for me.
If you had asked me at the time to explain what I meant by "save" I am not sure I could have answered the question correctly, but it did express how I felt. I was not saved that night although God did answer my prayer, some time after, at the open-air meeting.

But people were involved in leading me to Christ, and they were fishers of men. As a teenager I attended gospel meetings at the Methodist Central halls and Charlotte Baptist Chapel, and I had asked the Lord to save me and asked Him to come into my life, on more than one occasion, but I was not saved, nor was my life changed. The wind of the Spirit did not sweep into my life in the new birth, **until I believed in my heart the gospel message, and confessed this publicly; and then the miracle took place.**
1 Thessalonians 2;-13, was my experience:
"When we preached to you, you didn't think of the words we spoke as being just our own, **but you accepted what we said as the very Word of God – which, of course, it was – and it changed your lives when you believed it."** T.L.B.
There was no blinding flash or great emotional elation, but my life changed. The open air preacher was the late John Lawson, an open air evangelist, a real "fisher of men" and a man with a passion to win people for Christ through the preaching of the gospel, and he asked as he closed the meeting with an appeal, "Is there someone here who believes the Bible to be God's Word and that Jesus is the Son of God and died for you, and rose again from the dead, but you have never nailed your colours to the mast, and publicly acknowledged Him, and thanked Him for dying for you."
God was speaking to me through the preacher and I knew it, because I believed everything that was needed to be a real Christian but I had not publicly acknowledged this and wanted to go forward, but I was so very much afraid.
The thoughts that went through my mind at that time were, "These people are different from you. You will not be able to live like they do, for Christ." "If you become a Christian, people will make a fool of you."
I wanted more than anything else in the world to be a follower of Christ, and I remember saying in my heart, "Lord I will do anything you want me to do"; Like Saul of Tarsus on the road to Damascus when he said **"Lord what wilt thou have me to do?"**
Because I was so shy the hardest thing I think I have ever done in my life, even with some encouragement from my cousin George, who was standing beside me, was to walk into the ring and acknowledge publicly that I believed in the Lord Jesus Christ, and I wanted to follow Him. I was trembling like a leaf.
The text I was given that night was "That if thou shalt confess with thy mouth the Lord Jesus, and shalt believe in thine heart that God hath raised Him from the dead, Thou shalt be saved." Romans 10:-9. K.J.V.

My life was changed from that night on, because I believed in my heart that Jesus was God's Son and died for me, and because as the preacher put it, **I nailed my colours to the mast, by publicly acknowledging Christ.**
I had always believed the Gospel but not with my whole heart, that is I had never confessed this to others, and committed myself to following Him. With confession comes the assurance of salvation.

In the canteen at work the next day, a member of staff who had witnessed me going forward to make a public witness to the fact that I believed in Christ and was going to follow Him, said to the others in the canteen, "Jimmy has become a Holy Willie. I saw him go forward last night at the Mound."
I was embarrassed and did not know how to answer him, but it was not long before I was speaking to the men at my work about the Lord Jesus who had saved me, and now it was they who were embarrassed. I knew I had something that they did not have and needed, and I was not ashamed to witness for Him.
Jesus said, **"have faith in God."** that is to say, **put your trust in God.**
As I believe He does with everyone, God through various circumstances in my life spoke to me, and the Holy Spirit was certainly working powerfully, over a number of years through the Word of God I had been taught, and especially the hymns that conveyed the Gospel, but it was not to remove any unwillingness to come to Christ, or to take away any hatred or animosity either towards God or His people, because it did not exist.
I would, without doubt, have come to Christ when I was a child, if only someone had been willing to lead me to Him. There are not many among believers who are "fishers of men". There was never a time in my life when I hated God, and I know there are multitudes of others with exactly the same kind of experience, so far as their attitude towards God before they were born again is concerned.
In my thinking that would have been the height of stupidity and utterly futile to hate the One who created us!
Pink can only speak for himself, and I believe he is in a very small minority who have hated God before they were born again.

THE VAST MAJORITY OF CHRISTIANS COME TO CHRIST WHEN CHILDREN

It is a fact that most Christians are converted to Christ when they are children or in their teenage years, and children are not hostile to God.
Between seventy and eighty per cent of all Christians come to Christ in

childhood, or as teenagers and that most certainly is true also of those who go into full time service, whether missionary, evangelist, or pastor.
I doubt very much that the thirty or less percentage of people who come to Christ when adults, all hate God and are unwilling to be saved.

THE MIRACLE IN MR. FRASER'S LIFE WHEN HE BELIEVED

There was a man I had seen many times at the open air meetings at the Mound in Princes street, Edinburgh before and after I became a Christian, who had come to faith in Christ, and one summer evening after alighting from a bus, I met him at the East End of Princes Street, and said to him "I know you have become a Christian, but I do not know how and when, but would like to know."
I told him I was going to walk home, which meant walking to the West End of Princes Street, as I lived near Haymarket.
Mr. Fraser, for that was the man's name, said as it was a good night he would walk with me to the West End, and then walk to his lodgings in Calton Road, back at the East End of Princes Street, and would tell me during our walk how he was born again. He told me he was born a twin in the town of Inverness and as he grew up he had heard the gospel message, and when he became an adult he joined a police force in an Eastern country, and when he retired he came home to Scotland and had intended retiring to Inverness, but liked Edinburgh so decided just to stay where he was.
It was his custom when he first came to the City, because public houses (bars) were not open on a Sunday, to take a bus on a Sunday to a place like South Queensferry in order to go to a hotel and drink alcohol, because at that time no one could consume alcoholic drinks in a hotel bar on a Sunday without being a *bona fide* traveller.
One Sunday he decided to walk along Princes Street and he saw a large crowd of people at the Mound and went over to listen to the various speakers, and became interested in a group who were preaching the gospel and giving testimonies.
He became so interested in the Christian groups that from that time he spent all his Sundays listening to the Gospel at the Mound, and this went on for many months. He told me that one night he came away from the open air meeting after they closed at about ten thirty p.m. very disturbed by what he had heard, and he told me as we were walking on the shops side of Princes street, and pointing he said "I crossed the road there", and walked to my lodgings, and when I got home I locked the door and started to pray, and I wept like a child and cried to God to save me, as I wanted above anything else to become a Christian. I prayed for hours sometimes standing and sometimes kneeling.

The text the preacher closed with and had been preaching about was, "HIM THAT COMETH TO ME I WILL IN NO WISE CAST OUT". John 6:-37. At about 2:30 a.m. in the morning he said, "I heard the audible voice of God as clear as I hear your voice, saying" **"Take Him at His Word."** My thoughts instantly went to the text that the preacher had closed with, **"Him that cometh to Me I will in no wise cast out."**

Immediately I understood and took Christ at His Word and came to Him and I was born again. He said "I was filled with joy and felt like dancing, and I have never smoked a cigarette or taken an alcoholic drink since."
Mr. Fraser **was not** born again by the wind of the Spirit blowing on him when he prayed, **but was directed by God to take Christ at His Word and believe, and then he was regenerated the moment he turned to Christ and believed the miracle took place.**

"Being born again, not of corruptible seed, but of incorruptible, by the Word of God." 1 Peter 1:-23. K.J.V.

"Whereby are given unto us exceeding great and precious promises: that by these ye might be partakers of the divine nature." 2 Peter 1:-4. K.J.V.

"Believe on the Lord Jesus Christ, and thou shalt be saved, and thy house." Acts 16:-31. K.J.V.

"He that hath the Son hath life; and he that hath not the Son of God hath not life." 1 John 5:-12. K.J.V.

John 17:-3, tells us: "And this is eternal life: [it means] to know (to perceive, recognize, become acquainted with and understand) You, the only true and real God, and [likewise] to know Him, Jesus [as the] Christ, the Anointed One, the Messiah, Whom You have sent."
The Amplified New Testament.

Many people are waiting (especially in Calvinistic Churches) for God to burst into their lives like He did with Saul of Tarsus or like Mr. Fraser, but they fail to realise that Saul's or Mr. Fraser's experience did not save them. It was the fact that they believed in the Lord Jesus Christ that brought about regeneration. The experience only pointed or directed them to believe in Christ. Both could have been born again without any such traumatic experience through simply being obedient to Christ and believing on Him.

We are not saved by experiences but by Trust in Christ.

Chapter 15

IS REPENTANCE A GIFT FROM GOD?

J.W.Seaton sets out the five points in his booklet in the less obnoxious and abbreviated form of the TULIP.

"Total Depravity (i.e. Total Inability).

Unconditional Election.

Limited Atonement (i.e. Particular Redemption).

Irresistible Calling.

Perseverance of the Saints."

Among pastor Seaton's comments on the first point, "Total Depravity", he says, "The picture is one of death – spiritual death. We are like Lazarus in his tomb; We are bound hand and foot; corruption has taken hold upon us. Just as there was no **glimmer of life** in the dead body of Lazarus, so there is no **inner receptive spark** in our hearts. But the Lord performs the miracle -- both with the physically dead, and the spiritually dead.
The Bible teaches with absolute clarity that man, by nature, is dead; 'Wherefore, as by one man sin entered into the world, and death by sin; and so death passed upon all men, for that all have sinned.'" "It tells us that men are **bound,**" (and he quotes),
2 Timothy 2:-25-26, "In meekness instructing those that oppose themselves; if God peradventure will give them repentance to the acknowledging of the truth; And that they may recover themselves out of the snare of the devil, who are taken captive by him at his will." K.J.V.
Pastor Seaton is saying that men are bound like Lazarus was and are dead to God spiritually, in the same way as a corpse is to the world, which would mean they would be completely unaware of God, and therefore they would have no understanding of the Gospel which is spiritual.

THE QUESTION I WOULD ASK HIM IS.

HOW DO YOU GO ABOUT INSTRUCTING A CORPSE?

Only the living can be instructed; a physical carcass could not be taught. Why would Satan NEED TO BIND a spiritual carcass?

That is absurd and foolish and Satan is neither.
It is only the living that need to be bound to restrict their freedom of movement.
A corpse is not going anywhere, and is a threat to no-one.
The very fact that Satan needs to snare people is a clear indication that they are not spiritual corpses.
The Bible teaches us that man binds himself with his own sins.
"His own iniquities entrap the wicked man. And he is caught in the cords of his own sin." Proverbs 5:-22. N.K.J.V.

"An evil man will be caught in his wicked ways; the ropes of his sin will tie him up." Proverbs 5:-22. N.C.V.

Pastor Seaton also asks, what he believes to be a rhetorical question, "Can the bound free themselves?"
The answer is found in the text he has quoted, 2 Timothy 2:-25. "That they may recover themselves out of the snare of the devil." K.J.V. Not that God would recover them, but, **"That they may recover themselves out of the snare of the devil."**
So the bound according to the text he quotes can free themselves.

WHAT CALVIN TAUGHT ABOUT REPENTANCE

This is the text the Calvinists quote to say that God gives repentance to whom He will, arbitrarily, this being the outcome of their second point, "Unconditional Election".
Calvin himself taught that repentance is a "Special Gift" from God.
He writes as follows, "Moreover that repentance is **a special gift** of God, I trust is too well understood, hence the Church extols the goodness of God, and looks on in wonder, saying, "Then hath God also to the Gentiles granted repentance unto life." Acts 11:-18, and Paul, enjoining Timothy to deal meekly and patiently with unbelievers, says, "If God peradventure will give them repentance to the acknowledging of the truth, and that they may recover themselves out of the snare of the devil." 2 Timothy 2:-25-26.

In Acts 11:-18, in the King James Version, it tells us: "Then hath God also to the Gentiles granted repentance unto life."
The Gentiles are all people in the world who are not Jews!

So the text tells us that outside the Jewish people **all mankind throughout**

the world have been granted repentance!

The "Also," ("Then hath God also to the Gentiles granted repentance") clearly indicates that the granting of Repentance had been first given to the Jews, in exactly the same way.

If one interprets Acts 11:-18, in the same way as Calvin has with 2 Timothy 2:25, **that means that all Gentiles as well as Jews have been given repentance and are therefore believers in Christ, which of course is not the case.**
So Acts 11:-28, clarifies the interpretation of 2 Timothy 2:25 - 26, and shows us that the Calvinist exposition is wrong.

From 2 Timothy 2:-25 -26, the Calvinists draw the conclusion that the Lord gives particular individuals repentance at a specific time in order that they can be saved, and the assumption they draw from this is He withholds repentance from others.
Unlike 2 Timothy 2:- 25 - 26, which in the King James Version is ambiguous, and because of the way it is interpreted by Calvinists, it is in contention with the rest of Scripture on that subject.
The following interpretation of 2 Timothy 2:-25 - 26, from various translations establishes it in harmony with the other Scriptures on repentance, for example this is how it appears in the Amplified New Testament.
"He must correct his opponents with courtesy and gentleness, in the hope that God may grant that they will repent and come to know the Truth - that is, that they will perceive and recognize and become accurately acquainted with and acknowledge it."
The second part of the text explains how God will enable them to repent.

"He must always bear in mind the possibility that God will give them a different outlook, and that they may come to know the truth."
The J. B. Phillips translation. 2 Timothy 2:- 26.

Knox Translates the first part of 2 Timothy 2:- 26, thus: **"It may be that God will enable them to repent, and acknowledge the truth."**

"Be humble when you are trying to teach those who are mixed up concerning the truth. For if you talk meekly and courteously to them **they are more likely, with God's help, to turn away from their wrong ideas and believe what is true." 2 Timothy 2:-25. T.L.B.**

Throughout the Bible you find God calling upon people to repent through His servants, and God often chastises severely His people Israel in order to bring them to repentance, as in Psalm 78:-34-35: "When He slew some [of them, the remainder] inquired after Him diligently, and they repented and sincerely sought God [for a time]. And they [earnestly] remembered that God was their rock, and the Most High God their redeemer."
The Amplified Bible.
Also in Jeremiah 5:-3: "You have tried to get them to be honest, for you have punished them, **but they won't change!** You have destroyed them but they refuse to turn from their sins. **They are determined, with faces hard as rock, not to repent."** T.L.B.

You will not find anywhere in Scripture where God gives repentance to any person or group and certainly you will never read in Holy Writ a text that will corroborate the interpretation that Calvinists give of 2 Timothy 2:-25-26. Calvin's analysis of 2 Timothy 2:-25 is obviously wrong and at variance with the other Scriptures on repentance and, accordingly, a correct interpretation and understanding of the text must be in harmony with the rest of Scripture on this subject.

GOD COMMANDS JEZEBEL AND HER FOLLOWERS TO REPENT

Another contradiction to the Calvinistic belief that God gifts repentance is found in the book of Revelation where we read in the second chapter and verses 20 to 22 the following, "Notwithstanding I have a few things against thee, because thou sufferest that woman Jezebel which calleth herself a prophetess, to teach and seduce My servants to commit fornication, and to eat things sacrificed unto idols."
"And I gave her space to repent of her fornication; and she repented not. Behold, I will cast her into a bed, and them that commit adultery with her into great tribulation, **except they repent of their deeds.**" K.J.V.
The Lord is saying clearly in verse 21, "I gave her space (A Chance, Time, Opportunity, or Scope) to repent of her fornication; and she repented not. **"Repent" is an active verb** and God is placing the responsibility squarely on Jezebel and her followers to change their minds, and turn from their evil. Why did the Lord give Jezebel the chance and time to repent, and yet FAIL to give the gift of repentance, if man repents only because of God's intervention and in gifting the ability to repent? If the failure to repent was the result of God's Will, and His inactivity how could it possibly be said that He gave her the opportunity to repent?

THAT STATEMENT WOULD BE A LIE!

And if Jezebel's and God's servants' repentance was wholly the Lord's decision and not theirs, how could they possibly be responsible for repenting?

The Scriptures tell us clearly, **"It was impossible for God to lie."** Hebrews 6:-18. K.J.V.
"Which God, that cannot lie, promised." Titus 1:-2 K.J.V.

If we accept God's Word as the Truth, then Calvinists' teaching on repentance is complete nonsense! One person has said that theologians are a group of people who make simple things complicated, which is most certainly true of Calvinist theology, which, if believed, makes the Bible unintelligible.

THE MISCONCEIVED IDEAS OF WHAT GOD AND MAN DOES IN SALVATION

The incompetence because of man-made ideas to differentiate between the part that God plays from that which man plays in salvation, when it is so clearly defined in Scripture, has been and continues to be the stumbling block to finding in Calvinistic Churches the peace and Salvation that many are seeking. They are left in the misbelief that they must wait for God to give them faith and repentance, **when in reality God has already given them the faculty.** They have the ability, and God explicitly commands them to believe and repent.
1 John 3:-23, **"This is what God commands: that we believe in His Son, Jesus Christ, and that we love each other, just as He commanded."** N.C.V.
Acts 17:-30. **"As for the times of ignorance, God has overlooked them; but now commands mankind, all men everywhere, to repent."** N.E.B.

It is the misconceived idea that for man to have a part in his salvation would detract from the finished Work of Christ and deprive the grace of God of its rightful glory. But in actuality if men do not play their part, by believing and repenting there will be no glory given to God for the finished Work of Christ, because the grace of God will not be displayed and demonstrated in men's lives.

GOD WORKS THROUGH LAWS

There is the law of Gravity, the law of Aerodynamics, the law of Thermodynamics, the law of Harvest, and from Scripture we have, * "The law of Faith," * "The law of sin," * "The law of the Spirit," and* "The royal law." Laws are essential for order and stability and also predictability. *Romans 3:-27 7:-23 8:-2, also James 2:-8.

The law of Harvest is applicable in the spiritual realm and is often used in Scripture to encourage the sowing of the spiritual in our lives and to emphasize the need to use this law in order to obtain a spiritual harvest.

In Galatians 6:-7-8. "Do not be fooled: you cannot cheat God. People harvest only what they plant. If they plant to satisfy their sinful selves, their sinful selves will bring them ruin. But if they plant to please the Spirit, they will receive eternal life from the Spirit." N.C.V

GOD'S LAW GOVERNING REPENTANCE.

There is a procedure or law governing bringing people to repentance, and God will not bypass this as Calvinists seem to think, but will work through this law by His Spirit to bring the sinner to the point of repentance. But it is the Sinner who does the Repenting. If God gave repentance in the way the Calvinists believe, it would mean that God was doing the repenting for them, which is not so.

WHAT ACTUALLY IS REPENTANCE?

Basically repentance means, to have a change of mind, which in turn leads to a change of action. We change peoples' minds by reasoning with them and trying to persuade them from a particular line of thought and action to another way of thinking.

HOW THE APOSTLES WORKED TO BRING ABOUT REPENTANCE IN OTHERS

Paul explains how men are brought to repent (change their minds) of their sins and trust Christ, in 2 Cor 10:-4-5.

"For the weapons of our warfare are not physical (weapons of flesh and blood), but they are mighty before God for the overthrow and destruction of strongholds [inasmuch as we] refute arguments and theories and reasonings and every proud and lofty thing that sets itself

up against the (true) knowledge of God; and we lead every thought and purpose away captive into the obedience of Christ, the Messiah, the Anointed One." The Amplified New Testament.

THE POWER OF THE GOSPEL HAS ITS EFFECTS

Acts 24:- 24 - 25, Paul, in order to persuade his listeners to repent, reasoned with them, "And after certain days, when Felix came with his wife Drusilla, which was a Jewess, he sent for Paul, and heard him concerning the Faith in Christ." K.J.V.

"And as he" (Paul) "reasoned of righteousness, temperance, and of judgement to come, Felix trembled, and answered, Go thy way for this time; when I have a convenient season I will call for thee." K.J.V.

"But as he continued to argue about uprightness, purity of life – the control of passions – and the judgement to come, Felix became alarmed and terrified and said, go away for the present; when I have a convenient opportunity I will send for you."
The same verses from the Amplified New Testament.

THE GRACE OF GOD TOWARDS FELIX WAS NOT IRRISISTABLE

"Ye do always resist the Holy Ghost: as your fathers did, so do ye."
Acts 7:- 51. K.J.V.
A spiritual corpse would not be able to resist anything. This alarm and trembling was obviously the result of God speaking to Felix through His Word, and it was seen visibly. He would certainly never have heard the Lord if he had been dead to God spiritually (like a physical corpse) as Calvinists say all sinners are; nor would he have understood what Paul was speaking about. **But he did understand and he trembled.**
The Calvinists would have to say that the Lord gave Felix the New Birth experience first, so that he could hear the Lord speak to him. But if this is so He obviously did not in this case, impart repentance or faith, because there is absolutely no evidence that Felix did believe and repent. But he was brought to the place where he could have, because he had heard God's Word and God had clearly spoken to him. The believing and repenting (changing of his mind) was his decision. **God would not do it for him.**

Paul used the God given method or law to bring Felix to the place of repentance, he reasoned with him and proclaimed Christ in the power of the

Holy Spirit. The experience by Felix of terror and visible trembling seen by Paul and others, would not have happened without the means, the Message of the Gospel.
In 2 Corinthians 5:-11, we read, "Knowing therefore the terror of the Lord we persuade men." K.J.V.
You cannot persuade a spiritual corpse, nor can a carcass experience fear or terror!

APOSTLES DEBATED WITH RELIGIOUS, BUT NOT YET REGENERATED, JEWS

In Acts 17:-2-4,we also read: "And Paul, as his manner was, went in unto them, and three Sabbath days reasoned with them out of the Scriptures, Opening and alleging, that Christ must needs have suffered, and risen again from the dead; and that this Jesus, whom I preach unto you, is Christ." K.J.V.
The people Paul was instructing were not born again, although many would be good living, religious, and I have little doubt some would have been prayerful people who knew and believed the Old Testament, but needed to know that the Lord Jesus was indeed the Christ the promised Messiah and Saviour, in order to believe in Him and be saved.
Note. Some, if not many, would have been justified by faith, because they truly believed in the God of Israel and had repented. (See the chapter on Lydia). Paul reasoned with them from the Old Testament, persuading them that the Lord Jesus was indeed the one promised by God in the Old Testament, the Saviour.
Apollos did exactly the same for we read in Acts 18:-28. **"For he mightily convinced the Jews, and that publickly, shewing by the scriptures that Jesus was the Christ." K.J.V**

"For he powerfully refuted all the Jewish arguments in public debate, showing by the Scriptures that Jesus is indeed the Messiah."
The same verse in T.L.B.
The Lord instructs sinners through His servants to bring them to repentance. The Spirit of God takes the Word of God, and when heard and believed, through this makes the child of God.

THE TEACHING OF THE LORD JESUS CHRIST ON REPENTANCE

In Matthew 21:-28-31, Jesus said to the chief priests and elders of the people: "A certain man had two sons; and he came to the first, and said, Son, go work today in my vineyard. He answered and said, **I will not: but**

afterward repented, and went. And he came to the second, and said likewise. And he answered and said, **I go, sir: and went not**. Whether of them twain did the will of his father? They say unto him, The first. Jesus saith unto them. **Verily I say unto you, That the publicans and the harlots go into the kingdom of God before you." K.J.V.**

Did God have to give either of these sons a special gift of repentance so that they could **change their minds**, one to do his father's will and the other not to do it? This simple everyday story of young men changing there minds and either obeying or disobeying their father, Jesus likens to the publicans and harlots repenting and entering into the Kingdom of God, and Pharisees not. **"God commands all men everywhere to repent,"** (change their minds and turn to God). Acts 17:-30. "And this is His commandment, that we should believe on the name of His Son Jesus Christ, and love one another, as He gave us commandment." 1 John 3:-23. K.J.V.

The Lord will not hold man responsible for something it is impossible for him to do. It is foolish to believe that God would command people to do what they cannot do! It would also be wholly unjust. It is the straitjacket of the Calvinists' misbelief that puts them in such a ridiculous position, i.e. the spiritual corpse of man makes him incapable of doing anything, even denying his ability to change his mind, in order to be saved which is basically what repentance is. Because of His willingness to have all men repent and be saved, whatever lack there may be in man, the Lord supplies, through the Gospel message by the Spirit of God, so that man will be without excuse.

Romans 1:-16, "For I am not ashamed of the gospel of Christ: for it is the power of God unto salvation to every one that believeth." K.J.V.

FAITH MOVES MEN TO REPENTANCE

It is by the Word of God that faith comes, and repentance is made possible. Some believe that repentance comes before belief. But this is not so, the message comes first and, through this, understanding and faith (which is confidence) and the result or evidence of real faith (confidence) is repentance. "Faith without works is dead." James 2:-20; And Romans 10:-10, "For with the **heart** man believeth unto righteousness." K.J.V.

REPENTANCE IS THE RESULT OF BELIEVING

Repentance is generally motivated by the believing of the message. It is the acceptance of the message which is belief in it, and that should bring about the will for a change of mind, (repentance) and there has to be a belief towards the Lord Jesus in order to be born again. The preaching of Jonah at

Nineveh is an example. The Ninevites heard the message (accepted), believed it and the result was that they repented.

"CAN THE NATURALLY SINFUL CHANGE THEMSELVES?"

We find God's answer to pastor Seaton's question which he puts on page 6 of his booklet, "Can the naturally sinful change themselves?"
In Ezekiel 18:-27-28. "Again when the wicked man turneth away from his wickedness that he hath committed, and doeth that which is lawful and right, he shall save his soul alive." "Because he considereth, and turneth away from all his transgressions that he hath committed, he shall surely live, he shall not die." K.J.V.
The Lord's name is not mentioned in those two texts, just the wicked man and his reasoning (considereth) and his change of mind, repentance. We also read in Ezekiel 18:-24, "But when the righteous turneth away from his righteousness, and committeth iniquity, and doeth according to all the abominations that the wicked man doeth, shall he live?
All his righteousness that he hath done shall not be mentioned: in his trespass that he hath trespassed, and in his sin that he hath sinned, in them he shall die." K.J.V.
In Isaiah 55:-7, "Let the wicked forsake his way, and the unrighteous man his thoughts: and let him return unto the Lord; and He will have mercy upon him; and to our God, for He will abundantly Pardon". K.J.V.

THE EXAMPLE OF THE PEOPLE OF NINEVEH

Did not the people of Nineveh change themselves and turn from their wickedness with the Help of the message from the reluctant Jonah?
The Lord tells us in Matthew 12:-41, that, "The men of Nineveh shall rise up in judgement with this generation, and shall condemn it: because they repented at the preaching of Jonas; and, behold **a greater** than Jonas is here." K.J.V.
This statement and many others, would have been impossible to make if God was responsible for the gift of both faith and repentance! The people of Nineveh would not have repented without the preaching of Jonah. The desire and motivation to repent came through the message, the fear of impending judgement from the prophet, but it was their responsibility to believe it and repent, and Christ commends them for this.
Note. The Lord Jesus does not say that "It will be more tolerable (for Nineveh) at the day of Judgement," but that the people of that city will rise

up in judgement for they repented at the straightforward preaching of Jonah without any miracles or mighty works and a greater than Jonah is here." The inference Christ makes is that the wicked people of Nineveh would have responded to Christ's preaching in the way He desired, by believing Christ to be the Son of God, and changing their ways, by repenting of their sins, as they did with Jonah. "For what saith the Scriptures? Abraham believed God, and it was counted unto him for righteousness." Romans 4:-3

THE TRAGEDY OF FAITH WITHOUT REPENTANCE

It is possible to have faith without repentance, and Jesus refers to this in the gospels. Enough faith to partially accept the message and see Mighty Works, but without being willing to repent. Jesus makes this clear in Matthew 12:-41. He held the generation of people He preached to, responsible for their lack of repentance in response to what they had heard and experienced from the Lord Jesus Christ. We have the words of Christ, to confirm that men can - and the Lord expects them - to repent and change the way they live.

In Matthew 11:-20 to 23, we read: "Then began He to upbraid the cities wherein most of His mighty works were done, **because they repented not."** "Woe unto thee, Chorazin! woe unto thee Bethsaida! for if the mighty works, which were done in you, had been done in Tyre and Sidon, **They would have repented long ago in sackcloth and ashes."** K.J.V. Verse 23, "And thou, Capernaum, which art exalted unto heaven, shalt be brought down to hell: **for if the mighty works, which have been done in thee, had been done in Sodom, it would have remained until this day."** K.J.V.

GENTILE CITIES COMMENDED BY CHRIST FOR THEIR FAITH

Tyre, Sidon and Sodom were among the much despised and detested Gentiles, the ones not chosen. Jesus was highlighting the lack of Faith of the Elected people of Israel who, because of their background and knowledge of Scripture, and the preparatory work of John the Baptist, for the coming of Christ, should have Believed and Repented. The Gentiles would have done what the Jews should have done.

Unlike His own town of Nazareth, where He could do no mighty works because of their unbelief, (Mark 6:-3-6), the people in Chorazin, Bethsaida and Capernaum had faith enough in Christ to see mighty works performed, but they did not stop their sinning and Repent! What Jesus is saying is that the people in Tyre and Sidon and Sodom (also Nineveh) would have done what God wanted them to do and would have seen the mighty works as

evidence that Jesus was the Christ the Son of God, and believed in Him and Repented of their sins had they gone through the same experience as those in Chorazin, Bethsaida and Capernaum. See Note. **Jesus puts the onus on those who hear the gospel.**
The Lord is placing the responsibility for repentance squarely on those who hear the message and have seen the mighty works of God.
Would the Calvinist suggest that the Lord would have given Faith and repentance to the people of Tyre and Sidon, also Sodom, but not to those of Chorazin, Bethsaida,and Capernaum and still hold the people in those cities responsible for not repenting?

"But if you treat one person as being more important than another, you are sinning. You are guilty of breaking God's law." James 2:-9. N.C.V.

"For God judges all people in the same way." Rom 2:-11 N.C.V.

"For the Eternal our God knows nothing of injustice, nor of favouritism." 2 Chronicles 19:-7. J.M.V.

That being so, then the Lord cannot show favour and give faith and repentance to one but not to another.

Note. The words spoken by Christ about Tyre, Sidon, Chorazin, Bethsaida, and Capernaum, give us a window of understanding into the Majesty and comprehension of the one who created us and shows clearly that at the Judgment there will be perfect Justice because of the faultless and complete knowledge of Christ. Sodom would still have existed, had the people seen and experienced what the people of Capernaum had, because they would have responded in the way Christ had intended them to, for this was the whole reason for the mighty works, repentance, and belief in who Christ was, the Son of the Living God.
Those who die never having heard the gospel because no Christian has taken the message to them will be judged flawlessly, for the Lord knows what they would have done had they heard. No matter the multiplicity of circumstances, which could exist in our lives the Lord knows how we would react in them.
At the Judgment, there will be no mysteries, or questions of lack of evidence, for every secret thing in motive, thought, word, and deed will be made known, and clear to all.

CHAPTER 16

THE CALVINIST BELIEF THAT THE REAPER IN THE SPIRITUAL HARVEST IS THE HOLY SPIRIT!

A.W. Pink and many other Calvinists believe that the Holy Spirit is the reaper in God's harvest field, and this is the reason for the lack of enterprise in preaching and reaching people with the Good News of Christ, and for their not making appeals for people to come to Christ, either on a personal one to one basis or collectively, because they believe that they would be doing the work of the Holy Spirit. This is made clear in Pink's statement. "The New Birth is solely the work of God the Spirit and man has no part or lot in it."

The Holy Spirit is neither the sower of the seed nor the reaper of souls in God's harvest field, but the believers in Christ are.

Scripture informs us that there are sowers and reapers in God's Harvest, and the seed sown is the Gospel message, and there will be rewards for both, and the recipients are the believers who have laboured in the work of spreading the "Glad Tidings," and not the Holy Spirit, although the Holy Spirit is indeed involved. The Lord Jesus said to his disciples **"I will make you fishers of men."** *This was not said to the Holy Spirit but to the disciples!*

WHAT HAPPENS WHEN CALVINISTS DO PREACH THE GOSPEL

Calvinists may preach the Gospel, and in so doing throw out the fishing net or line, but they never pull them in. They expect the fish to jump into the boat. It is lunatic of a fisherman to cast a line or net but never pull it in, even when he knows that there could be something on the line or in the net. It is senseless to expect the fish to jump into the boat, and a majority of Calvinists believe that the 'fish' will do this without even anyone fishing, **because it is God the Holy Spirit that does everything.**

Matthew 9:-37-38. "The harvest truly is plenteous, but the labourers are few; Pray ye therefore the Lord of the Harvest, that He will send forth labourers into His harvest." K.J.V. The Lord Jesus is not speaking about the Holy Spirit but Believers in Christ! John 4:-36-37. "And he that reapeth receiveth wages, and gathereth fruit unto Life Eternal: that both he that soweth and he that reapeth may rejoice together. And herein is that saying true. One soweth, and another reapeth." K.J.V.

"How beautiful are the feet of them that preach the gospel of peace, and bring glad tidings of good things!" Romans 10:-15. K.J.V.

"He that winneth souls is wise." Proverbs 11:-30. K.J.V.

"And they that be wise shall shine as the brightness of the firmament; and they that turn many to righteousness as the stars for ever and ever." Daniel 12:-3. K.J.V.
WILL IT BE THE BELIEVERS, OR THE HOLY SPIRIT WHO WILL BE REWARDED IN THE HARVEST OF SOULS INTO GOD'S KINGDOM?

THE WAY GOD ADDS TO THE CHURCH AND BRINGS ABOUT REGENERATION

In the book of Acts chapter 8 from verses 26 to 40, we read about the coming to Christ of the Ethiopian eunuch, and how he was converted to Christ. Philip was told by the angel of the Lord to go down towards the South to the road that goes from Jerusalem to Gaza, and run alongside the chariot of the Ethiopian eunuch, and he heard him reading from Isaiah 53:-7, and asked him if he understood what he was reading. His reply was: "How can I, except some man should guide me? Then Philip opened his mouth, and began at the same Scripture, and preached unto him Jesus." K.J.V.
As they journeyed they came to a certain water, "And the eunuch said, See, here is water; what doth hinder me to be baptized?" K.J.V.
"And Philip said, if thou believest with all thine heart, thou mayest. And he answered and said, I believe that Jesus is the Son of God." K.J.V.
DID MAN HAVE NO PART OR LOT IN THE REGENERATION OF THE ETHIOPIAN EUNUCH?

WAS THE ETHIOPIAN REGENERATED BY THE WIND OF THE SPIRIT BLOWING ON HIM BEFORE HE HEARD AND BELIEVED THE GOSPEL MESSAGE?

WOULD THE EUNUCH HAVE BEEN BORN AGAIN WITHOUT PHILIP PREACHING THE GOSPEL TO HIM?

THE ANSWER TO THESE QUESTIONS IS NO, NO, NO.

If we as individuals are to be successful in winning people for Christ, the same principles must be followed. We must be in tune with God and obedient to what He tells us to do.

“As God’s fellow workers we urge you not to receive God’s grace in vain,” 2 Cor 6:-1. N.I.V.

“For we are fellow workmen - joint promoters, laborers together - with and for God;” 1 Cor 3:-9. The Amplified New Testament.

THE GOSPEL IS “THE POWER OF GOD UNTO SALVATION”

It is the Gospel that is “The power of God unto salvation to everyone that believeth,” Romans 1:-16 .K.J.V, and not the Holy Spirit without the message (Christ the Word), for the Holy Spirit does not work independently of the Word, either in conviction of sin or the New Birth. Just as the Lord Jesus did not work independently of His Father!
In John 8:-28-29 , “Then ye shall know that I am He, and that I do nothing of Myself; but as My Father has taught me, I speak these things. And He that sent Me is with Me: the Father hath not left me alone: for I do always those things that please Him.” K.J.V.

In John 12:-49, “For I have not spoken of myself; but the Father which sent Me, He gave me a commandment, what I should say, and what I should speak.” K.J.V.
“The things I taught were not from myself. The Father who sent me told me what to say and what to teach. And I know that eternal life comes from what the Father commands. So whatever I say is what the Father told me to say.” John 12:-49-50. N.C.V.
This is the example the Lord Jesus gives believers who would serve God and seek to further His cause and kingdom.

WE CAN ONLY BE REGENERATED - BORN AGAIN THROUGH BELIEVING

People are not regenerated - born again before they believe in Christ as Calvinists insist. But by believing, and this is why the preaching of the Gospel is imperative, in order that people believe in Christ and through believing be regenerated – born again.
“This means that you are all children of God through faith in Christ Jesus.” Galatians 3:-26. N.C.V.
In John 20:-31, we read, “But these are recorded so that you will believe that He is the Messiah, the Son of God, **and that believing in Him you will have**

life." T.L.B.
"Those here written have been recorded in order that you may hold the faith that Jesus is the Christ, the Son of God, **and that through this faith you may possess eternal life by His name." John 20:-31. N.E.B.**

"Tell me this one thing: how did you receive the Holy Spirit? Did you receive the Spirit by following the law? **No, you received the Spirit because you heard the Good News and believed it."** Galatians 3:-2. N.C.V.
T.L.B. interprets 1 Thessalonians 2:-13 as follows: "When we preached to you, you didn't think of the words we spoke as being just our own, but you accepted what we said as the very Word of God - which of course, it was - **and it changed your life when you believed it."**

"That when you received the message of God [which you heard] from us, you welcomed it not as the word of [mere] men but as what it truly is, the Word of God, which is effectually at work in you who believe – exercising its [superhuman] power in those who adhere to and trust in and rely on it." 1 Thessalonians 2:-13. The Amplified New Testament.
This text teaches that the word of God works and is only activated and effectually at work in those who believe, and as we are regenerated through the message of the Gospel through believing, as our Lord insisted, the new birth can only take place when people trust in Christ, and not before. These Scriptures make it clear that regeneration - new birth - does not come before one believes in Christ.
WHO IS RIGHT THE LORD JESUS AND SCRIPTURE OR THE CALVINIST?

THE MAN THAT IS REGENERATED HAS NOTHING TO DO WITH IT

Pink in his book "The Sovereignty of God" goes on to say: **"Birth altogether excludes the idea of effort or work on the part of the one who is born."**
"Personally we have no more to do with our spiritual birth than we have with our natural birth."
THIS IS UNBIBLICAL NONSENSE, WHICH WE SHALL CLEARLY SEE. People are involved in natural and spiritual birth.

With natural birth you have no antecedent, but with the second birth you do, you are already alive physically, in other words you have to have a birth before you can have a second birth, so it is not exactly the same. Far from it. In natural birth there are two people involved before conception can take place and a child be born; and of a truth God is involved, for the Scriptures tell us, "Children are a gift from God." Psalm 127:-3. T.L.B.
Without people taking part there would be no gift from God, either in children or eternal life, for this is how God in His Sovereignty has planned it. In Physical birth people must be involved, otherwise conception would not take place. Likewise in the second birth people are involved in sowing the good News of the Gospel, which is the seed for the conception of the second birth.
Before you can have the regeneration, new birth, take place in man you must have the sower of the seed, (The Gospel Message), and the reaper. Evangelists are reapers, and we are all told to "Do the work of an Evangelist." Regeneration takes place when the person believes, the message and repents of his sins, and in so doing welcomes Christ into his life.

JESUS EXPLAINS TO NICODEMUS HOW TO BE BORN AGAIN

It is true that in natural birth, because there is no antecedent, the one born has no say as to whether he is born or not, but this is not so in the second birth, as Jesus makes clear from what He said to Nicodemus.
The conversation with Nicodemus would indicate that he would be acutely involved with his being born again, by the questions he asked and the answers the Lord gave him.
"How can a man be born when he is old? can he enter the second time into his mother's womb and be born?" John 3:-4. K.J.V.
"Jesus answered, except a man be born of water (Natural Birth) and of the Spirit he cannot enter the Kingdom of God." K.J.V.
He also said to Jesus **"How can these things be?"** (How can you be born again) verse 9 of John 3.
"How can this happen?" is how the N.C.V. interprets the same phrase.
In answer to Nicodemus's question, **"How can this happen?"** the Lord Jesus explains to him how to be born again, through a simple Old Testament story and conveys to Nicodemus **the sheer simplicity of how he can be born again,** verses 14 - 16 of John 3.
"And as Moses lifted up the serpent in the wilderness, even so must the Son of man be lifted up: that whosoever believeth in Him should not perish but

have eternal life."
"For God so loved the world, that He gave His only begotten Son, that whosoever believeth in Him should not perish, but have everlasting life." K.J.V.
Nicodemus would have to look to Christ "The Lamb of God that taketh away the sin of the World" and believe, and accept God's Word, and he would be saved and born again.
The Lord Jesus makes it explicit how to experience the new birth, in verses 15-16-18 and 36, by believing and it would appear from Scripture that Nicodemus was obedient.
If the person who is born again has no part or lot in the process of his new birth what was the purpose of the Lord's conversation with Nicodemus?

'WHOSOEVER WILL MAY COME' WHAT IT MEANS TO THE CALVINIST

Pink goes on to say: "But does the Scriptures say 'Whosoever will may come?' "It does. Does this signify that everybody has the will to come?" "What of those who won't come? 'Whosoever will may come' no more implies that fallen man has the power to come, than 'Stretch forth thine hand' implied that the man with the withered arm had the ability within himself to comply."
"In and of himself the natural man has power to reject Christ: but in and of himself he has not the power to receive Christ. AND WHY?"
"Because he has a mind that is "Enmity against" Him. (Romans 8:-7) "Because the carnal mind is enmity against God."
"Because he has a heart that hates Him." (John 15:-18) "If the world hate you, ye know that it hated me before it hated you."
"Man chooses that which is according to his nature, and therefore before he will ever choose or prefer that which is divine and spiritual, a new nature must be imparted to him; in other words he must be born again."

The reason he gives for the lost not being able to accept Christ is that the lost are dead spiritually! Calvinists also tell us that because of this the lost are also deaf and blind to spiritual things, so the lost cannot repent or believe, for the same reason. Pink also tells us, **"And no corpse can re-animate itself."**
So how can a spiritual carcass reject Christ? He is dead!

He also tells us that man can reject Christ but he cannot accept Him.
This is illogical and makes no sense.
Rejecting Christ is based upon a choice between two decisions, **accepting or rejecting.** John 12:-47 - 48.
One has to be able to do either, or it isn't a viable choice.

In other words one cannot reject Christ unless one has the ability and opportunity to accept Him.

Before Christ can be rejected he must first be offered as the Saviour, and that offer must be genuine. Before a woman can Reject an offer of marriage, she has to have had a proposal of marriage and, if the woman were dead she would be in no position either to have a proposal made to her, or to accept or reject such a proposal, unless she were resurrected first.
So with the Calvinist's spiritual carcass of lost man!

This idea that man has the ability to reject Christ, but not accept him, is a figment of their imagination.

CONFUSION IN THE DOCTRINE OF "UNCONDITIONAL ELECTION"

The Calvinists have another problem, in "Unconditional Election." If God intended men to reject Christ because they were not elected (Chosen), and Christ had not died for them, resulting in no provision having been made for their salvation, how could God justly condemn them to hell for this rejection, when they are doing what God intended them to do, and it was not possible for them to do anything else?

WHERE IS THE JUSTICE IN THIS?

WHERE IS THE LOGIC IN THIS KIND OF BEHAVIOUR?

SCRIPTURE TELLS US, "SHALL NOT THE JUDGE OF ALL THE EARTH DO RIGHT?" - NOT ACCORDING TO THE CALVINIST!

CHAPTER 17

ELECTION IS NOT ON ACCOUNT OF OUR BELIEVING

Another extract from Pastor Seaton's booklet informs us that: "Election is not on account of our believing, but our believing is on account of our being elected." (Being given eternal life first.) "Ordained to eternal life". This is perhaps the most frequently quoted verse used by Calvinists in order to prove their belief that regeneration - new birth comes before faith in Christ and repentance. The full quote of "Ordained to eternal life" is from Acts 13:-48, and from the K.J.V. and is as follows:
"And when the Gentiles heard this, they were glad, and glorified the word of the Lord: and as many as were ordained to eternal life believed."

Bishop Ellicott's Commentary on this verse is as follows:
"'As many as were ordained to eternal life believed.' **'better as many as were disposed for.'** The words seem to the English reader to support the Calvinistic dogma of divine decrees as determining the belief or unbelief of men, and it is not improbable, looking to the general drift of the theology of the English church in the early part of the seventeenth century, that the word 'ordained' was chosen as expressing that dogma...**The Greek word, however, does not imply more than that they fell in with the divine order which the Jews rejected."**

The Calvinist theologian Albert Barnes, in his well-known commentary, deals with the verse in a similar way: "There has been much difference of opinion in regard to this expression. One class of commentators have supposed that it refers to the doctrine of election - to God's ordaining men to eternal life; and another class, to their being disposed themselves to embrace the gospel - to those among them who did not despise and reject the gospel, but who were disposed and inclined to embrace it.
The main inquiry is, what is the meaning of the word rendered ordained? The TASSO **properly means to place; to place in a certain rank or order – It does not properly refer to an eternal decree, or directly to the doctrine of election;** although it may be inferred from it; **but it refers to their being then in fact disposed to embrace eternal life.** It refers not to an eternal decree, but that then there was such an influence as to dispose them, or incline them, to lay hold of salvation."

Albert Barnes and Bishop Ellicott, would wholly agree with the rendering of the same text by The Living Bible, and the Emphasized New Testament, which are as follows:
"When the Gentiles heard this, they were very glad and rejoiced in Paul's message; and as many as wanted eternal life, believed. So God's message spread all through the region." T.L.B.

Joseph B. Rotherham, in his Emphasized New Testament, translates the same verse thus: "And they of the nations hearing this, began to rejoice and to be glorifying God, and they believed - as many as had become disposed for life age-abiding."

Dr. Arthur Pierson, who succeeded C.H.Spurgeon as minister of the Metropolitan Tabernacle, wrote: "Some misconceptions, though often corrected, keep reappearing with surprising vitality....Hence the preeminent importance of getting and holding that true meaning of any particular passage which is consistant with the teaching of Scripture as a whole. **We may well mistrust any interpretation of a text which is not in harmony with the general tenor of the inspired Word."**
If you are among those not chosen who is responsible?

A friend of mine after listening to a young preacher telling how glad he was that the Lord had chosen him for salvation before the foundation of the world, asked him what message he had for those who were not chosen, and the thought had apparently never crossed his mind.
If it is impossible for one to be saved unless one has been chosen, one obviously cannot be held responsible!

THE CONSEQUENCES OF CALVINISTIC DOCTRINE

When Calvinists claim that regeneration is given arbitrarily by God, with man having no part or lot whatsoever in it, not even the recipient, and that faith and repentance for salvation are gifts from God, and only imparted to the sinner at the time he is saved, **they are maintaining that sin, unbelief and the repudiation of Christ is the result of the inaction of God in withholding these gifts.** So through their theology they transfer the responsibility which Scripture makes plain is man's, **solely to God**, while at the same time they insist that man is completely responsible, and will be condemned for his lack of faith, and repentance and the rejection of Christ.

Calvinist theologians, as did Augustine and Calvin before them, spend much of their time struggling with this very problem, one of their own making, trying to square the circle of the theological dilemma they are in.

One of the exponents and apologists of Calvinism writes as follows, "On the one hand, we want to maintain the freedom of God in election, and on the other hand, we want to avoid any conclusion which would make God the cause of sin." **They should know that because of their thesis the task they have is impossible.**

THEIR DOCTRINE IS FULL OF IMPLICIT AND RADICAL CONTRADICTIONS

God issues a universal invitation, they say, and then they prohibit this by arbitrary interdiction or exclusion.
They tell us that man is dead to God just as a corpse is to its surroundings and yet say man can know the will of God, and worship Him!

The lost are spiritually dead to God like a carcass is to its habitat, but has the astonishing ability to be aware of God and hate Him.
This same spiritual corpse can reject but cannot accept Christ.
How is it possible for a carcass to accept or reject anything?

That God "Commandeth all men everywhere to repent." But then they say this is unachievable and impossible for man, because he has not got this ability, since he lost his free will at the fall, until the gift is given from God. They would teach that the way to be saved is to "Believe on the Lord Jesus Christ and thou shalt be saved."
Yet they tell us it is unattainable, and beyond the bounds of possibility for man to believe in Christ, until God regenerates him and then gifts him faith and repentance in order to be saved.
Calvinists would preach John 3:-16. "For God so loved the world, that He gave His only begotten Son, that whosoever believeth in Him should not perish, but have everlasting life." K.J.V.
But they say that God does not love the world, and that Christ did not die for all mankind but only for the few whom God loves!

They hold this thesis (Monergism) and are faced with the problem of their own creation, **the Impossible task of how to relieve God of the**

responsibility of sin, unbelief and the rejection of Christ.

Note. Monergism: Means God alone is involved in salvation; Synergism is where others also play a part.

CHAPTER 18

THE CALVINIST ON FAITH

Calvinists tell us that God gives at the time of salvation the faith to individuals to believe in Christ and be saved, and they quote Ephesians 2:-8 and tell us that faith is the gift mentioned in the text and not salvation.
"For by grace are ye saved through faith: and that not of yourselves: it is the gift of God." Ephesians 2:-8. K.J.V.
But Calvin himself does not agree with this interpretation, so it can be said to be going beyond what he taught.
Calvinists normally quote verse eight only, and then claim that faith is what is gifted in this verse.
But when we include verse 9, "Not of works lest any man should boast," we see clearly that salvation is the gift, not faith, and the verses compare Grace with Works, and salvation is the gift by grace and not faith.

Dr. Alexander MacLaren, in his commentary on this verse says, "These words, 'It is the gift of God', have often been quoted as if they referred to faith, which is mentioned just before. But that is a plain misconception of the apostle's meaning, and is contradicted by the whole context.
It is not faith, which is the gift of God, but it is Salvation by Grace. That is very plain if you will read on to the next verse – 'not of works lest any man should boast.' What is it, which is not of works? Faith? Certainly not: nobody would have thought it worth while to say that faith is not of works, because nobody would have said that it was.
The two clauses – 'not of yourselves,' 'not of works,' necessarily refer to the same thing, and if 'not of works' refers to Salvation, so must 'not of yourselves.' Thus the apostle's meaning is that we get Salvation not because we work for it, but because God gives it to us as a free gift for which we have nothing to render, and which we can never deserve."
Other Scripture would back this interpretation. "When people sin, they earn what sin pays - death. But God gives us a free gift - life for ever in Christ Jesus our Lord." Romans 6:-23. N.C.V.
"And if by grace, then is it no more of works; otherwise grace is no more grace". Romans 11:-6. K.J.V.
"The people of Israel tried to follow a law to make themselves right with God. But they did not succeed, because they tried to make themselves right by the things they did instead of trusting God to make them right."
Romans 9:-31-32. N.C.V.

If both salvation, (which is most certainly a gift) and faith were gifts from God it would read in the plural, not in the singular; "they are the gifts of God." Ephesians 2:-8-9, as Translated by the N.C.V. is as follows: "I mean that you have been saved by grace through believing. You did not save yourselves: it was a gift from God. It was not the result of your own work, so you cannot boast about it."

CALVINISTS' ROBOT-LIKE MAN: FAITHLESS AND WITHOUT A WILL

This interpretation of faith being gifted by God at one's conversion, reflects Calvinists' belief that man can do nothing for, or contribute anything to, his salvation - not even **belief**, because he is **dead spiritually** like a corpse, so God must give the new birth first, then faith and repentance, so that one can be saved.

This presupposition of man being gifted "saving faith" at a particular time specifically for salvation would only be correct if man were robotic.

They are again ignoring the fact that man has a **will**, and also **reason**, and is not a **robot**.

Scripture repudiates the idea that faith for man's salvation is a special kind of Faith, and gifted to him by God at the time he is born again, just like someone would hand over a present.

Jesus said, **"Ye will not come unto Me that ye might have life."**

In John 20:-25, Thomas said to the other disciples, "Except I shall see in His hands the print of the nails, and put my finger into the print of the nails, and thrust my hand into His side, **I will not believe."** K.J.V.

What was it that Thomas would not believe?

He would not believe Christ could have risen from the dead!

Christ did not give Thomas faith to believe in Him! But he did give him evidence, which made his faith possible and valid, because faith is simply a response to information.

The conclusion is clear. Thomas had the ability to believe but would not until he had some convincing evidence for it. He wanted confirmation of the fact before he would believe.

To presume that man's will is not involved in believing in Christ is nonsense, when Scripture would deny this.

"And if any man hear my words, and believe not, I judge him not: for I came not to judge the world, but to save the world. **He that rejecteth Me, and receiveth not My Words,** hath one that judgeth him: the Word that I have

spoken, the same shall judge him in the last day." John 12:- 47- 48. K.J.V.
One cannot reject or receive without the use of the will!

THE CALVINISTS' DEAD ROBOTIC MAN REFUSES TO BELIEVE

A. W. Pink asks us, "Why is it that all are not saved, particularly all who hear the gospel? Do you still answer, because the majority, refuse to believe? Well that is true, but it is only part of the truth. It is the truth from the human side. But there is a Divine side too, and this side of the truth needs to be stressed or God will be robbed of His glory. The unsaved are lost because they refuse to believe; the others are saved because they believe. But why do these others believe? What is it that causes them to put their trust in Christ?"
"Who maketh thee to differ from another? And what hast thou that thou didst not receive? now if thou didst receive it, why dost thou glory, as if thou hadst not received it? (1 Cor 4:-7)." " 'Faith is God's gift,' and 'All men have not faith' (2 Thess 3:-2) therefore we see that God does not bestow this gift upon all. Upon whom then does He bestow this saving favour? And we answer, upon His own elect – 'As many as were ordained to eternal life believed (Acts 13:-48).' Was it because God foresaw they would believe? No; for how can those who are 'Dead in trespasses and sins' believe in Christ? How could God foreknow some men as believers when belief was impossible to them?"
He tells us "The unsaved are lost because they refuse to believe."
"Faith is God's gift" and "All men have not faith" **"belief was impossible to them."**
Pink also says, "If Faith were a natural product of the human heart, the exercise of a principle common to human nature, it would never have been written, **'all men have not faith.'** (2 Thess 3:-2)."

HOW CAN THE LOST BELIEVE WHEN THEY HAVE NOT GOT THIS ABILITY?

How can the lost refuse to Believe, if they have not the capability to do so? If they have the capacity to believe then they can refuse to believe, but, if they don't have that capacity, it is not possible for them to refuse to believe! It is as ridiculous as asking a corpse to get up and walk!
Life is expressed in movement and activity and therefore faith cannot be expressed in believing if that ability does not exist in man!
As he says himself, (because of their misbelief) **the lost have no faith so this makes it impossible for them to believe.**
This surely is complete nonsense.

Pink is trying to convince his readers that all men who are unregenerate have no faith, and therefore it is essential for God to gift that Faith in order that they be saved, and uses five words from the text in 2 Thess 3:-2 "All men have not faith" as so-called Biblical evidence.
If his interpretation were true that would make the Bible erroneous, which it is not. "All men have not faith" does not mean as he implies, that all men cannot believe (have faith) or that the ability to have faith (trust) does not exist in all men, for it most certainly does!

The N.C.V. interprets the verse thus, "And pray that we will be protected from stubborn and evil people, **because not all people believe."**

James Moffatt translates the latter part of 2 Thess 3: verse 2 as follows, "And that we may be delivered from perverse and evil men – **for the faith is not held by all."**
Meaning the Christian faith, and that all men do not believe in Christ.
This I believe to be the true interpretation, because faith (trust) is common to all men, but the text is speaking about faith in Christ.

IS FAITH TRULY A GIFT FROM GOD?

I would take issue with Pink, not in the fact that we have nothing that we have not received, which would include man's capability to believe, but in his understanding of the gift of faith, which he infers is given by the Lord at a specific time in order for an individual to believe in Christ and be saved. He also tells us that the unsaved have no faith, by which to trust Christ.
This is total nonsense.
Faith in a person is basically the ability to have confidence in that individual, and that capability is universal.
James tells us that "Every good gift and every perfect gift is from above, and cometh down from the Father of lights, with whom is no variableness, neither shadow of turning." James 1:-17. K.J.V.

IS FAITH GIVEN BY GOD AND, IF SO, WHEN?

Indeed Faith is a gift, or, to be more accurate, the ability to Trust is a gift given by God, in the same sense that life itself is, and health, sight, hearing, intelligence, talent, and aptitude are, and the capacity to trust (faith) is a component of our nature, and an integral part of life for all mankind everywhere.

WHEN ARE ALL THESE GIFTS GIVEN TO US?

Surely with the gift of life itself, they are all in place at our birth. Some if not all gifts like physique, intelligence, talents, the capacity to trust and abilities which are manifest in an aptitude for a particular task or activity are latent and are given to each one in varying degrees and which like our physical body, develop as we grow up.
"Because **your faith groweth exceedingly**, and the charity of every one of you all towards each other aboundeth;" 2 Thess 1:-3 K.J.V.

"Because **your faith is growing more and more**, and the love every one of you has for each other is increasing." 2 Thess 1:-3. N. C. V.

FAITH IS THE MOTIVATING FORCE BEHIND ALL HUMAN ACTIVITY!

Belief (faith, confidence) is the catalyst of behaviour!
Faith is the motivation of all decisive action, and is at the very heart of every level of human activity, be it a very small every day task, a baby's first step, or the many decisions we all have to make every day, to the vast business venture or enterprise, and is in essence the ability to accept, use and practise. Faith is the vision that sees clearly the advantageous end result can be achieved, and it is faith that motivates the work necessary to achieve the desired final result. Faith is the eye that sees the way out of seemingly insurmountable difficulty, and the way of solving what appear to be impossible problems. When it is absent Despair takes its place!
Faith is the hand that takes, that makes, that uses, and creates.

"We pray that with His power God will help you do the good things you want **and perform the works that come from your faith."**
2 Thessalonians 1:-11. N.C.V.

THE BUSINESS WORLD IS RUN ON TRUST

The whole of the business world is run on trust, and everyone is involved in business in one way or another, and without faith the world of commerce would come to a grinding halt. Life itself is made up of relationships, and they are bonded together by faith (trust) and without faith relationships could not occur or remain.
The optimist has hope, which can lead to the exercise of faith, but the pessimist has doubts, sometimes born of fear and this can lead to unbelief

which kills faith. Faith calms anxiety, quenches fear, and provides confidence and assurance and, while man is in "The land of the living" and active, **he has no other option but to exercise faith, because without it normal life could not exist.**

Faith is life: which can only be expressed in movement and action!

Life in the physical body is only understood and recognized when there is movement and action. No movement or activity and a person is declared dead. So also with Faith. "Faith without works is dead."

"Just as a person's body that does not have a spirit is dead, so faith that does nothing is dead!" James 2:-26. N.C.V.

Mark says in Chapter 2:-5, **"When Jesus saw their faith**, He said unto the sick of the palsy, Son thy sins be forgiven thee." K.J.V.

SO TO SAY THAT ALL MEN HAVE NOT FAITH IS ILLOGICAL AND NONSENSE. **Pink's teaching on faith is erroneous.**

ENTERPRISE SEEN AS THE EVIDENCE OF FAITH

We can use what God has given us and put it to good and constructive use, or misuse and abuse the gifts He has afforded us. As we exercise our faith, intellectual, and physical abilities, gifts and talents, we increase them many times over, and likewise the reverse is true.

Surely in the Gospels the Lord Jesus illustrates the fact that we need to use what God has given us to the full, as is shown in the parables of **the Talents** and also of **the Pounds**. In the parable of the Talents each individual did not receive the same number of Talents, and this is true of everyone, so far as abilities and gifts are concerned. But in the parable of the Pound everyone received the same, which would correspond with each one of us receiving a life, and using it, or not, for His Kingdom.

In both parables it is the failure in the use of faith, which is seen in the deficiency of enterprise that is condemned and punished.

What we do not use we lose.

This was part of the teaching of the Lord Jesus.

Calvinists, although they have no Scriptural basis for their doctrine, believe that man is completely passive in salvation and in order to be saved he has to wait to receive regeneration from God, then what they term **"saving faith"** and repentance, is given at a specific time so that an individual can believe in Christ and be saved.

Such a phrase or term as "saving faith" is never used in Scripture, and if **the faith that saves was a special kind of faith Scripture would say so.**
Did not the Lord Jesus say in Mark 11:-22, "Have faith in God", which is the same as saying put your trust in God, and this cannot be done unless we have the ability to trust, which we undoubtedly all have.

THE PEOPLE WITH THE GREATEST AMOUNT OF GOD GIVEN FAITH!

Scripture teaches that one particular group of people and the very largest grouping on the face of the earth, have an abundance of faith, and this common faith is directly related to salvation and entrance into the kingdom of God. The Lord Jesus Christ tells us in Luke 6:-20,
"Blessed are ye poor: for yours is the kingdom of God." K.J.V.

"Happy you people who are poor, because the kingdom of God belongs to you." The same verse in N.C.V.
James explains the reason why this is so and tells us in chapter 2:-5: "Hath not God chosen the poor of this world rich in faith, and heirs of the kingdom which He hath promised to them that love Him." K.J.V. (Heirs because of their faith)

"God chose the poor of the world to be rich with faith and to receive the kingdom God promised to those who love Him." The same text in the N.C.V.
Heirs are those who have rights because they are born into the family, and **faith** exercised in Christ is the very requisite needed to give anyone the right to become a child of God and to enter into His Kingdom, Heirs because of their faith!
As it says in John 1:-11-12, "He came unto His own, and His own received Him not. But as many as received Him, to them gave He the power to become the sons of God, even to them that believe on His name." K.J.V.
Galatians 3:-26, **"For ye are all children of God by faith in Christ Jesus."** K.J.V.
"But His own people did not accept Him. **But to all who did accept Him and believe in Him He gave the right to become children of God."**
John 1:-11-12. N.C.V.

"This means that you are all children of God through faith in Christ Jesus." Galatians 3:-26. N.C.V.
The people who are wealthy in faith are the poor, and James does not say

that the poor will be rich in faith but that they are **at present rich in faith,** although they are poor in material things and most likely poorly educated, and possibly poor also in spirit though they are already **rich in faith,** the **common ordinary faith that can save,** and the vast majority of the poor have not as yet heard the gospel and been given the opportunity to use the **abundant faith** that they have.

Faith in essence is the confidence to accept and use and put into practice!

SO OF ALL THE PEOPLE IN THE WORLD THE POOR HAVE THE GREATEST ABILITY TO ACCEPT CHRIST BECAUSE THEY ARE RICH IN FAITH!

THE DISCIPLES ARE REBUKED FOR NOT USING THEIR GOD GIVEN ABILITY TO BELIEVE

If faith is a gift from God given only to specific individuals, and only at a particular time, why did Christ rebuke the disciples **for their lack of faith** when they woke Him up in the ship during the storm? "And He said unto them, **why are ye so fearful?" "How is it that ye have no faith?"** (trust). Mark 4:-40. K.J.V.

"Why are you afraid? Do you still have no faith?" Mark 4:-40. N.C.V.

Christ expected the disciples, because of the mighty works and miracles they had seen Him do, to have had trust in Him.

If the Lord is the giver of faith surely it was His fault for not giving them the faith (confidence) in Him? His questions would have been sheer mockery, as well as being pointless, and there was not a word that Jesus uttered that was unimportant or needless.

Jesus said in Matthew 12:-36, "That every idle word that men shall speak, they shall give account thereof in the day of judgement." K.J.V.

DISCIPLES REBUKED FOR NOT BELIEVING THE BASICS OF THE FAITH

There are those who would say that this particular incident of censure for lack of faith, has nothing to do with the salvation of the soul and can be discounted. This is debatable.

But there are other instances where the disciples were reprimanded for the absence of trust, and this had to do with the fundamentals of the Christian faith, that is, believing that Christ is the Son of God, died for our sins, and rose from the dead.

The very things we must believe in order to be Christians.
Jesus reprimanded the two disciples on the road to Emmaus, when He said, **"O fools and slow of heart to believe** all that the prophets have spoken: Ought not Christ to have suffered these things, and to enter into His Glory. And beginning at Moses and all the prophets, He expounded unto them in all the Scriptures the things concerning Himself."
Luke 24:-25-26-27. K.J.V.
This rebuke was groundless if they had no ability by which to believe in Christ.

WHY DID JESUS GO THROUGH THE SCRIPTURES: THEN REVEAL HIMSELF?

Why did Christ not just reveal himself to the disciples, without going through the Scriptures with them? Jesus did this to lay a solid foundation for their trust in Him, for believing Jesus was the Christ and had died for them and was risen from the dead, fixing this firmly in their minds by anchoring these facts in the authority of Scripture and thereby giving them a solid basis to believe in Him. He revealed Himself through the written authoritative Word before confirming this by their experience of seeing the Risen Christ. By doing this Christ is emphasizing the importance of the authority of Scripture over experience! Experience is secondary. "Faith cometh by hearing and hearing by the word of God." Romans 10:-12 K.J.V.

Why did Jesus rebuke Thomas, in John 20:-25-27 ?
Did not Jesus say to Thomas **"Be not faithless but believing?"** K.J.V.

The New Century Version interprets the last part of verse 27, as follows **"Stop being an unbeliever and believe."**
Christ was putting the onus on Thomas to believe!

Just as He did with the other disciples, Mark 16:-14, "Later Jesus showed himself to the eleven apostles while they were eating, and he criticised them because they had no faith. **They were stubborn and refused to believe those who had seen Him after He had risen from the dead." N.C.V.**
If Jesus were the giver of Faith, this would not have been said.

The conjecture is clear, the ability to trust and believe was there but had to be exercised. There is not one Scripture to back up the claim that God gives people special faith to believe in Christ and repent, in the same sense and way that the Calvinists would have us believe.

THE WOMAN WHO PUT FORWARD A REASON (LOGIC) WHICH STRENGTHENED HER CAPACITY TO BELIEVE, WHICH IS THE ABILITY TO RECEIVE.

The woman from Canaan put forward a reasoned argument why Jesus should heal her daughter, which was part of the basis of her faith (trust) that Christ would concede to her prayer. The Lord granted her request and complimented her on her trust in Him by saying, **"Great is thy faith: be it unto thee as thou wilt."** K.J.V.

The story is found in Matthew 15:-21-28. Verses 25 to 28 say:
"Then the woman came to Jesus again and bowed before Him and said, 'Lord, help me'! Jesus answered, 'It is not right to take the children's bread and give it to the dogs.' The woman said, 'Yes, Lord, but even the dogs eat crumbs that fall form their masters' table.' Then Jesus answered, **'Woman, you have great faith! I will do what you asked.**' And at that moment the woman's daughter was healed." N.C.V.

FAITH, BELIEF OR TRUST COMES THROUGH A PROCESS

Belief results from an assessment of the pros and cons. If the cons are more convincing than the pros, the result is unbelief, and *vice versa*. Belief which leads to faith (trust) is the result of a mental process.

PLACES WHERE FAITH IS SAID TO BE A SPECIAL GIFT

There are a few places in Scripture that I can think of, or others that appear to, that mention faith, as a gift. For example Philippians 1:-29, "For unto you it is given in the behalf of Christ, not only to believe on Him, but to suffer for His sake." K.J.V.
Other translations make clearer the true meaning of "given" which is used in the King James Version.
The Greek word which is not the word usually used for given or gift, has the meaning of "as a privilege".

"For you have been granted the privilege not only of believing in Christ but also of suffering for Him." The New English Bible.
The Jerusalem and the Weymouth Translations use the word "Privilege" in the same text. **"God gave you the honour not only of believing in Christ but also of suffering for Him." N.C.V.**

Also in 2 Peter 1:-1: "To them that have obtained like precious faith with us through the righteousness of God and our Saviour Jesus Christ:" K.J.V.

The Bible makes clear how we obtain this "like precious faith."
Romans 10:-17, "So then faith comes by hearing and hearing by the Word of God." N.K.J.V.

In 1 Corinthians 12, and also in chapter 13. In chapter 12 it says, *"To another **Faith**, by the same Spirit; to another the gifts of **Healing** by the same Spirit: verse 10. To another the working of **Miracles**, to another **Prophecy**, to another **Discerning of spirits**; to another divers kinds of **Tongues**; to another the **Interpretation of tongues.**" K.J.V.
These are gifts given to believers for service.
The gifts of the Spirit are given after a person becomes a Christian.
*This undoubtedly is a special gift of faith and is post-salvation and really means that God gave them the confidence or help needed to believe and to trust Him to do things in His service they asked Him for.

We have the example of George Muller, William Quarrier and James Hudson Taylor to name just a few among many in recent Church history. We increase our faith the more we get to know the Lord. "But they that do know their God shall be strong and do exploits." Daniel 11:-32. K.J.V.
The gift of faith was not given to every believer, but just to some, as were the other gifts. Most Calvinists believe in any case, that the gifts listed in 1 Corinthians 12 died with the apostles, which would also mean the gift of faith.

ACCORDING TO CALVINISM, GOD MUST DO EVERYTHING

The Synod of Dort pronounced that, "Man's natural state was a state of Total Depravity and therefore there was a Total Inability on the part of man to gain or contribute to his own Salvation."
This in theological terms is called Monergism. God does everything in salvation and man plays no part at all.
The theological term for the participation of man in salvation, is Synergism, defined by one Calvinist theologian as "The idea of co-operation." But it means much more than that, its meaning is "Free will to select from alternatives."

DOES THE LORD JESUS CHRIST DO EVERYTHING?

In John chapter 2, we have the first recorded miracle of the Lord Jesus Christ in the story of the changing of water into wine at the wedding in Cana of Galilee. Mary brought the problem to Christ and said, "They have no wine."

and after Jesus' answer, she then turned to the servants and said, **"Whatsoever He saith unto you do it."** K.J.V.
Why did Mary say this?
Because she did not expect Jesus to do everything Himself!

MARY'S LARGE FAMILY

After Joseph died Jesus being the first born would have become head of the family which was large, for we are told in Matthew 13:-55-56.
"He is just the son of a carpenter. His mother is Mary, and his brothers are, James, Joseph, Simon and Judus. And all His sisters are here with us." N.C.V. Apart from Jesus and Mary there were at least six others in the immediate family, and possibly more. Mary would bring her problems to Him, and I have no doubt with such a large family the difficulties were many, and this I believe became a habit, and she found that Christ could always solve the problems. But Mary knew from experience that He would not do everything Himself.

GOD WILL NOT DO FOR US WHAT WE ARE CAPABLE OF DOING OURSELVES

When Jesus was at the grave of Lazarus, He asked Martha to have the stone that barred the entrance to the tomb removed.
He did not do it Himself although He could have.
He would not physically, or by some miracle do for others what He had already given them the ability to do.
But after He was obeyed, what was impossible for them, He did. He brought Lazarus back from the dead.
Mary's practical experience was obviously similar because she said to the servants, "Whatsoever He saith unto you do it." K.J.V.

SHE ANTICIPATED THAT CHRIST WOULD ASK THEM TO DO SOMETHING.
He did not say to the servants get out of the way and I will do everything.
No, He asked them to fill the waterpots with water.
Jesus could have done this Himself but He didn't.
The movement towards a miracle would have been stopped if they had been unbelieving and disobedient.

"And He did not many mighty works there because of their unbelief"
Matthew 13:-58, K.J.V.

After they had filled the waterpots to the brim, He asked them for even greater faith, (confidence in Him). He commanded them to draw out the water and pour it out for wine. The progress towards a miracle would have ceased even at this late stage if they had questioned or doubted Jesus.
They could have said, we are not going to make fools of ourselves, it is still just water. We can't pour that out for wine, and there would have been no miracle. It was water when they drew it out, it was water when they carried it into the marriage feast, but the Lord performed the miracle as they poured it out.

FAITH AND OBEDIENCE REWARDED

Because of their faith, and unquestioning obedience, they were brought into the scope of the miraculous. **Did the servants perform the miracle?**

No, but they did everything else.

Did they contribute (were they partly responsible for) or participate in the bringing about of the miracle? **Yes, most certainly.**
They had confidence in Him and obeyed Christ. Without this there would have been no miracle! They were instrumental in the bringing about of the miraculous, although it was Jesus who performed the miracle.
This is a principle that is seen throughout the Scriptures.
The almighty power of God travels along the road of faith, on the vehicle of obedience to His Word.

A few of the translations would give credence to the belief that the changing of the water into wine was done at the last moment.
The Jerusalem Bible interprets John 2:-8-9, as follows, "'Draw some out now' He told them 'and take it to the steward'. They did this; the steward tasted the water, and it had turned into wine. Having no idea where it came from – only the servants who had drawn the water knew."

"Then He said to them, 'Now take some out and give it to the master of the feast.' So they took the water to the master. When he tasted it, the water had become wine. He did not know where the wine came from, but the servants who had brought the water knew." The same verses in the N.C.V.

FULL OBEDIENCE COMES BEFORE SALVATION IN 2 KINGS 5

There is also another reason I am convinced that the water that Jesus

changed into wine was not changed until the servants went in with the water to the marriage feast and were asked for wine, and that is the story of the healing of Naaman.
If Naaman had been healed when he walked into the river, or after he had dipped under the water the first time, he would most likely have come up out of the river and gone home, thinking there was no need for him to go under the water seven times. I believe and have no doubt that he looked at his leprosy not only the first time, but each time he went down and came up, as most of us would have done, to see if he had been made whole, or if there was any improvement; and there was no change in his condition even after the sixth dipping; his leprosy was not reduced, it was still the same. It was not until he fully obeyed the Lord that he was healed.
He was told to dip seven times under the river and he would be healed. Faith is a practical thing. If it is not, it is of little use, and we would see no miracles worked out in our own lives. But God does not do everything for us. In almost all situations we play a part.
There must be obedience on our part, and if we don't play a part it is likely there will be no miracle. Obedience and Trust in Him must be exercised.
1 Corinthians 3:-9, **"For we are labourers together with God."** K.J.V.

" We are workers together with God." 2 Cor 6:-1. N.C.V.

2 Corinthians 6:-1. **"We then as worker together with Him."** K.J.V.

THE SHEER SIMPLICITY OF THE GOSPEL OBEYING AND TRUSTING

The story of Naaman is an Old Testament illustration with a New Testament application, showing the simplicity, and principles involved in Salvation, of obedience and trust as an essential part in receiving (wholeness) salvation.
The Bible does not say that the Lord gave Naaman special faith, in order to do an extremely simple thing so that he could receive his (salvation) wholeness. The same applies to New Testament Salvation.
2 Kings 5, Naaman was not healed in the way he expected, and was almost not healed at all, because of a preconceived idea of how he should be made whole. Would God have healed him, if he had gone back to Syria as he had intended, and not been obedient to the command of God?

I think not! Did he then work for his salvation?

Many Calvinists writers would say he did, if you believe what they write, and apply it to Naaman, and his healing.

Naaman did what God told him to do - a very simple thing that a four year old could have done!

Did Naaman heal himself?   NO.

Did he work for his (salvation) wholeness by dipping under the water seven times?

Did he then because it was his own faith and not faith specially given to him by God at the time, work for his salvation?

Did he participate or contribute anything to bring about the miracle?

Yes, of course, he believed and obeyed God.

Although what he did was simple and insignificant it was proof of the faith and trust he had in God's Word, and without it the miracle would not have taken place.

THE OLD TESTAMENT STORY USED BY JESUS TO ILLUSTRATE THE GOSPEL

When the children of Israel were bitten by the serpents in the wilderness, Moses interceded for them, and was commanded by God to make a brass serpent, put it on a pole and lift it up, and if those who were bitten, would look to the serpent they would be healed.
Just a look, that is all they needed to be healed; so simple a little child could have done it.
Were those who refused to believe and obey God's Word healed?
The answer is no, because the healing was conditional on their looking.
God did not heal them unconditionally.
Nor did He do the looking for them.
Did the people who believed and obeyed God and were healed, heal themselves?   The answer is, NO.

Did they work for their (salvation) healing?

Did they participate or contribute anything to bring about their healing?

Yes, most certainly, they obeyed God and looked.
Without their obeying God and looking, they perished.
The miracle of the new birth is the same.

Did the Israelites need some special kind of faith from God for them to believe Moses and look? No, it was simple everyday faith.
This is the very story Jesus used to show Nicodemas the sheer simplicity of how to be born again.
"And as Moses lifted up the serpent in the wilderness, even so must the Son of man be lifted up: That whosoever believeth in Him (Looks to Christ) should not perish, but have eternal life."

"For God so loved the world, that He gave His only begotten Son, that whosoever believeth in Him should not perish, but have everlasting life." John 3:-14 -15-16. K.J.V.

In his commentary Dr. Alexander MacLaren, tries to explain what is meant by faith in Christ. I quote:
"Those who know what is meant by faith in a promise, know what is meant by faith in the Gospel. Those who know what is meant by faith in a remedy, know what is meant by faith in the blood of the redeemer. Those who know what is meant by faith in a physician, a friend or an advocate know what is meant by faith in the Lord Jesus Christ."

A MODERN ILLUSTRATION

An Evangelist was having meetings in the south of England and was in bed and breakfast lodgings and was not given any hospitality in the way of meals, and after a few days he was very hungry. As he walked down a street in the town he told the Lord he was hungry and that he had no money and asked God to provide for him as He had promised.
As he was walking past a restaurant the Lord told him to go in and have a meal, and He would provide the finance. He obeyed the Lord and went in and, as God was going to provide, he had the best on the menu.
He finished his meal, received the bill, and was waiting for the Lord to supply the needed money in some wonderful way. He waited as long as he possibly could, and then with fear and trembling he went reluctantly to the counter, still looking for the Lord to show His hand, and then timidly he passed the check over the counter.
The girl behind the counter looked up, and as she looked at him said, are you the person who is having the meetings in such and such a hall, and he said he was. Then she said, looking at the check, "I will pay for your meal."
He breathed a sigh of relief, and thanked the Lord for His faithfulness.

CHAPTER 19

THE FOOLISH DOCTRINE THAT FAITH IS WORKS

Perhaps in recent past history no one has been foolish enough to say that faith is works, but this is not now the case, because the Calvinist says exactly that. This old Calvinist heresy has been resurrected and propagated by a number of Reformed writers who equate an act of faith with a work of the law. From the book "The Sovereignty Of God" by Arthur W. Pink on page 50, the writer makes this amazing statement:
"The basis on which God elected this **'remnant' was not faith forseen in them, because a choice founded upon the foresight of good works is just as truly made on the ground of works as any choice can be,** and in such a case it would not be 'of grace'; for, says the apostle, 'if by grace, it is no more of works: otherwise grace is no more grace;' which means that grace and works are opposites." He clearly states that faith is works!

THEIR UNDERSTANDING OF "UNCONDITIONAL ELECTION" REGARDING FAITH

Another Reformed writer James Dick writing in the Bulwark magazine comments as follows: "Nothing is more common among professing Christians than the admission that we are saved by grace. **And yet the error is very prevalent that faith is properly a condition of salvation; that is, it is something that we are to do ourselves, on the ground of which we are saved. Faith, according to this view, is a certain work performed, entitling us to the offered salvation**, and, therefore, salvation is not wholly of God's grace, but partly of man's merit. For so long as a man thinks that faith is something in his own power, to be performed by himself, before God will save him, **he is seeking life 'by the works of the law.'** It is true that faith on the part of the hearer of the gospel is necessary to salvation, **yet it is not a condition of salvation, for there are no conditions."**

TRUST IS INDEED AN ACT OR WORK AND A CONDITION OF SALVATION

Scripture teaches that faith is indeed a condition of salvation. "Sirs, what must I do to be saved? And they said, Believe" (trust) "on the Lord Jesus Christ, and thou shalt be saved, and thy house." Acts 16:-30-31. K.J.V.
Calvinists, Insist that if faith (confidence) is something that I do, and it is my own faith, **then that means I am saved by my works.**

Another Calvinist writer tells us that this would make us our own Saviour. Nonsense. If I have faith in a doctor to operate on me, in order to save my life, does that make me my own doctor, and therefore my own saviour?
My trust in a doctor or surgeon does not add anything to the ability or skill of the physician, but it does bring me into a position of being helped by him.

TRUSTING IN CHRIST IS NOT ADDING TO SALVATION

My faith in Christ does not add anything to the salvation He has purchased for me, which is complete and finished, but it makes possible my personal salvation, because it allows Christ to save me. This is the condition of salvation and I participate by believing in Christ, and I am jointly responsible, because I believe. **If I do not believe in Christ, I will perish. Believe is an active verb and is something that we do.**

FAITH IS NOT WORKS BUT THE TASK OR ACT OF BELIEVING IS!

For instance if a person is afraid to travel on a bus, train, or airplane and you manage to persuade him that it is safe and no harm will come to him, he has to believe you and then he must (trust) commit himself to the driver or pilot, "Faith without works is dead;" getting on the means of transport is something that he has to do. The person would not have to work his way to his destination, but he would have to trust the driver or pilot to get him there. If this is not done then he cannot believe you.
It is the same with salvation.

WHAT THE LORD JESUS TEACHES IN JOHN'S GOSPEL

I do not believe the Lord Jesus teaches that faith is works, but He does tell us in John 6:-27-29, **that we have to work at believing,** (trusting Him) and encourages us to do exactly that. Even if one interprets these texts to mean that Jesus is teaching that faith is works it is obvious that the Lord Jesus Christ, unlike the Calvinists, found that it did not Conflict, Contradict, or Compromise in any way the doctrine of Justification by Faith, and God's free gift of salvation. So the Lord Jesus Christ fully sanctions it! In fact this is the only way to obtain salvation!

WAS JESUS TEACHING THAT MEN SHOULD WORK FOR THEIR SALVATION?

"Stop toiling and doing and producing for the food that perishes and decomposes in the using; but strive and work and produce rather for the lasting food which endures continually unto life eternal. The Son of man will give (furnish) you that, for God the Father has authorized and certified Him and put His seal of endorsement upon Him. They then said, What are we to do that we may [habitually] be working the works of God? – What are we to do to carry out what God requires? Jesus replied, this is the work (service) that God asks of you, that you believe in the One Whom He has sent – that you cleave to, trust, rely on and have faith in His Messenger." John 6:-27-28 -29. The Amplified New Testament.

Jesus quite clearly tells us to work at believing and that believing is a work we do. "'This is the work that God requires: believe in the One whom He has sent.'" John 6:-29 N.E.B.

"Jesus answered, 'The work God wants you to do is this: believe the One He sent.'" John 6:-29. N.C.V.

In 1 John 3:-23 we read, **"This is what God commands: that we believe in His Son, Jesus Christ,** and that we love each other, just as He commanded." N.C.V. **This is something that we are commanded to do!**

WORK FOR THE FOOD THAT IS ETERNAL BY BELIEVING

The Lord Jesus also tells us about the rich farmer who pulled down his barn to build a larger one to hold his bountiful harvest. "But God said unto him, Thou fool, this night thy soul shall be required of thee: then whose shall those things be, which thou hast provided?" **"So is he that layeth up treasure for himself, and is not rich toward God."**
Luke 12:-20-21. K.J.V.
The Lord Jesus was highlighting what the rich man should have done, but had failed to do.
He should have been striving to produce the lasting food, which endures continually unto life eternal. "Seek ye first the kingdom of God, and His righteousness; and all these things shall be added unto you."
Matthew 6:-33. K.J.V.

CHRIST'S OLD TESTAMENT ILLUSTRATION

"Your fathers did eat manna in the wilderness, and are dead. I am the living bread which came down from heaven: if any man eat of this bread, he shall live for ever: and the bread which I will give him is my flesh, which I will give

for the life of the world." John 6:-49-51. K.J.V.
The key verse in understanding the above texts and what the Lord Jesus means is (verse 63): "It is the spirit that quickeneth; the flesh profiteth nothing: the words that I speak unto you, they are spirit, and they are life." K.J.V.

BELIEVING IN CHRIST IS SOMETHING WE DO

The Lord Jesus clearly teaches us that believing in Him is something we do, and is therefore a work, and that we should labour at it! Although faith (trust) is not works the focusing or act of trusting Christ is. It is the transferring of our trust (faith) from religion, good works or whatever we trust in, to Christ.

WE SHOULD FEED SPIRITUALLY ON CHRIST EVERY DAY

By believing and paying attention to what the Lord Jesus taught and applying it to the way we live, **that is working at believing in Christ.** "Work out your own salvation in fear and trembling." Phil 2:-12. Because our salvation is Christ and because He dwells within us, this means working the Living Word (Christ) out in our daily life. Feeding on His Word, which is something we do, day by day and not neglecting this "Great Salvation." Hebrews 2:-3. The Living Bread Christ "This bread is my flesh." John 6:-51. N.C.V.

THE MANNA AND QUAIL HAD TO BE GATHERED AND PREPARED

Just as the Israelites in the desert were given manna and quail for their physical salvation, which they had to gather daily, and they had to catch, kill and prepare the quail, before eating, so we have to work at partaking of Christ, the living bread.
The salvation was provided for the Israelites but there was a certain amount of work involved in gathering and preparing, as well as eating their (food) salvation.

FAITH IS THE HAND THAT RECEIVES THE GIFT OF SALVATION

This is something we do and continue to do, just as we do not live our whole life on one meal, but continue throughout our life to eat and drink, so in the spiritual life we must, as the Lord Jesus tells us, continue to believe in Him and feast on Him the Living Bread (His Word) day by day.
The Bible teaches us that faith (trust) is not works, but that (The works of) righteousness are imputed to those who believe, nevertheless believing in Christ is something we do.

In Galatians 3:6 we read, "Even as Abraham believed God, and it was accounted" (Imputed) "to him for righteousness." K.J.V.

The New Century Version, translates the text thus: "The Scriptures say the same thing about Abraham: "Abraham believed God, and God accepted Abraham's faith, and that faith made him right with God."
Whose faith did God accept? Abraham's own personal faith (Trust)!

WHAT WAS THE MESSAGE OF THE REFORMATION?

The central message of Martin Luther's Reformation doctrine was Justification by faith, and not works, **that is confidence in Christ to save, instead of confidence in works to save**, which is Scripturally correct. So how is it possible that those who claim to be of the Reformed faith now say that faith is works? They say that if it is my own personal faith then it is works. Where is the Scriptural basis for such a statement?
When time and time again Jesus said to those He healed, "Thy faith hath healed thee," or "Thy faith hath saved thee" or "according to thy faith be it unto thee?" Not the faith that I am giving thee, "But thy faith."
The Calvinists turn the sheer simplicity of the glorious gospel into a complex labyrinth of complete nonsense.
"He that believeth on Him is not condemned: but he that believeth not is condemned already, because he hath not believed in the name of the Only Begotten Son of God." John 3:-18. K.J.V.

IF WE NEGLECT: WE DO NOT DO SOMETHING WE SHOULD BE DOING

In Hebrews 2:-3, We read, **"How shall we escape, if we neglect so great salvation?"** K.J.V. We neglect by not doing something that we should do. Believing is something Christ commands us to do and we are encouraged by Christ to work hard at believing in Him and to put as much effort into it as we do into our daily work. "And this is His commandment, That we should believe on the name of His Son Jesus Christ, and love one another as He gave us commandment." 1 John 3:-23. K.J.V.

USING WHAT WE HAVE AND TRUSTING JESUS TO DO THE MIRACULOUS

In Matthew 14:-27-28, When the disciples were in the storm on the sea of Galilee, and Jesus approached the ship walking on the sea, and called out to

them, "be of good cheer; it is I; be not afraid." K.J.V.
"And Peter answered Him and said, Lord, if it be Thou, bid me come unto Thee on the water. And He said, come." K.J.V.
Why did Peter say, "Lord if it be thou, bid me to come unto thee on the water?" Possibly because Peter knew that if it was Christ and He invited him to come, he would be able to do the astonishing miracle that Jesus was doing, because the ability to achieve what the Lord asked would be given, if he attempted to respond to the invitation.

WE DO WHAT IS POSSIBLE IN ORDER FOR GOD TO DO THE IMPOSSIBLE

The Lord will not do for us what He has already given us the ability to do. For instance He did not miraculously convey Peter to Himself without Peter walking, nor did he do the walking for him. Peter had that faculty, but He enabled him to do something that no other man has ever done, walk on water. Between the possible, walking, and the impossible, walking on water, was trust in Christ's Word, and through this, obedience made the IMPOSSIBLE, POSSIBLE.
Peter had to do what was possible for him to do, **walk**, in order that the Lord could do **for Peter the impossible**. The power of Christ's Word was only activated and proved when Peter attempted to do what Christ asked him to do, and it could have been put to the test in no other way!

There was participation, the combination of the practical physical ability of Peter combined with his faith (trust) in the miraculous ability of Christ.

DID PETER PERFORM THE MIRACLE BY DOING WHAT CHRIST ASKED?

Peter's faith was in the word **"come"**, and all the power and authority of the Almighty was behind that invitation, as with all his invitations, and Peter knew through seeing Christ dealing with others, that if the Lord invited him to **come**, even though it was humanly **impossible**, the ability was inherent in the command, because of the person who gave it.
All Peter had to do was to act in response to the invitation and the ability to come to Christ would be given. The Lord does not command all men everywhere to repent without enabling them to do what He asks. That would be grossly unjust. Did Peter perform the miracle by walking? **No. But if he had not walked there would have been no miracle!**
This incident happened before Peter was born again - regenerated.

He did participate and contribute towards the miraculous even although he did not perform it! It is true with all the invitations and also with the command to all men to repent, given by the Lord.
If we make an attempt to respond, this shows we have faith, (confidence) however small, in His Word and the ability is given, no matter how impossible it may appear to be, as Peter found out to his, and the other disciples', amazement. **This is why repentance is possible to all men.**
It is through man using the inbuilt ability to obey and trust, which is common to all men and placing this in the message of the Gospel of Christ, that men come **to believe**, and the miracle of regeneration takes place.

THROUGH FAITH ALONE: BUT IS FAITH ALONE ?

The saying of Martin Luther, that, "We are saved by Grace Alone, Through Faith Alone, By Christ Alone," is not altogether true, Because, the faith that saves is never alone, and if it is alone it is not faith. Faith produces (action) repentance, and the Lord Jesus, Paul and James agree on this. Scripture never says "By faith alone" in fact it contradicts this statement, but it does say we are saved by faith and "not of works."

THE ETHOS AT THE TIME OF MARTIN LUTHER

The times in which Martin Luther lived were called the Dark Ages and for a very good reason. We must remember the great darkness of the religious climate and atmosphere of the times in which Luther found himself, when considering how he came to make this statement. The doctrine and tyrannical rule of the Church of Rome was universally accepted. The religious belief and practices of the day were that salvation was by Good Works Plus the Mediation and Rituals of the Roman Church and forgiveness of one's sins could be had through indulgences, which could be bought at a price from the Roman Catholic priests who sold them. The whole emphasis of Rome on salvation was on Doing Good Works and obeying the Papacy. Once he found salvation through faith in Christ, and that Christ alone was the way of salvation, Martin Luther had to emphasize the fact that salvation was by Faith in Christ, without the addition of Good Works or obedience to the hierarchy of the Papacy.
Perhaps what Martin Luther had in mind when he said "by faith alone" was the thief on the cross beside Jesus, who called out "Lord remember me when Thou comest into Thy kingdom." The thief was saved by faith in Christ, as he was passing out of this life. But, had he been given a pardon and taken down from the cross and lived, his faith in Christ would have undoubtedly been evidenced in a changed life.

Note. An elderly pastor of a Protestant Church in Czechoslovakia, which existed before the mainstream Reformation, and which was part of what was sometimes referred to as the "Rival Church," read some of Martin Luther's writings and wrote to him to rebuke him for his disregard of "fruits worthy of repentance" and told him "Nohow and never will you be able to ascribe Justification to faith alone, for you have the Scripture against you." There were many such Churches throughout Europe which existed long before the mainstream Reformation, who we are told were decidedly predisposed to the book of James, and who stuck tenaciously to Scripture in their manner of lifestyle and worship. It is well known that Luther disliked particularly the book of James and also the Epistle to the Hebrews.

REAL FAITH IS NOT INVISIBLE BUT CAN BE SEEN

The first Three gospels give the account of the healing of the paralysed man and all verify that Jesus saw their faith, (the faith of the four who carried the sick man) and Mark says in Chapter 2:-5, "When Jesus saw their faith, He said unto the sick of the palsy, Son, thy sins be forgiven thee." K.J.V. The men's faith was seen by their action in bringing the sick man to Christ, and through their faith salvation was given to the man with palsy, as well as healing. Jesus confirms the argument, which James puts forward in his epistle.

WOULD NINEVEH HAVE BEEN SAVED IF THEY HAD NOT REPENTED?

The same is true with the people at Nineveh. **They were not saved by faith alone**, because faith is never alone, but the evidence of faith wrought in their lives, through a complete change of behaviour. God watched that city for forty days and saw a transformed community, which was the proof that they had faith in what God had said and for that reason (their repentance) He did not destroy the city.

"And God saw their works, that they turned from their evil way; and God repented of the evil, that he had said that he would do unto them; and he did it not." Jonah 3:-10. K.J.V.

"Ye see then how that by works a man is justified, **and not by faith only."** James 2:-24. K.J.V.

JAMES ARGUES THIS POINT OF SEEING FAITH BY PEOPLES' WORKS

"So you see that people are made right with God by what they do, **not by**

faith only." James 2:-24. N.C.V.
"Friend of God. Ye see that a man is justified on the principle of works, and not on the principle of faith only." The same verse from J. N. Darby. James argues this point of seeing faith in works in his epistle in chapter 2:-18: **"Yea, a man may say, Thou hast faith, and I have works; shew me thy faith without thy works, and I will shew you my faith by my works."** K.J.V.
"Someone might say, 'You have faith, but I have deeds.' Show me your faith without doing anything, and I will show you my faith by what I do."
The same verse from the New Century Version.
Faith without works is not faith but wishful thinking dressed up as faith. Proverbs 13:- 4, "The soul of the sluggard desireth, and hath nothing:" (Wishful Thinking) "but the soul of the diligent shall be made fat." (faith) K.J.V. Where there is faith there is activity.

FAITH IF IT EXISTS SHOWS ITSELF

"Shew me thy faith without thy works." James was asking the impossible because faith cannot be seen without works. Jesus confirmed this when it was said, "When Jesus saw their faith, He said unto the sick of the palsy, Son thy sins be forgiven thee." K.J.V.
Was this not the reason Christ said, **"Wherefore by their fruits ye shall know them?"** Matthew 7:-20. K.J.V.

Faith is like life itself, it cannot be said to exist without some kind of action or movement. It cannot exist without expressing itself.

FAITH AFFECTS THE MIND, WILL AND EMOTIONS

Faith involves the **intellect, emotion, and the will,** as illustrated in Hebrews 11:-7: "By faith Noah, being warned of God," **intellect enlightened,** "moved with fear"- **emotions stirred**, "prepared an ark"- **the will exercised**.

WE ARE NOT SAVED BY WORKS PRODUCED BY FAITH

We are not saved, nor can we ever be saved by the works of faith, "For with the heart man believeth unto righteousness," but by trust in Christ, since the works of faith in anyone's life are incomplete and imperfect, but the works that must show themselves, if faith exists, are proof or evidence that it is faith and not just wishful thinking.

The perfect Righteousness of Christ is imputed to us when we believe in

Christ that He is the Son of God and died for us and rose again from the dead; and the life of Christ is evidenced in our life by the Lord working out His life through us. If some of this imputed righteousness is not evidenced through the recipient, it is unlikely it has been imputed.

WE ARE ALL ON THE SAME LEVEL: SINNERS SAVED BY GRACE

There is no such thing as a first, second or third class Christian, so far as salvation is concerned, for the mature and godliest saint who has walked with the Lord for fifty or more years is as dependent upon the blood of Christ and the Grace of our dear Lord, for the forgiveness of his sins, as is the new convert. To put it another way we are all in the same lifeboat.

THOSE THINGS THAT ACCOMPANY SALVATION

In Hebrews 6:-9 we read of those things that accompany salvation, "But, beloved, we are confident of better things concerning you, yes things that accompany salvation, though we speak in this manner." The N.K.J.V.

"I am confident that you are producing the good fruit that comes along with your salvation." The same verse from The Living Bible.
The validity of the faith that saves is clearly seen in the production of a changed life. Jesus said "Ye shall know them by their fruits." Matthew 7:-16. K.J.V.

An acquiescent belief or mental acceptance of the truth of the gospel is not sufficient although it is necessary and is a step in the right direction, but it is the belief of the heart that saves, the faith that produces repentance.
Peter preached, "Repent ye therefore and be converted that your sins may be blotted out." Acts 3:-19.

A MODERN ILLUSTRATION

A church elder in a country church in Scotland attended a tent mission, and his life was changed. Sometime after the mission his grandson was stopped on the street by someone who asked him; "What has happened to your grand-daddy, he seems changed since the mission?"
The wee boy answered, "he has had his religion moved eighteen inches." What on earth do you mean by that? The boy replied, "he has had it moved fae his heid tae his heirt." (from his head to his heart).
When we believe in our heart, that is the faith that saves and it is seen by everybody because it brings about repentance.

CHAPTER 20

ELECTION TO SALVATION, FOREKNOWLEDGE, PREDESTINATION.

The writer W. J. Seaton, a Baptist minister, in his booklet called "The five points of Calvinism", under the heading of "Unconditional Election," states: "What was the doctrine that Jesus preached in the synagogue at Nazareth but the doctrine of the Unconditional Election?
'And I tell you, many widows were in Israel in the days of Elias...but unto none of them was Elias sent save unto a woman of Sarepta...and many lepers were in Israel in the days of Eliseus...and none of them was cleansed saving Naaman the Syrian." [Luke 4.25 - 27].
"We know the outcome of our Lord's preaching of that message.
'They led him to the brow of the hill that they might cast him down headlong.' "He also tells us, "Election is not on account of our believing but our believing is on account of our being Elected... 'Ordained to eternal life' [Acts 13:- 48]."

WERE NOT THE JEWISH PEOPLE CHOSEN (Elected) BY GOD?

How can he speak of these two incidents as "Unconditional Election" when the nation of Israel at the time of the two prophets were The Lord's (elected) Chosen People, as were the Pharisees and Jews to whom Jesus was speaking.
Psalm 105:- 6, "O ye children of Abraham His servant, ye children of Jacob His Chosen." K.J.V.
Deuteronomy 7:- 6, "For thou art a holy people unto the Lord thy God: the Lord thy God hath **chosen thee to be a special people** unto Himself, above all people that are upon the face of the earth." K.J.V.

GOD'S ELECTED PEOPLE REJECTED GOD'S PLAN FOR THEM!

The people Jesus was speaking to in Luke 4:- 25 -27, were God's Chosen people the Israelites, they did not believe because they were elected (or chosen) they rejected Christ and His salvation.
In Luke 7:- 30, we are told: "But the Pharisees and the lawyers [of the Mosaic Law] annulled and rejected and brought to nothing God's purpose concerning themselves, by [refusing and] not being baptized by [John]." The Amplified New Testament.

Later on in the book of Acts chapter 13:-46, the chosen Jews again reject the gospel message preached by the apostles. "Then Paul and Barnabas waxed bold, and said, It was necessary that the word of God should first have been spoken to you: but seeing ye put it from you, and judge yourselves unworthy of everlasting life, lo, we turn to the Gentiles." K.J.V.
Why was it "necessary" that God's message should be spoken to the Jews first? Was it not because they were God's special chosen (elected) people?
It would appear that, although the Lord chose the children of Israel, they had not chosen or elected to follow and obey the Lord.
To say that because a person is elected he will automatically believe in Christ is nonsense.

GOD'S WILL IS THAT THE WORLD SHOULD BE SAVED!

In John 3:-16-17, God chose (elected) the world to be saved.
Verse 17 says: "For God sent not His Son into the world to condemn the world; but that the world through Him might be saved." K.J.V.

"And He – that same Jesus Himself – is the propitiation (the atoning sacrifice) for our sins, and not for ours alone **but also for [the sins of] the whole world."** 1 John 2:-2. The Amplified New Testament.
The Lord Jesus in John 3:-16-17, and in 1 John 2:-2, is comprehensive in His election of those to be saved.
It is through the atoning sacrifice that Christ elects, although this is All Embracing, its outworking and effectiveness is Conditional on believing.
God has chosen (elected) the world to be saved and His Son made the atonement with His own blood.
JESUS WAS HIGHLIGHTING THE FAITH OF THE UNELECTED

The key verse to understanding the two incidents mentioned in the passage quoted is verse 24: "And He (Jesus) said, Verily I say unto you, No prophet is accepted in his own country." K.J.V.
Both of the miraculous incidents mentioned in the verses he quoted were performed on people who **were not numbered among the Chosen of Israel. This was the very point the Lord was underlining.**
But they were among the despised, and detested, the unclean pigs and dogs of Gentiles, and it was the impartiality of Jesus, and His **commendation** of the Unelected Gentile's Faith that infuriated the Pharisees.
I quote, "We know the outcome of our Lord's preaching of that message.

'They led him to the brow of the hill that they might cast him down headlong.'"
Unlike the Chosen of Israel they believed and trusted the word of the prophet of the Lord. This was the reason the Jews were so angry with Christ. **So it was the unelected who believed, which is the opposite of what pastor Seaton claims.**
How much further can you go than the very opposite of what the Lord Jesus taught?

FAITH: THE HAND THAT TAKES IMPUTED RIGHTEOUSNESS

Paul, the apostle, speaks about this same factor (faith) in Romans 9:-30-32, when speaking about the Jews and the Gentiles.
"Those who are not Jews were not trying to make themselves right with God, but they were made right with God because of their faith. The people of Israel tried to follow a law to make themselves right with God. But they did not succeed, because they tried to make themselves right by the things they did **instead of trusting in God to make them right**." Romans 9:-30-32. N.C.V.
If you put these texts, Luke 4:-25-27, in their context, you will find that Jesus was not teaching "Unconditional Election," **for such a thing does not exist except in the minds of Calvinists,** and there is no Scriptural basis for this. In fact the opposite is true.

THE CALLING OF ABRAHAM AS UNCONDITIONAL ELECTION

I quote from the same article by W.J.Seaton, "The story of the Bible is the story of unconditional election. It is strange that those who oppose themselves to this doctrine fail to recognise this."
"Some believers have difficulty in believing that God could pass by some and choose others, and yet they have no apparent difficulty in believing that God called Abraham out of heathen Ur of the Chaldees and left others to their heathenism".
The inference the "Pastor" makes is, that Abraham was heathen, before God called him, and that God's call was "Unconditional Election" (choice) on the part of the Lord.
Acts 7:-2, "The God of glory appeared to our Father Abraham when he was in Mesopotamia, before he dwelt in Haran." N.K.J.V.
Was Jacob, Moses, Gideon, David or Solomon heathen before God appeared

to them? It is sheer speculative presumption to assume that God arbitrarily chose Abraham, when he has no biblical evidence for this.

THE BIBLE REVEALS THAT ABRAHAM CAME FROM A GODLY FAMILY

In Genesis 31:-53, Jacob said to his uncle Laban, "The God of Abraham, and the God of Nahor, the God of their fathers, judge betwixt us." K.J.V.

"Let the God of Abraham, who is the God of Nahor and the God of their fathers, punish either of us if we break this agreement." Genesis 31:-53. N.C.V.

Nahor was a brother of Abraham, and their father's name was Terah. Abraham's grandfather was also called Nahor.

Abraham's brother Haran's son, Lot, was referred to as "A Just and a righteous man," in 2 Peter 2:-7-8.

It would appear from Scripture that Abraham came from a godly family, and was familiar with and had knowledge of God and was not one of the heathen, as his suggestion would infer.

If Abraham only got to know God when He appeared to him and called him out of the Ur of the Chaldees, then the same would have to be true of all the rest of the family. So Abraham, Nahor, Haran, Lot, and Terah were all worshippers of the true God. Why did Abraham send his servant to get a wife for Isaac from among his own people?

Was it not that he wanted Isaac to marry a believer and not a heathen girl?

WHAT FOREKNOWLEDGE MEANS ACCORDING TO CALVINISTS

Regarding Romans 8:-29-30, "For whom He did foreknow, He also did predestinate to be conformed to the image of His Son,...Moreover whom He did predestinate, them He also called: and whom He called, them He also justified: and whom He justified, them He also glorified."

1 Peter 1:-2, "Elect" (chosen) "according to the foreknowledge of God the Father, through sanctification of the Spirit." K.J.V.

W. J. Seaton informs us that, "God's foreknowledge is spoken of in connection with a people and not in connection with any action which people performed."

What Scriptural basis has he for such a statement?

FOREKNOWLEDGE HAS TO DO WITH PEOPLES' ACTIVITY OR LACK OF IT

All the statements made by the Lord Jesus pertaining to what was going to happen to individuals or groups of people had to do with what they had done or omitted to do, and the subsequent consequences. Here are a few examples of many in the Gospels. In Matthew 11:- 20 - 22 we read, "Then began He (Jesus) to upbraid the cities wherein most of His mighty works were done, **because they repented not**: Woe unto thee, Chorazin! woe unto thee, Bethsaida! for if the mighty works, which were done in you, had been done in Tyre and Sidon, **they would have repented long ago in sackcloth and ashes."**
"But I say unto you, It shall be more tolerable for Tyre and Sidon at the Day of Judgment, than for you." K.J.V.
Matthew 11:- 23 -24, "And thou, Capernaum, which art exalted unto heaven, shalt be brought down to hell: for if the mighty works, which have been done in thee, had been done in Sodom, **it would have remained until this day."**
"But I say unto you, That it shall be more tolerable for the Land of Sodom in the day of judgement, than for thee." K.J.V.

IT WAS THE UNELECTED WHO BELIEVED

Note. Tyre, Sidon and Sodom were Gentile cities. They were not among the chosen people, and yet the Lord tells us they would have done what they, the chosen people should have done but failed to do, and that was to believe that Jesus was the Christ and Son of God, and to repent of their sins. **Again, highlighting the faith of the unelected, and the lack of trust and obedience of the chosen people of God.**

In Matthew 10:- 42, "And whosoever shall give to drink unto one of these little ones a cup of cold water only in the name of a disciple, verily I say unto you, he shall in no wise lose his reward." K.J.V.
Also in Matthew 26:- 34, "Jesus said unto him (Peter), Verily I say unto thee, That this night, before the cock crow, thou shalt deny Me thrice." K.J.V.
In the Old Testament, in Isaiah 57 and the first verse we are told why God very often takes the righteous from the earth. "The righteous perisheth, and no man layeth it to heart: and merciful men are taken away, none considering **that the righteous is taken away from the evil to come."** K.J.V.
The foreknowledge (which is prevision) of God most certainly has to do

with what men will or will not do, and it is purely wishful thinking to believe otherwise.

CALVINISTS EQUATE FOREKNOWLEDGE WITH PREDESTINATION

The word election is employed freely as a substitute for the word predestination, or as meaning exactly the same, from a different viewpoint. The reasoning behind this is to establish the doctrine of variableness as a characteristic of God, when God is invariable in nature.

Romans 9 is referred to as confirming this, and the text so frequently and triumphantly quoted as conclusive evidence, is: "As it is written Jacob have I loved, but Esau have I hated."

The choice of Jacob to be the father of God's people Israel instead of Esau, was the consequence of foreknowledge (prevision) and not predestination. This is clear if you read the Genesis account of the two brothers. (This is covered more fully in another chapter in this book).

THEY HAVE TO REVERSE THE BIBLICAL ORDER TO SUIT THEIR THESIS

The dogmatic five point Calvinist, in order to accommodate his doctrine, has to reverse the Biblical order in 1 Peter 1:-2, from that of, **"Elect according to the foreknowledge of God" to that of "Foreknowledge according to the election of God."**

And they equate foreknowledge with predestination, which is wrong.

The Calvinist author, when speaking about God in another publication, makes the statement: "He knows, and foreknows, all things, and his foreknowledge is foreordination."

But Calvin himself put it the opposite way round, "God foresees future events only by reason of the fact that he decrees that they take place."

Although the consequences of both statements are the same, the end result is stoical and in line with Muslim teaching which is basically fatalistic. It is preordained. "What is for you will not go past you!" "If your number is on it, you will be sure to get it." "Our destiny is written in the stars": so believe the modern day pagans, when the first thing they look at in their tabloid newspaper is the horoscope.

QUESTIONS PROVOKED BY IRREVOCABLE PREDESTINATION

What is the purpose of Prayer, when every individual has been foreordained to suffer the pains of hell, **not for any wrong he has done,** or else is eternally blessed in heaven, not for any good he has done?

What use is there in prayer if our destiny has already been decided and that unalterably?

If, as the Calvinists say, salvation of the elect is absolutely unconditional, then without the Gospel the elect are already saved.

The preaching of the Gospel to the elect would be superfluous to their salvation and would be of no help to the unelected who are damned already.

What is the purpose of the Final Judgment when from all eternity every individual man's status and condition has been fixed and that irrevocably so?

Augustine and Calvin's doctrine turns the Judgment day into something meaningless.

What essential obligation is there to morality when all man's accomplishments have been predetermined?

If man's life is foreordained to be what he demonstrates it to be, why in plain justice, should he be punished in this or the next world for Theft, Lies, Adultery, Dishonesty, Murder, or any other sin?

No matter how much they surround their arguments with clouds of verbiage, the advocates of unchangeable predestination cannot escape the clear conclusion that, **if it is accepted, then human responsibility ceases to exist.**

THE DOCTRINE OF FOREORDINATION A THREAT TO MORALS

Augustine, Bishop of Hippo, was forced to admit that the doctrine of Predestination was a danger to morals and, as a result his advice was that it should be preached with restraint. Augustine mentioned in his writings (De Dono Perseverantice) of a monk known to him who committed some misdemeanour and who, when brought to account for this and reprimanded, replied: "Whatever I am now that God had predestined that I should be."

Augustine commented, "This man certainly did say what was true."

MAKE YOUR CALLING AND ELECTION SURE

W. J. Seaton writes as follows: "Surely, instead of arguing against these things, we should be doing what the Holy Spirit through the apostle Peter commands us to do: 'Give diligence to make your calling and election sure.'"

How do you make your calling and election sure, if as they say, we are Unconditionally Elected to salvation by God and we play no part in this whatsoever? As he says on the same page, "Election is not on account of our believing, but our believing is on account of our being elected – 'ordained to eternal life.'"

According to their doctrine it is God, not we, who makes sure our calling and election and it has nothing whatsoever to do with man!

To quote from the Westminster Confession of Faith, **"Some men and angels are Predestinated unto everlasting life, and others fore-ordained to everlasting death." That God, "Unchangeably ordains whatsoever comes to pass."**

There could be nothing more fatalistic than the above statement!

CHAPTER 21

FOREKNOWLEDGE IN SCRIPTURE COMES BEFORE PREDESTINATION

In the Chambers Biographical Dictionary when speaking about James Arminius, it says: "Selected to defend Beza's doctrine of predestination, he soon came to adopt the opinions he had been commissioned to refute. Arminius asserted 'that God bestows forgiveness and eternal life on all who repent of their sins and believe in Christ; He wills that all men attain salvation, and only because He has from eternity foreseen the belief or unbelief of individuals, has He from eternity determined the fate of each – Thus rejecting the high Calvinistic doctrine of absolute predestination or election."

GOD PREDESTINES GOOD OR BAD BEHAVIOUR: NOT MEN

Foreknowledge is not predestination, but from man's point of view foreknowledge (prevision) is being forewarned of decisions and actions the results of which are predetermined by God to lead to destruction or conversely decisions and actions foreordained by God which will lead to life. It is man's actions that determine his predestination either to Life or destruction. In Jeremiah 26:-13 it says: "Now therefore, amend your ways and your doings, and obey the voice of the Lord your God; **Then the Lord will relent concerning the doom that He has pronounced against you."** N.K.J.V.

All who will trust and believe in Christ are predestined to salvation and because of God's foreknowledge He knows who will trust Christ.

It is the result of the action people take that is predetermined, not the people themselves. They are not foreordained as the Calvinists believe to take that action, and there is no Scriptural basis for this belief. Foreknowledge along with predestination can only exist in the context of time, and can only be comprehended in the same framework.

THE JEWISH BELIEF IN CONDITIONAL PREDESTINATION

Unlike Augustine and Calvin's irrevocable predestination, which was pagan in its origin, and anti-Jewish, because conditional predestination was a doctrine held by the Hebrews and approved and adopted by the early

Christian Church. So this is truly an apostolic doctrine.
They believed that God laid down the general lines of a man's life, decided where and when he should be born and in what social situation, along with his inherited capabilities, and faculties. But it has been left to man's free will to use and profit by what God has placed at his disposal. The Lord Jesus illustrated this in the parable of the Talents and the Pounds!

CONDITIONAL PREDESTINATION ILLUSTRATED IN THE STORY OF NINEVEH

We have an example of conditional predestination in the story of Jonah. The Lord issued through Jonah a decree of destruction against Nineveh, yet He reversed that decree, because He saw that the people of Nineveh repented in sackcloth and ashes. So the destruction of the Ninevites which was their destiny, decreed by God, was changed because the circumstances changed, due to the Ninevites repenting of their wickedness. So this makes it clear that it was the results of their behaviour that was predestined and not them.

A PROMISED DECREE OF BLESSING STOPPED BECAUSE OF SIN

God dealt with the Israelites in the same way as He did with the Gentiles, and there was no favouritism on the part of God because they were His chosen people and His decrees and promises were conditional.
In 1 Samuel 2:-30-31: "So the Lord, the God of Israel, says: 'I promised that your family and your ancestor's family would serve me always.' But now the Lord says: **'This must stop! I will honour those who honour Me, but I will dishonour those who ignore Me.** The time is coming when I will destroy the descendants of both you and your ancestors." N.C.V.

ZEDEKIAH'S PREDESTINED CHOICE OF GOOD OR EVIL

When King Zedekiah, during the siege of Jerusalem asked Jeremiah's counsel and what God would have him do, Jeremiah replied: "'This is what **the Lord God All powerful**, the God of Israel says: 'if you surrender to the officers of the king of Babylon, your life will be saved. **Jerusalem will not be burnt down and you and your family will live.** But if you refuse to surrender to the officers of the king of Babylon, Jerusalem will be handed over to the Babylonian army and they will burn it down. And you yourself

will not escape from them.'" Jer 38:-17-18. N.C.V.
The decree was set out for Zedekiah. It was his choice; if he surrendered he and his family and the city would be saved, but if he did not he would suffer the consequences. The result of Zedekiah's choice is found in
Chapter 39:-6-7.
"At Riblah the king of Babylon killed Zedekiah's sons and all the important officers of Judah as Zedekiah watched. Then he put out Zedekiah's eyes. He put bronze chains on Zedekiah and took him to Babylon." N.C.V.
Zedekiah's destiny along with his family's and the city of Jerusalem were due entirely to his decision, because it was the result of this decision that was predestined, and he had foreknowledge of this. It was the result of what Zedekiah did that was predestined, not his family, the city, or himself.

ANOTHER EXAMPLE OF CONDITIONAL PREDESTINATION.

After the murder of Gedaliah and his company by Ishmael son of Nethaniah, the remnant of the Israelites who survived came to Jeremiah and asked him to pray to the Lord for them, "So pray that the Lord your God will tell us where we should go and what we should do." N.C.V. Jer 42:-3. They also vowed solemnly to do whatever God told them to do. Jer 42:-5-6. God told them through Jeremiah to stay in Israel and all would be well. But if they went down to Egypt, "Then it shall come to pass, that the sword, which ye feared, shall overtake you there in the land of Egypt and the famine whereof ye were afraid, shall follow close after you there in Egypt; and there ye shall die." Jer 42:-16. K.J.V.
They broke their word and went to Egypt and suffered the consequences. The full story is found in Jeremiah 42 to 44.
They themselves were not foreordained to destruction by God, but the outcome of their actions were, and again they had foreknowledge of this. There is life eternal for those who accept and trust Christ, but those who reject Him will perish. John 1:-12 and 3:-16.

GOD'S GRACE SHOWN TO WICKED AHAB BECAUSE HE HUMBLED HIMSELF

Another example of God's decree being changed although this time not a complete reversal, is found in 1 Kings 21 and from verse 17 to the end of the chapter. I quote from verse 25 to 29, which was part of the message
Elijah was given by God to give to Ahab. "But there was none like unto

Ahab, which did sell himself to work wickedness in the sight of the Lord, whom Jezebel his wife stirred up. And he did very abominably in following idols, according to all things as did the Amorites, whom the Lord cast out before the children of Israel. And it came to pass, when Ahab heard those words, that he rent his clothes, and put sackcloth upon his flesh, and fasted, and lay in sackcloth, and went softly. And the word of the Lord came to Elijah the Tishbite saying, Seest thou how Ahab humbleth himself before me? **Because he humbleth himself before Me, I will not bring the evil in his days:** but in his son's days will I bring the evil upon his house." K.J.V. **The Lord changes his decree because "Ahab is now sorry for what he has done."** Verse 29. N.C.V.

A DECREE REVERSION BECAUSE OF THE KING AND LEADERS REPENTING

In 2 Chron 12:-5 -7 we find another instance of Conditional Predestination when a decree of destruction from God through the prophet Shemaiah is reversed because of the repentance of the leaders and the king of Israel. Shemaiah informs Rehoboam, "This is what the Lord says: 'You have left me, so now I will leave you to face Shishak alone.'" 'Then the leaders of Judah and King Rehoboam were sorry for what they had done. They said, 'The Lord does what is right.' When the Lord saw that they were sorry for what they had done, the Lord spoke his word to Shemaiah, saying, 'The King and the leaders are sorry. **So I will not destroy them but will save them soon. I will not use Shishak to punish them in My anger."** N.C.V. The decree of death and destruction issued by God through Shemaiah to Rehoboam was changed due to God's mercy being shown in response to their decision and action to repent. Thus proving along with the other examples expounded from Scripture that **the decrees of God are not irrevocable.** It is the result of things we do or omit to do that is predestined and not people. Conditional Predestination is Scriptural, and was taught by the Jews and accepted by the early Church.

GOD CHANGES HIS DECREE OF DEATH IN ANSWER TO PRAYER

Isaiah said to king Hezekiah. **"Thus saith the Lord, set thy house in order; for thou shalt die, and not live.** Then he turned his face to the wall, and prayed unto the Lord, saying. I beseech thee, O Lord remember now how I have walked before Thee in truth and with a perfect heart, and have done that

which is good in Thy sight. **And Hezekiah wept sore."**
Before Isaiah had gone out of the king's courtyard the Lord spoke to him and sent him back to Hezekiah **with a changed decree.** "Thus saith the Lord, the God of David thy father, **I have heard thy prayer, I have seen thy tears:** behold I will heal thee: on the third day thou shalt go up unto the house of the Lord. And I will add unto thy days fifteen years." 2 Kings 20:-1-2-3-5-6. K.J.V. Clearly the decrees of God are not irrevocable and on occasions can be changed through prayer.
There are other instances in the Old Testament, which could be cited.

CHRIST TAUGHT CONDITIONAL PREDESTINATION

Conditional Predestination is found also in the teaching of Christ. Jesus said, "And thou Capernaum, which art exalted unto heaven, shalt be brought down to hell: for if the mighty works, which have been done in thee, had been done in Sodom, it would have remained until this day." Matthew 11:-23. K.J.V.
Why was it decreed by the Lord Jesus that Capernaum would be cast into hell? Because they would not repent, and if they had repented the decree would have been reversed. Given the same opportunity as Capernaum the Sodomites would have believed and repented and thus the sentence of Judgment would not have been executed on them. **"Sodom, it would have remained until this day."**

So Predestination in Scripture is quite clearly conditional.

THE ELECT ARE CORPORATE NOT PARTICULAR AND ONLY EXIST AS ELECT "IN CHRIST" WHO IS THE ELECT OF GOD

Election and predestination in Scripture are always understood "In Christ" which is corporate, and not particular.
All who are outside of Christ are **elected to salvation**, but we are the elect **only "In Christ"** (when we believe in Christ) **For Christ is the elect of God. "Behold My Servant Whom I have chosen, My Beloved in and with Whom My soul is well pleased and has found its delight."**
The Amplified New Testament. Matthew 12:-18.

"In Christ we were chosen to be God's people." Eph 1:-11. N.C.V.

No one is ever chosen before they are in Christ and we are only in Christ when we believe in Him. In other words Scripture never tells us that we are chosen for salvation (that is to be in Christ) before we believe in Him, or that God has predestined us to believe in Christ! **Christ is the Elect of God** and we become also among the elect only when we believe in Him.

UNDERSTANDING WHO ARE REFERED TO IN THE PERSONAL PRONOUNS

I believe to get a correct appreciation of many passages in Scripture including Ephesians 1:-3-6, depends entirely on how one understands the personal pronouns, " We" and "Us". Both of these pronouns in this passage refer to believers in Christ.* In legal documents a noun is often used instead of a pronoun in order to avoid any misunderstanding, and if we substitute the appropriate noun, which is "believers", for the pronouns, we shall see quite clearly that the reference is not to certain individuals being predestinated to salvation, but to **believers being predestinated to adoption,** to wit, the redemption of our body" (Romans 8:-23.)

*In the following passage I have put the appropriate noun, which is believers, in brackets beside the pronoun, to illustrate my point.

"Blessed be the God and Father of our Lord Jesus Christ, who hath blessed" (believers) "us with all spiritual blessings in heavenly places **In Christ:** According as **He hath chosen"** (believers) **"us in Him before the foundation of the world**, that" (believers) "we should be holy and without blame before Him in love: Having predestinated" (believers) **"us unto the adoption of children** by Jesus Christ to Himself, according to the good pleasure of His will, To the praise of the glory of His grace, wherein He has made" (believers) "us accepted in the beloved." Ephesians 1:-3-6. K.J.V.

The expression "in Christ" or its equivalent, occurs no less than ten times in the first thirteen verses, and is the key to the understanding of the passage. Who are "We?" Those "Who first trusted in Christ" (verse 12); and when did we join that number? "After that ye believed" (verse 13).

*The elect are always referred to in the plural: not as individuals, but as a class, and no one is among the elect until that person believes in Christ. The elect are seen "In Christ" only because of the foreknowledge (Prevision) of God.

A young man joins the army, and six months later his regiment is posted to Northern Ireland, a move, which had been decided upon by the War Office six months before the young man joined. The recruit could say quite truthfully:

"It was decided a year ago that we should be posted here," but he could

not say, "I", because at the time he had not enlisted.
"Elect" does not mean "elected", or we should have to include the Lord Jesus (1 Peter 2:-6.) **"Behold, I lay in Sion a chief corner stone, elect, Precious:" And the angels** (1 Timothy 5:-21)
"I charge thee before God,.....and the elect angels." We are only **"elect"** when we are "In Christ," **who is God's Elect.**

"He hath chosen" (believers) "us in Him before the foundation of the world." Ephesians 1:4 K.J.V.

FOREKNOWLEDGE MEANS TO KNOW IN ADVANCE

To facilitate their unscriptural doctrine on election the Calvinists have to change the universally accepted meaning of the word Foreknowledge, to mean something other than knowing in advance, or they say foreknowledge equals predestination. 2 Peter 3:-17, clearly illustrates the fact that foreknowledge is not predestination. "Ye therefore, beloved, seeing ye know these things before, beware lest ye also, being led away with the error of the wicked, **fall from your own steadfastness"**. K.J.V.
Foreknowledge helps us avoid the Predestined Results of sin.

WHO ARE THE CHOSEN REFERED TO IN JOHN 15:-16?

Another Scripture which is misapplied and, because of this, is misunderstood is John 15:-16: "Ye have not chosen me, but I have chosen you, and ordained you, that ye should go and bring forth fruit, and that your fruit should remain." K.J.V.
This was spoken by the Lord Jesus only to the eleven disciples on their way from the upper room to the garden of Gethsemane.
Earlier in John 6:-70-71, He had said: "Have I not chosen you twelve, and one of you is a devil? He spake of Judas, being one of the twelve." In Luke 6:-13 it tells us: "He called unto Him his disciples, and of them He chose twelve, whom He named apostles," and Mark 3:-14: "He ordained twelve." K.J.V.
Calvin writes in his Institutes: "He elsewhere numbers Judas among the elect, although he 'is a devil.' **This refers only to the office of apostles,** which...still does not contain in itself the hope of eternal salvation."
Yet in the very same chapter he states: "We therefore find Christ's statement to His disciples, 'You did not choose me, but I have chosen you' **generally**

valid among all believers."

Such contradictions and inconsistencies in his own teaching are common in Calvin's writings and also among the writings of his followers.

THE RESULT OF FALSE TEACHING

Recently a friend and fellow Evangelist told me he was teaching a group of children and gave an invitation for anyone who wanted to accept Christ and become a Christian to speak to him after the meeting. A boy of thirteen did come forward to speak and told him that, "we do not choose Christ but that Christ chooses us and we have to wait until He calls us and gives us eternal life."

Once again a soul has been hoodwinked out of his salvation and put into the straitjacket of Calvin's erroneous and sterile doctrine!

"He came to what was His own, yet His own folk did not welcome Him. **On those who have accepted Him, however, He has conferred the right of being children of God."** John 1:-11-12. J.M.V.

"Him that cometh to Me I will in no wise cast out." John 6:-37. K.J.V.

"And if anyone hears My words and does not believe, I do not judge him; for I do not come to judge the world but to save the world. **He who rejects Me,** and does not receive My words, has that which judges him – the word that I have spoken will judge him in the last day." John 12:-47-48. N.K.J.V.

Believing is Receiving.

"Whereby are given unto us Exceeding Great and Precious promises: **that by these ye might be partakers of the Divine nature.**" 2 Peter 1:-4 K.J.V.

Partaking is something that we do.

FOREKNOWLEDGE IS NOT FOREORDINATION NOR PREDESTINATION

A number of years ago we were told through the media that if we looked up into a certain part of the sky on a particular day and time we would be able to see Haley's comet, weather permitting.

The men of science with great accuracy had the foreknowledge of the day and time the comet would appear, but their foreknowledge was not foreordination, in fact they had nothing to do with the comet's emergence, nor could they have prevented its appearance.

CHAPTER 22

ANOTHER WAY OF LOOKING AT THINGS

Though there are other theories, possibly the most widely held view of space and the universe is that of a vast endless expanse which is the home of innumerable galaxies containing stars, and planets, which have their being and activity within it, and time is looked upon as a continuous line in which countless events have and are and will take place, and they are considered as Absolutes and not as a concept. They are conceived as not being part of nature but rather as an everlasting receptacle of nature.
Cosmology from a Christian standpoint would be that all the universe and the concept of time and space are part of nature and dependant upon God.
Albert Einstein in his theory of relativity brought a better understanding of space and time, for he formulated the belief that time is not an absolute.

ALL EXISTENCE, PAST, PRESENT, AND FUTURE, IS SIMULTANEOUS TO GOD

So far as man is concerned there is no such thing in his experience, as a universal **"now"** which could apply to all existence, past, present and future, because of his place in time and space.
If objects are moving at a very high speed relative to each other, at velocities nearing the speed of light, their time frames are altogether different.
At the speed of light time would stand still, which would mean that one could live forever. Accordingly if one were able to exceed the velocity of light one would go back in time.
Space and time together are referred to scientifically as "The space-time continuum" (in which we live etc.).
Albert Einstein believed that the velocity of light was an absolute and therefore could not be exceeded.

SCIENTISTS QUESTION THE SPEED OF LIGHT BEING AN ABSOLUTE

At the present time some scientists have questioned whether the speed of light is absolute and cannot be exceeded.
There is thought that there may be something like a light barrier.
The speed that light travels at, is said to be 186,000 miles per second.

It is also believed that no material could exist, as such, once it reached the speed of light, as it would change into pure energy, which as light would be everlasting.
Note. Einstein believed the universe to be curved, but recently his findings have been brought into question, because of experiments which have found the universe to be flat and expansion going on infinitely.

PROBLEMS WITH SPACE TRAVEL AT SPEEDS NEARING THAT OF LIGHT

If the possibility ever existed for men to be launched into space in vehicles able to travel at speeds nearing that of light to investigate part of the universe, and their travelling was of a brief length of time (that is so far as the astronauts were concerned), so that what appeared to the astronauts to be just a few days, they would find when they returned that the earth had aged thousands of years, and their families, homes, and neighbourhoods and what had been so familiar to them would have been lost in the distant past, **although they themselves were only a few days older.**
One day travelling out into space at a velocity approaching that of light, and one day back, would in our earth time be approximately **Equivalent to two thousand years.**

WITH THE LORD ONE DAY IS AS A THOUSAND YEARS

In 2 Peter 3:-8. "But beloved, be not ignorant of this one thing, **that one day is with the Lord as a thousand years, and a thousand years as one day."** K.J.V.
The Bible tells us in 1 John 1:-5, "God is light and in Him is no darkness at all." K.J.V.
"For a thousand years in Thy sight are but as yesterday when it is past, and as a watch in the night." Psalm 90:-4. K.J.V.
Although, so far as man is concerned, there is no universal "NOW", which would apply to all existence, this is not true of God.
Jesus said to the Pharisees in John 8:-58, "Before Abraham was, I AM". The ever present (Now) I AM.
All past and future are one and **a universal now** (I AM) to God.
*Because God views the world from a different perspective and is not locked into time and space like man, but is in a different dimension, and what man views as past and future, **is to the Lord an ever present now."**

As we are creatures of time, God has to speak to us in the context of time which is understandable to us; so when the terms, **"Foreknowledge," "Predestination"** are used, they do not imply that God "Foreordains" all things in the same way and sense that Calvinists and Muslims believe.

But God has given man the ability to choose, and in spite of all that man does against the will of God, and because He is Sovereign, He overrules and uses it for His own purpose.
The crucifixion of Christ is an example.
NOTE, When Adam and Eve were in the Garden of Eden, God was in this sinless couple, and pervaded every part of their being, **and yet the Lord gave them the ability to choose.** They were not robotic.

We read in God's Word, in Revelation 13:8, **"The lamb slain from the foundation of the world."** K.J.V., and in Ephesians 1:- 4: "He chose" (believers) "us as His own in Christ before the foundation of the world."
R. F. Weymouth Translation.

HOW THE LORD GOD ALMIGHTY LOOKS AT THINGS

Christ's atoning sacrifice on the cross is an ever present fact to the Lord, as it was even from the creation of the world, just as the trust of believers and the absence of trust in unbelievers. All **things past** and **future** are an ever present **"now"** to the **Great I AM**. See note 2.
Consequently God's election to salvation and eternal life of those who believe could not be before their earthly existence or prior to their faith in Christ, just as Christ's crucifixion could not come before His incarnation and earthly ministry.
Rev 13:- 8 "The lamb slain from the foundation of the world."

THE CRUCIFIXION IS NOT ISOLATED FROM THE REST OF CHRIST'S LIFE

The crucifixion cannot be separated from the incarnation and earthly work of the Lord Jesus Christ, and made an isolated fact as most of us are inclined to do in our thinking, when looking at Rev 13:- 8.
If the slaying of Christ was "From the foundation of the world", so were all the other events, the incarnation, and the different stages and development of the life and work of Christ, the miracles and the lives of all who were

touched by the life of Christ. The perfect life of the Lord Jesus on earth, as well as His ministry were all necessary for the salvation of mankind, and culminated in the Crucifixion, Resurrection and Ascension of our Lord.
If this is so, then it necessarily follows that each person's whole life, with all its decisions, mistakes, joys and grief, belief or unbelief in Christ from the cradle to the grave in God's sight are all one unabridged present happening, even from the foundation of the world, no matter in what century one may happen to sojourn in time, and because of this understanding of how God views things, both foreknowledge and predestination, which can only exist and be understood in the framework of time is a resultant factor as, I believe, Scripture clearly states and does not predispose or influence in any way the freedom of men's actions, or contravene their ability in making choices. All the past and future is an ever present now to the Great I AM.

THERE IS NO HISTORY WITH GOD AND HE HAS NO HISTORY

Because God is the Great I AM, with God there is no such thing as history and God has no history. The I AM is eternal and in Him is eternity.
Eternity is certainly not to be understood as Calvinists constantly insist, as the endless existence of time!
Eternity is a different dimension wherein exists the spiritual .

We have eternal life only when we have Christ, for in Him is Eternal Life. The material universe is transitory and will pass away, but the unseen spiritual universe is eternal.
"And this is the record, that God has given to us eternal life, and this life is in His Son. He that hath the Son hath life; and he that hath not the Son of God hath not life." 1 John 5:-11-12. K.J.V.

ETERNITY CANNOT BE SPENT

Eternity cannot be spent, because it has nothing whatsoever to do with time. Time has to do with the material universe, those things, which can be seen, and the things that are seen are transitory and only temporary. "For the things which are seen are temporal; but the things which are not seen are eternal." 2 Cor 4:-18. K.J.V.
But in time we spend our life. Our being really consists of our becoming, a travelling along the line of time leaving behind yesterday and in so doing part of ourselves and looking forward to the morrow. God does not

remember what we did last month or last year, or foresee what we will do tomorrow and next month, because from His dimension, which is outside of time, He clearly and simply sees us doing them. In the Lord's sight the whole of our life is seen to Him in Parallel and is complete, but in the truest sense, God knows our actions only when we have done them.
It has to do with the I AM-NESS OF GOD, THAT ALL THINGS PAST PRESENT, AND FUTURE ARE AN EVER PRESENT NOW TO THE LORD ALMIGHTY.

Note 2,

THE TESTIMONY OF A MAN WHO WENT TO HEAVEN AND CAME BACK

A number of years ago, an interview was broadcast on BBC 4, and repeated on "Pick of the Week," of the experience of Edmund Wilbourne, a *Church army Captain of the Church of England, and the contents of the interview were also reported in the press.
Before the BBC interview Captain Wilbourne asked a colleague for his advice as to whether he should go ahead with the broadcast, and he was told, "As an evangelist it is your task to tell people how to die, not how to live."
He told the BBC interviewer how he had been dead for three hours, and had gone to Heaven, and returned to be reunited with his body again in a Manchester mortuary. One of the statements he made was that,
"WE ALL ARRIVE IN HEAVEN AT THE SAME TIME.THERE IS NO TIME IN HEAVEN."
"I sat up (in the mortuary) and asked where I was and it was the attendant who nearly had a heart attack! In fact I had to comfort and look after him. After a very short time I felt very weak and must have fainted for the next thing I knew was that I woke up in the hospital ward, where I had a long haul back to health."
The event happened over forty-five years ago, and Edmund Wilbourne related how he had developed pneumonia and pleurisy as a young Church Army Student, (in the Church of England.) I was taken to Crumpton Hospital near Manchester, and put on the critical list. This was in the days before the miracle drugs, which we have today. Although I was unconscious for much of the time I was able to hear the conversations going on around me and was aware of a great deal of activity.
I heard someone praying. "After a time I seemed to stop fighting and stood

outside my body. A cord seemed to link my soul and body and I watched as a nurse shaved me, in preparation for the mortuary, and the attendant stood by with his trolley." "My body was lifted on to the trolley, and it was at this point that I began to hiccup and the cord was severed. I found myself in Heaven where there was light and peace, music, love and a great deal of beauty. The light was so intense that at first I could hardly see, and there was purposeful activity and a great deal of JOY. "There was a loving welcome and I recognized people."

"IN HEAVEN THERE IS NO SENSE OF TIME AND BECAUSE OF THIS EVERYONE DIES AT THE SAME MOMENT. EVERYONE WAS AT A PERFECT AGE--NOT OLD OR UNDER AGE."

"I felt truly alive as I have never been before or since. My past made perfect sense and the dark and light strands of life's tapestry revealed a perfect pattern."
"Then I saw the Lord Jesus with the scars of the crucifixion on His body and I can hear my laughter at the thought that these scars were the only man made thing in heaven." "Jesus who was my Saviour on earth and was now my Lord in heaven laughed too. I wanted to stay for ever." "Heaven was a place of perfection where human characteristics were recognizable."
"I was aware of a voice getting louder and louder and raucously filling the whole of Heaven." "Oh God, don't let him die! Don't let him die! he has work to do for You. It was my old landlady's voice."

"I had been dead for three hours and here I was back again in answer to old Miss Green's prayer. I learned later that she had knelt to pray for me at the side of my bed, saying, O God, don't let him die."
*The Church army is an organization within the Church of England, which is run on similar lines to the Salvation Army.

THE LESSON FROM THIS TESTIMONY

The authenticity of this testimony is, I believe, confirmed by Scripture - that all events in history and in the future are happening in God's sight at the same time. To put it another way all time past, present and future are running simultaneously, or in Parallel.

CHAPTER 23

PHARAOH'S HEART BEING HARDENED BY GOD

The hardening by God of Pharaoh's heart has often been used by unbelievers to attack the Bible and show from Scripture that God is unjust, and because God hardened Pharaoh's heart, He was responsible for Pharaoh's sin, and that it was wrong of the Lord to hold him accountable for his rebellion and to punish him for this sin.

Many young Christians have also been perplexed by this seemingly unjust behaviour on the part of God. Calvinists are not at all disturbed by this, which, to their way of thinking, fits in with the Calvinist system of apartheid theology, that God is sovereign, and He hates one and loves another for no particular reason and the Lord can do whatever He pleases, whether it is unjust or not, and by so doing they discredit the justice of God. The Lord will say to the Calvinist what He said to Job in Job 40:- 8, **"Will you seek to discredit my Justice? To justify yourself."** J. M. V.

Scripture tells us in Psalm 145:-17:

"The Lord is [rigidly] righteous in all His ways, and gracious and merciful in all His works." The Amplified Bible.

"Truly God will never do wrong; the Almighty will never twist what is right." Job 34:-12. N.C.V.

SURELY GOD'S JUSTICE UNLIKE MAN'S IS FLAWLESS

If man's sense of justice, (which is but a reflection of God's perfect Justice and part of the image of God in man), regards this as unjust and is offended at the idea of the Lord hardening Pharaoh's heart and raising him up specifically for the purpose of his destruction, mainly because this conclusion does not balance and reconcile the Love of God for all mankind with the Justice of God and as a result renders the thesis Calvinists put forward as ambiguous. There must therefore be a reasonable and Biblical answer to this problem where these two attributes of the Almighty are brought together in harmony.

"Shall mortal man be more just than God? Shall a man be more pure than his maker?" Job 4:-17. K.J.V.

Calvinists overlook the fact that God cannot act against His character. **God cannot do evil, be unjust, or lie.**

To be correct, the interpretation of the events about Pharaoh in Exodus, as well as those in Romans 9, must be in harmony with the character of God, which is Love, Holiness, Justice and Righteousness, and to be in conflict with this dishonours God.
"God is Love" 1 John 4:-8 and 16. The very essence of God is love and as God is infinite so is His love, and this is expressed in every aspect of His Character and purpose. Someone has defined love, **"As a desire and an active working for the advancement and prosperity of others."**

For God to take a man and to harden that man's heart and by so doing, to make him go against God's will, would be an action on the Lord's part that would be impossible to reconcile with what we know to be justice. But when we study carefully what the Scriptures actually say and also what God is reported as saying, and the framework in which they were said, the difficulties no longer exist.

WHAT IS ACTUALLY SAID ABOUT THE HARDENING OF PHARAOH'S HEART

In Exodus 4:-21 we read of the prophecy the Lord gives that He will harden Pharaoh's heart, God's foreknowledge telling Him exactly what response He would receive from Pharaoh when asked to let the Israelites go, before there is any action on the part of the Lord actually to harden Pharaoh's heart. Between Exodus chapter 7 and 9, six times we are told that Pharaoh hardened his heart, or his heart was hardened, before we are told the Lord hardened Pharaoh's heart.
But in the King James Version we read in Exodus 7:- 13, "And He hardened Pharaoh's heart, that he harkened not unto them."
Most, if not all, modern translations correctly translate this verse, as in the N.C.V. **"Still the king was stubborn and refused to listen to Moses and Aaron, just as the Lord had said."**

"And Pharaoh's heart grew hard, and he did not heed them, as the Lord had said." The N.K.J.V. Exodus 7:-13.

"But the Pharaoh was obdurate and would not listen to them, just as the Eternal had predicted." The same verse from the J.M.V.
Moses and Aaron appeared before Pharaoh and presented God's message: "Thus saith the Lord God of Israel, let My people go, that they may hold a

feast unto me in the wilderness," and Pharaoh replied, "Who is the Lord, that I should obey his voice to let Israel go?" K.J.V.

Pharaoh was an oppressive cruel tyrant, subjecting the Israelites to the most awful bondage, suffering and death, and God looked down upon His people, heard their cries, and in His mercy determined to deliver them. Exodus 2:-25, also 3:-7-8.
Pharaoh in his pride and rebellion defied God and gave himself to even more evil oppression of the Israelites, once God through Moses and Aaron started the process of delivering His people and because of Pharaoh's stubbornness the Lord increased His judgments on Egypt.

WHY DID GOD HARDEN PHARAOH'S HEART?

God had given Pharaoh six opportunities to believe and repent and thereby save himself and his people from even severer judgment, and when God hardened Pharaoh's heart He was simply following His common practice of dealing with men. God's method is, **if man chooses error, and persists in it, to give him up to his error.** Romans 1:-21-28, also Rev 22:-11.

In Psalm 81:-11-12 it says, "But my people would not heed my voice, And Israel would have none of me. So I gave them over to their own stubborn heart, To walk in their own counsels." N.K.J.V.

Also 2 Thessalonians 2:-9-12.
"Because they did not receive the love of the truth, that they might be saved. And for this reason God will send them strong delusion, that they should believe the lie, that they all may be condemned who did not believe the truth but had pleasure in unrighteousness." N.K.J.V..

"They will die, because they refuse to love the Truth (If they loved the truth, they would be saved.) For this reason God sends them something powerful that leads them away from the truth so they will believe a lie. So all those will be judged guilty who did not believe the truth, but enjoyed doing evil." 2 Thessalonians 2:10-12: N.C.V.
This text is a guide as to how God deals with those who reject His Truth and is applicable to all ages as well as the present dispensation, and those who hear the gospel and refuse the Truth: the Lord Jesus Christ, as **the Way, the Truth and the Life and persist in it**, God gives them over to their own way

and sends delusions: so that they are led into believing false doctrine and religions, such as Romanism, Russelism, Spiritualism, Mormonism, Christian Science, etc.

CHAPTER 24

PARALLEL LINES

A Calvinist minister sent a copy of his church magazine to a friend of mine, which contained a very Calvinistic sermon and an announcement that he had a new grandson, named Paul, and requesting prayer that he may grow up to emulate the great apostle. My friend wrote to him in a courteous and kindly way, and asked him how we could offer that prayer when, as far as we knew, the new baby may have been "Fore-ordained" to "Everlasting death" long before he was born.

The minister wrote in answer to my friend: "Election and human free-will are like two railway lines; they are complementary and equally essential, but try and remove them from a parallel position to a union is to spell spiritual confusion and disaster."

THE PARALLEL LINE REASONING OF CALVINISTS

Calvinists get the idea from an optical illusion and explain it thus: If you look along two railway lines which go in a strait line into the distant horizon you will see them merge in the distance, and "Election and human free-will" are like parallel lines which go into infinity and merge, and in Eternity these two contradictions are reconciled and come together. Their idea is illusionary and their conclusion sheer fantasy.

A mathematician as well as common sense will tell you, that it is impossible, if lines are parallel, ever for them to meet no matter how far into infinity they go. If they meet they cannot be parallel.

If you really believe it, how can you reconcile the Calvinist idea of predestination to salvation, which is described as **"God's eternal and unchangeable decree"** with free-will or a desire to pray for the salvation of someone near to you.

If it is **unchangeable** then you are wasting your time, if God has already made up His mind about the matter, and that loved one has been appointed to damnation, and if God has appointed him to life, then it will happen whether you pray or not.

IS THERE A MORE FATALISTIC DOCTRINE THAN CALVINISM?

He mentions the "free will of man" and yet in one of the points of Calvinism we are told **that man lost his** "free will" in the fall, and because of this man is a spiritual corpse. It is in their belief that man has no free will! This is one of their arguments for "Unconditional Election"

If contradictory statements are like parallel railway lines, they must be mono-rail, with traffic going in opposite directions.

How can contradictory statements be "complementary"?

To say, as the Westminster Confession of Faith does, "In the gospel God declares His love for the world and His desire that all men should be saved;" Then in the same book they say, "They who are elected...... are redeemed by Christ.....Neither are any other redeemed by Christ, but the elect." In other words, God loved and Christ died for only a few, the Calvinists so called elect, and not the world.

EXPOUNDING THE DOCTRINE OF "UNCONDITIONAL ELECTION"

Dr. Hodge says in "Evangelical Theology," p121, when speaking about the new birth in men: "If God begins the work, if our believing follows His quickening, then it is God, not man, who makes the difference between the quickened and the unquickened. If we believe, it is because we have been first quickened." (been born again).

But on page 393 he says: "We are told to believe in Christ or we shall be damned. We are told to take our lives in our hands and make every sacrifice to preach the gospel to every creature in this life, in order that they may be saved."

These statements are not complimentary, they are contradictory.

SO WE CANNOT BE SAVED UNLESS WE BELIEVE, AND WE CANNOT BELIEVE UNLESS WE ARE ALREADY SAVED.

You cannot be on both the strait and narrow way and also on the broad road at the same time. You cannot be traveling **east** and also be traveling **west** at the same time.

"Election and human free will" are not parallel lines and there is no problem in Scripture reconciling the two, if you accept the fact of the foreknowledge of God, (which Calvinists do not) and that the elect are only the elect In Christ and this is corporate and not particular.

The Bible tells us in 1 Peter 1:- 2. "Elect" (chosen) "according to the foreknowledge of God the Father, through sanctification of the Spirit."

K.J.V. The problem exists only in the man-made theology of Calvinism.

THE CONTRADICTIONS IN THE DOCTRINE OF CALVINISM

This parallelism is very evident in Calvin's writings and his followers and also in the Westminster Confession, which is self-contradictory, as they switch from categorical Scriptural statements and then to Calvinistic theories, which are in conflict and impossible to reconcile.
The Westminster Confession of Faith states:
"In the gospel God declares His love for the world and His desire that all men should be saved; reveals fully and clearly the only way of salvation; promises eternal life to all who truly **repent** and **believe** in Christ; invites and commands all to **embrace** the offered mercy; and by His Spirit accompanying the word pleads with men to **accept** His gracious invitation. It is the duty and privilege of everyone who hears the gospel immediately to **accept** its merciful provisions; and they who continue in impenitence and unbelief incur aggravated guilt **and perish by their own fault."**
(CF:10:-2-3).

That is perfectly Scriptural, and could have been written by any New Testament writer, by John Wesley, D. L. Moody, William Booth, Campbell Morgan or James Arminius, **but if you turn over a couple of pages to 12:-2, we see it contradicted. There the one who hears the gospel is "altogether passive."**

In the paragraph above we have **four active verbs** applied to sinners who hear the gospel; He must **"repent," "believe," "embrace,"** and **"accept,"** or **"perish by his own fault."**
If sinners remain **"altogether passive,"** and God does not choose to save them, **how can it possibly be their own fault?**

THE PROBLEM CALVINISTS HAVE

Calvinists have the great problem of wanting to be seen to be true to the Word of God, and preach the Gospel of Christ and at the same time teach Calvinism which is diametrically opposed to the teaching of Christ, and this is the reason they continually and consistently contradict themselves. **They want to stick firmly to Calvinist Tradition, which is man-made, and be true to the gospel of Christ, which is impossible.**

They have the same problem the Pharisees had. Jesus said to them, **"And why do your traditions violate the direct commandments of God?"** Matthew 15:-3, T. L. B.

CHAPTER 25

LYDIA, "WHOSE HEART THE LORD OPENED"

Calvinists point to this incident as proof that man is passive in salvation and that it is God by His "irresistible grace" that forces His way into peoples' lives.

"And a certain woman named Lydia, a seller of purple, of the city of Thyatira, which worshipped God, heard us; whose heart the Lord opened, that she attended unto the things which were spoken of Paul." Acts 16:-14. K.J.V.

"ALL THAT THE FATHER GIVETH ME SHALL COME TO ME"

There must have been many thousands who have been saved by claiming the promise in John 6:37: "Him that cometh to me I will in no wise cast out," but some have been unnecessarily hindered by the first part of the verse: "All that the Father giveth me shall come to me." **Who are they?** We have the answer in verse 45: "Every man therefore that hath **heard**, and **hath learned** of the Father, cometh unto me." In John 17:-6 we have the clear statement: **"Thine they were, and thou gavest them Me."** K.J.V.

They were true believers, justified by faith, as Abraham was (Gen 15:-6) and among them were people like Lazarus whom Jesus mentions in Luke 16:-19-31 in the story of the rich man and Lazarus who, when he died, "was carried by the angels into Abraham's bosom:" and also Nathanael "Behold an Israelite indeed, in whom there is no guile." (John 1:-47).

This is further emphasized in John 8:-42-47: "Jesus said unto them. "If God were your Father, ye would love me," and "He that is of God heareth God's Words: ye therefore hear them not, because ye are **not of God.**"

Lydia was another example. She was already a true believer, and it is not said of her "whose heart the Lord opened to receive salvation."

Because she was already **"of God,"** her heart was receptive to Paul's teaching about the Lord Jesus Christ, like the two disciples on the road to Emmaus. Timothy's mother and grandmother were probably in the same class (2 Tim.1:-5), as were **"much people"** in Corinth (Acts 18:-10), also Apollos (Acts 18:-24-26), and the twelve disciples of John the Baptist at Ephesus (Acts 19:-1-7).

"One of the listeners was a woman named Lydia from the city of Thyatira whose job was selling purple cloth. She worshipped God, and He opened her mind to pay attention to what Paul was saying." Acts 16:-14. N. C. V.

A comparable verse is found in Luke 24:-45 which is: **"Then opened He their understanding, that they might understand the Scriptures."** K.J.V. **"Then Jesus opened their minds so that they could understand the Scriptures."** The same text from the N.C.V.

Psalm 110:-3, **"Thy people shall be willing in the day of Thy power."** K.J.V.
"May the God of our Lord Jesus Christ, the glorious Father, grant you the Spirit of wisdom and revelation for the knowledge of Himself, **illuminating the eyes of your heart** so that you can understand the hope to which He calls us." Ephesians 1:-17. The James Moffatt translation.

Note. Many of the Jewish people believed wholeheartedly in the true God, the God of Israel and were obedient to the light they had, but many did not believe, like the rich man in the story of the rich man and Lazarus. Those who were believers in the God of Israel, like Lazarus, had God as their Father, and were justified by faith. It is evident that all who were the Father's would believe the Gospel of the Lord Jesus Christ, because they welcomed God into their lives by believing His Word, as the Bible confirms. "Ye believe in God, believe also in Me." John 14:-1 K.J.V.

"'They will all be taught by God.' 'Everyone who listens to the Father and learns from Him comes to Me." John 6:-45 N.C.V.

"In John 17:-6 **"They belonged to You, and you gave them to Me, and they have obeyed Your teaching."** N.C.V.

There must have been many thousands who were spoken to by God through the ministry of John the Baptist, and who were brought to believe in the true God, the God of Israel, and who repented and were baptized by John, and thereby were prepared to receive the Messiah, the Lord Jesus Christ. Another example is found in Acts 10 in the story of Cornelius and his household.
Acceptance of God's truth as we hear it is the imperative prerequisite for perceiving and receiving additional truth.

CHAPTER 26

THE EXTREMES IN CALVINIST DOCTRINE

Dr. A. A. Hodge in a chapter on predestination in Evangelical Theology page 124 says "God works in man freely and spontaneously to will according to his good pleasure." (Phil.2:-13). But that is not what Paul wrote. The text has no relevance to "man" in general, **but only in the believers.** The verse says, "As ye have always obeyed......work out your own salvation in fear and trembling. For it is God which worketh in you both to will and to do His good pleasure." Phil 2:-13. K.J.V.

God is able to work in us because Christ has been welcomed and dwells in us by His Spirit, but that is no guarantee of success, else why the "fear and trembling."

"This is the will of God even your sanctification." But is every believer fully sanctified? You cannot work out what is not already in you. Christ is our salvation and dwells within all believers and His life is worked out in our lives. Christ is Present in all believers, Prominent in some, and Preeminent in a few, and this is determined by how believers allow Christ to be worked out in their lives. Christ does not dwell in unbelievers.

SPIRITUAL DEATH IS THE ABSENCE OF GOD IN ONE'S LIFE.

Dr. Hodge followed Calvin in this teaching.

Calvin taught: "Whatever things are done wrongly and unjustly by man, these very things are the right and just work of God."

Also as previously quoted from the Institutes, "All are not created on equal terms, but some are preordained to eternal life, others to eternal damnation; accordingly, as each one has been created for one or other of these ends, we say that he has been preordained to life or to death."

Calvin as evidenced in his writings, believed and also quoted what Augustine wrote: "Who does not tremble at these judgments with which God works in the hearts of even the wicked whatever He will, rewarding them none the less according to desert? ...God works in the heart of men to incline their wills just as He will, whether to good for His mercy's sake or to evil according to their merits."

When these doctrines are so spelled out in all their crudity, there are those who will object that this is "Hyper-Calvinism" but this is what Calvin taught. If this is "Hyper-Calvinism" we shall have to rename the author John Hyper-Calvin.

Can this, in honesty be called, "Doctrines of Grace"!

WHERE IS THE SCRIPTURAL WARRANT FOR THESE STATEMENTS?

This would mean that God was working in people like Thomas Hamilton in March 1996 at Dunblane in order to perpetrate evil, when he murdered 16 small children and their teacher. You can also add people like the torturers of the Roman Catholic Inquisition, Stalin, Hitler, Himler, Saddam Hussein and all those that come to mind who are or were particularly evil and they tell us that God was the one who was and is perpetrating the evil through them. What blasphemy!

Scripture tells a different story:

"That ages-old serpent, who is called the Devil and Satan, he who is the seducer (deceiver) of all humanity the world over." Rev 12:-9.

The Amplified New Testament.

Augustine and Calvin's conclusion that God perpetrates evil through man, is not the answer to the question so often asked: "Why does God allow evil?" They go very much further!

"No, never will God do an evil deed, never will the Almighty act unjustly." Job 34:-12. J.M.T.

James wrote: **"And remember when someone wants to do wrong it is never God who is tempting him, for God never wants to do wrong and never tempts anyone else to do it."** James 1:-13. T.L.B.

"A man must not say when he is tempted, 'God is tempting me' For God has no dealings with evil, and does not Himself tempt anyone."

The same text from J. B. Phillips translation.

ARE NOT AUGUSTINE AND CALVIN COMMITTING THE UNPARDONABLE SIN?

In Matthew 12:- 24, the Pharisees accused the Lord Jesus of casting out demons by Beelzebub and by so doing they were committing the unpardonable sin, by attributing to Satan the work of the Spirit of God through Jesus, as Jesus tells them in Verse 31. Surely Augustine and Calvin are doing the same, by attributing the evil deeds of men and the work of Satan, to the work of God's Spirit? Psalm 145:- 9 tells us: "He is good to

everyone; He is merciful to all he has made." N.C.V.
Calvinists want us to believe that God is like a lunatic potter, who makes vessels for the purpose of destroying them.
Geoffrey Wilson quotes Calvin as saying that "the ungodly themselves have been created for the specific purpose of perishing," and Arthur Pink claimed that it is God who fits them for destruction. According to them, God goes further than tempting people; He makes them sin, so that He can have the pleasure of punishing them.
We are asked to believe that God is at present engaged in "Manufacturing" billions of "vessels" ready for a stupendous smash-up, but these "vessels" are sentient creatures, who are going to be "made subject to death with all miseries, spiritual, temporal and **eternal**" (CF 6:6), including countless babies born to starving mothers, who have never known anything but pain and misery, and are then precipitated out of the "frying pan into" hell fire, "for the glory of (God's) sovereign power over His creatures...to the praise of his glorious justice" (CF 3:7).

MAN PLAYS A PART IN WHAT KIND OF VESSEL HE WILL BECOME

"True Wisdom has two sides." Job 11:-6. N.I.V.

They overlook the fact that man does play a part in what kind of vessel he will become, by refusing to believe or by believing in the Lord Jesus Christ and working Christ out in his life and for what purpose he will be used by God. In 2 Timothy 2:-20-21:
"But in a great house there are not only vessels of gold and silver but also [utensils] of wood and earthenware, and some for honorable and noble [use] and some for menial and ignoble [use]. So whoever cleanses himself [from what is ignoble and unclean] – who separates himself from contact with contaminating and corrupting influences – will [then himself] be a vessel set apart and useful for honorable and noble purposes, consecrated and profitable to the Master, fit and ready for any good work." The Amplified New Testement.
"For this is the will of God, even your sanctification." 1 Thess 4:-3. K.J.V.
So the result is dependant not solely on God or solely on man but on both. We are workers together with God. 1 Cor 3:-9, **"For we are labourers together with God:"** also 2 Cor 6:-1, **"We then as workers together with Him."** K.J.V.

APPENDIX
Notes and comments on Chapter 10.

JESUS GIVES US A LOOK BEHIND THE CURTAIN OF DEATH

In Luke 16:-19-31, Jesus tells us: "And it came to pass, that the beggar died, and was carried by the angels into Abraham's bosom: the rich man also died and was buried; And in hell he lift up his eyes, being in torments, and seeth Abraham afar off, and Lazarus in his bosom." K.J.V.

Just as a nomad tent-dweller does not cease to exist when he leaves his tent and moves on, so man when he moves out of his earthly TENT (Tabernacle) does not cease to exist.

WERE THEY COMPLETELY OBLIVIOUS OF THEIR SURROUNDINGS?

The body they left behind was but the house they had lived in; it was not the person. The real person - the lasting part of the individual, the soul and spirit was very much aware of the environment they found themselves in. Jesus refers to the Person of Lazarus being carried by the Angels into Abraham's bosom. It is the spirit of man that makes him conscious of God and of spiritual things, so after physical death it would be the spirit of man that would be the functioning part of the Soul and Spirit. Simply because he would find himself in a completely spiritual environment. "The natural man" (body and soul) "receiveth not the things of the Spirit of God:........because they are spiritually discerned." 1 Cor 2:-14. K.J.V. I believe the soul sees material things through the eyes of the physical body, but the spirit of man sees the unseen spiritual things, in the spiritual world.

SIGHT, FEELING, HEARING, PRAYER, LOVE AND CONCERN AFTER DEATH

In fact the rich man could see, feel pain, hear, understand, communicate, remember, have concern for others, and pray. He prayed that Lazarus might put water on his tongue to ease him of his torment. He also prayed for his five brothers. All the faculties he had when in his body he had when he was separated from his body.

I AM SURE THE RICH MAN WISHED IT HAD NOT BEEN SO.

THE REPLICA OF BODY IN THE SOUL

It would appear from Scripture that the body is a physical replica of the soul and spirit and a material extension of it and that the soul and spirit has similar members and characteristics to that of the body. According to Luke 16 and the story of the Rich man and Lazarus, it has eyes and can see, and also hear, therefore must have ears or the equivalent, and has a tongue, so presumably has a mouth. It has a memory, and must therefore have the spiritual equivalent of a brain.

Continuing notes and comments on chapter 10.

It must also have Love, since the Soul and Spirit of the rich man expressed concern for his brothers, and feeling, which can experience comfort or pain. The Soul and Spirit also have the ability to communicate to others in the spiritual realm. When the Lord Jesus spoke about man's heart in Luke 6:-45, I believe He was speaking about the counterpart of the physical, the heart of the Inner Man, The Soul and Spirit. **"A good man out of the good treasure of his heart bringeth forth that which is good; and an evil man out of the evil treasure of his heart bringeth forth that which is evil: for of the abundance of the heart his mouth speaketh."** K.J.V.

THE ANALOGY OF THE HAND AND THE GLOVE

The analogy, which comes to mind, although inadequate, is that the body is like a glove in which the soul and spirit are temporarily housed to enable us to live in this present material world. Although Paul, in Romans 7:-18, speaks about there being "No good thing in the flesh," and refers in Philippians 3:-12, to our present bodies as "Our vile body," the Soul and Spirit are precious, and are housed in the body. Jesus asked, "For what is a man profited, if he shall gain the whole world, and lose his own soul? or what shall a man give in exchange for his soul?" Matthew 16:-26. K.J.V.

BELIEVERS RECEIVE A NEW BODY AT THE RESURRECTION

We are also told that for the Christian, the body is the Temple of the Holy Ghost. In 1 Corinthians-3:-16: "Know ye not that ye are the Temple of God, and that the Spirit of God dwelleth in you?" K.J.V.

In 1 Corinthians 6:-13: "Now the body is not for fornication, but for the Lord; and the Lord for the body." K.J.V.

The flesh is mortal, and the container, or as the Bible puts it, an earthen vessel, tabernacle, or tent, of the soul and spirit which continue on. Nevertheless, man is incomplete without his body, but this will be rectified at the first resurrection, when the believer will receive a changed body, **"That it may be fashioned like unto His glorious body."** Philippians 3:-21. K.J.V.

Note, In Genesis God created man first of all materially out of the dust of the earth, breathed into his nostrils, and then man became a living soul. So it would appear the complete man (soul), is body, soul and spirit.

Also in John 5:-28-29, "Marvel not at this: for the hour is coming, in the which all that are in the grave shall hear His voice, And shall come forth; they that have done good, unto the **resurrection of life**; and they that have done **evil**, unto **The resurrection of damnation."** K.J.V.

Continuing the notes and comments on chapter 10.

The believer will be given a Glorified Body like unto Christ's. "It is sown in corruption; it is raised in incorruption: It is sown in dishonour; it is raised in glory; it is sown in weakness; it is raised in power: it is sown a natural body; it is raised a spiritual body." 1 Cor 15;- 42- 44. K.J.V.

In Revelation 20:-14 We read about the second death: "And Death and Hades were thrown into the lake of fire. The lake of fire is the second death." N.C.V.

Although there may be references in Scripture when the word death is referring to a dead body, as in contemporary life, the teaching of Scripture is clear, that death is caused through separation.

Genesis 35:-18, speaks about Rachel's death as follows: "And it came to pass, **as her soul was departing**, (for she died) that she called his name Benoni: but his father called him Benjamin." K.J.V.

Spiritual death is separation from God by sin. Isaiah 59:-1-2,

"Behold, the Lord's hand is not shortened, that it cannot save; neither His ear heavy, that it cannot hear: **But your Iniquities have separated between you and your God,** and **your sins have hid His face from you,** that He will not hear." K.J.V.

James 2:-20, says, "But wilt thou know, O vain man, that faith without works is **dead**." K.J.V.

THE SEPARATION OF WORKS FROM FAITH.

NOTES ON CHAPTER 11

Note. In Romans 5 verse 18 the phrase **(Pantas anthropous)** occurs twice. This undoubtedly means **"all men"**. In verse 19, however, the word (Polloi) (meaning **"many"**) occurs twice. Polloi is the root of our word, Poly (many). The salient phrase could be translated: **"So also, by the obedience of the righteous One shall many be established."** This would mean that, though the Propitiation was adequate for All **(Pantas)**, the establishment, or salvation, is only to the Many (Polloi) who accept the overture of the atonement.

CHAPTER 12

COMMENTS ON THE CHANGE IN C. H. SPURGEON'S CALVINISTIC BELIEFS.

Spurgeon's Calvinistic views changed considerably after the visit of D. L. Moody and Sankey. Moody through his preaching "expounded unto him the way of God more perfectly." Acts 18:-26. In his magazine: Sword and Trowel for November 1876 he wrote: "We rejoice to mention that during the last few months we have met with more converts from Messrs Moody and Sankey's meetings than in all the time before. Some of our brethren have also made the same observation....We expressed our disappointment very plainly some time ago, because we met with so few decided conversions, and it is therefore with the utmost pleasure that we intimate more pleasing things." But did those "more pleasing things" meet with the approval of the Calvinists? Spurgeon wrote: "I recollect great complaint being made against a sermon of mine, 'Compel them to come in,' which I spake with much tenderness for souls. That sermon was said to be Arminian and unsound. Brethren it is a small matter to me to be judged of men's judgment, for my Master has set His seal on that message."

"I never preached a sermon by which so many souls were won to God, as our Church meetings can testify; and all over the world, where the sermon has been scattered, sinners have been saved through its instrumentality; and, therefore, if it be vile to exhort sinners, I purpose to be viler still."

Strangely enough, Spurgeon still claimed to be a Calvinist! – but that did not save him from ostracism, which continues to this present day.

In a well-known Calvinist magazine they commented on the fact that Spurgeon "Did not assess the extent to which the whole evangelical outlook for a long time to come was to be influenced by 'Moodyism'.
In this misjudgment Spurgeon was not alone...His brother, James, who was called upon to give the address on 'Particular Redemption' at the time of the opening of the Tabernacle in 1861, was no longer of the conviction thirty years later." Unfortunately, the only leader at the Tabernacle who was not delivered from this sterile doctrine, was J. W. Harrald, who was responsible for the editing and publishing of Spurgeon's sermons.

In Edinburgh in the public book-room of one of our biggest Calvinist denominations, they had on the wall a large framed picture of a ship representing the world, which was sailing to destruction, and among the worldly attractions and side shows on the deck was C. H. Spurgeon preaching to a group of people. That was how the Calvinists regarded him at the time. A comment was made to the man in charge, and he made a joke of it.

Spurgeon himself said when he started his college: **"I thought the Calvinism of the theology usually taught to be very doubtful, and the fervour of the generality of the students to be far behind their literary attainments."**
How could any intelligent person be fervent in evangelism if he believed that all his efforts could not affect the eternal destiny of a single soul?

Notes and comments on chapter 14
"LOST MAN'S CARNAL LIFE."

THE CARNAL MAN CAN HAVE A SPIRITUAL REVELATION.

In Matthew 16: verses 15 to 17, when Jesus asked His disciples, "But whom say ye that I am?" Peter answered "Thou art the Christ the Son of the Living God." K.J.V.
"Jesus answered and said unto him, blessed art thou, Simon Bar-jona: for flesh and blood hath not revealed it unto thee, but My Father which is in heaven." K.J.V.
This was a spiritual revelation given to Peter by God (through what he had seen of Jesus and heard from Him), even though Peter was carnal in his outlook, God revealed this Great spiritual Truth to Peter's spirit through the Spirit of God. A few verses later (verse 21), Jesus tells His disciples that He

is going to Jerusalem to suffer and be killed and be raised on the third day. Verse 22, "Then Peter took Him, and began to rebuke Him, saying, Be it far from thee, Lord, this shall not be unto thee."

Verse 23, "But He turned, and said unto Peter, **get thee behind Me Satan**: thou art an offence unto me: for thou savourest not the things that be of God but those that be of men." (The natural man). K.J.V.

"But He turned and said to Peter, 'Get behind Me Satan! You are a stumbling block to Me; **for you are not setting your mind on God's interests, but man's**.'" Matthew 16:-23. N.A.S.B.

Jesus never rebuked anyone in such a way, or referred to anyone as Satan, except Satan himself, not even wicked king Herod whom he called a fox.
It was because of Peter's carnal (natural man) outlook that this very severe rebuke was given. Even though Jesus said to him "Flesh and Blood hath not revealed this unto thee" and complimented Peter on his Spiritual Revelation from God, that He was, "The Christ the Son of the living God". He also said, **"For you are not setting your mind on God's interests, but man's."** Matthew 16:-23. N.A.S.B.

PETER "THE NATURAL MAN"

This statement put Peter on the "Natural Man" level, ("But the Natural man receiveth not the things of the Spirit of God: For they are foolishness unto him: neither can he know them, because they are spiritually discerned."
1 Cor 2:-14. K.J.V.)
Because Peter was living on the "Natural Man" level he looked upon the cross as foolishness and did not understand or discern the spiritual implications of what Jesus had said, even though God had just a short time before revealed a great spiritual truth to him, by His Spirit to Peter's spirit.
"For the preaching of the cross is to them that perish foolishness; but unto us which are saved it is the power of God." 1 Cor 1:-18, K.J.V.
Speaking to Peter Jesus said, "But I have prayed for thee, that thy faith fail not: and when thou art converted, strengthen thy brethren." Luke 22:-32. K.J.V. The act of repentance and being converted are synonymous.

JESUS EXPLAINS TO HIS DISCIPLES HOW TO BECOME SPIRITUAL

The Lord gives Peter and the other disciples a clear answer to the lack of spiritual understanding. In verse 24, immediately following the rebuke to Peter, Jesus says: **"If any man will come after Me, let him deny himself, take up his cross and follow Me."** K.J.V.

When the Lord Jesus says, **"If any man", He means exactly that and not any man who is born again, as Calvinists would claim.**

SPIRITUAL TRUTH IS REVEALED BY HIS SPIRIT THROUGH THE WORD

Spiritual truths are revealed to us through God's Word by His Spirit, but we have to be in the correct frame and focus of mind with a humble spirit to receive them. God is not partial in His revealing of spiritual truth, but only those who meet the right criteria will have spiritual truth made clear to them.
"God resisteth the proud, but giveth Grace unto the humble." K.J.V. James 4:-6 and 1 Peter 5:-5.
"For thus saith the high and lofty One that inhabiteth eternity, whose name is Holy; I dwell in the high and holy place, with him also that is of a contrite and humble spirit, to revive the spirit of the humble, and to revive the heart of the contrite ones." Isaiah 57:-15. K.J.V.

CONCLUSION

As we have journeyed through the origins of Calvinistic teachings and examined what these teachings are, we have seen that the form in which they have come down to us owes not a little to the Council of Dort with its formulation of the "Five Points", condemning the vast majority of mankind to a lost eternity - an eternity in Hell - whilst a favoured minority, selected arbitrarily by God, are destined for an eternity in the blessedness of Heaven, whatever good or evil they may have done.

It leaves but little certainty that one is of the elect and gives not a glimmer of hope to one who is not.

Yet as we have examined the Scriptures, we find a different teaching emerges - a true Gospel of Hope. The word "WHOSOEVER" in Scripture means just what it says and, if you should be one of those that the teaching of Calvinistic predestination has cast into doubt and uncertainty, take heart for the "WHOSOEVER" in Scripture includes you. John 3:-16 means you; you are in the "WHOSOEVER" of that verse.

Dear reader, just trust the simple words of Scripture and "Believe on the Lord Jesus Christ and thou shalt be saved." Belief in Calvin's teaching cannot save you.